Phenomenology
Second Edition

Phenomenology
An Introduction

Stephan Käufer and
Anthony Chemero

polity

First published in 2015 by Polity Press
This edition published in 2021 by Polity Press

Polity Press
65 Bridge Street
Cambridge CB2 1UR, UK

Polity Press
101 Station Landing
Suite 300
Medford, MA 02155, USA

ISBN-13: 978-1-5095-4065-5
ISBN-13: 978-1-5095-4066-2 (pb)

A catalogue record for this book is available from the British Library.

Library of Congress Cataloging-in-Publication Data

Names: Käufer, Stephan, author. | Chemero, Anthony, 1969- author.
Title: Phenomenology : an introduction / Stephan Käufer and Anthony Chemero.
Description: Second edition. | Cambridge, UK ; Medford, MA, USA : Polity Press, 2021. | Includes bibliographical references and index. | Summary: "The much-anticipated second edition of this celebrated introduction to phenomenology"-- Provided by publisher.
Identifiers: LCCN 2020047814 (print) | LCCN 2020047815 (ebook) | ISBN 9781509540655 | ISBN 9781509540662 (pb) | ISBN 9781509540679 (epub)
Subjects: LCSH: Phenomenology.
Classification: LCC B829.5 .K38 2021 (print) | LCC B829.5 (ebook) | DDC 142/.7--dc23
LC record available at https://lccn.loc.gov/2020047814
LC ebook record available at https://lccn.loc.gov/2020047815

Typeset in 10 on 12.5 Sabon LT Pro by
Servis Filmsetting Ltd, Stockport, Cheshire
Printed and bound in the UK by TJ Books Ltd

The publisher has used its best endeavours to ensure that the URLs for external websites referred to in this book are correct and active at the time of going to press. However, the publisher has no responsibility for the websites and can make no guarantee that a site will remain live or that the content is or will remain appropriate.

Every effort has been made to trace all copyright holders, but if any have been overlooked the publisher will be pleased to include any necessary credits in any subsequent reprint or edition.

For further information on Polity, visit our website: politybooks.com

Contents

Detailed Contents

Acknowledgments

We have been fortunate to study and discuss this material with many teachers and colleagues who have shaped our understanding of phenomenology. In particular we wish to thank Bert Dreyfus, Dagfinn Føllesdal, Bill Mace, Mike Turvey, and Fred Owens for teaching us much of the material in this book. We are also grateful to Mike Anderson, Chris Baber, Ed Baggs, Louise Barrett, Abeba Birhane, Bill Blattner, Taylor Carman, Dave Cerbone, Amanda Corris, Steve Croker, Steve Crowell, Elena Cuffari, Fred Cummins, Rick Dale, Hanne De Jaegher, Ola Derra, Ezequiel Di Paolo, Dobri Dotov, Catarina Dutilh-Novaes, Tom Froese, Shaun Gallagher, Melina Gastelum, Beatrice Han-Pile, Harry Heft, Manuel Heras-Escribano, Dan Hutto, Jenann Ismael, Mark James, Scott Jordan, Chris Kello, Sean Kelly, David Kirsh, Julian Kiverstein, Jonathan Knowles, Tomasz Komendzinski, Mariusz Kozak, Miriam Kyselo, Wayne Martin, Samantha Matherne, Teenie Matlock, Jakub Matyja, Marek McGann, Jonathan McKinney, Richard Menary, Marcin Miłkowski, Ronny Myhre, Erik Myin, Lin Nie, Mark Okrent, Jacek Olender, Kevin O'Regan, Isabelle Peschard, Marek Pokropski, Vicente Raja, Mike Richardson, Erik Rietveld, Etienne Roesch, Komarine Romdenh-Romluc, Joe Rouse, Gui Sanches de Oliveira, Miguel Segundo Ortin, Charles Siewert, Michael Silberstein, Paula Silva, Michael Spivey, Pierre Steiner, John Sutton, Iain Thompson, Bas van Fraassen, Witold Wachowski, Jeff Wagman, Ashley Walton, Mike Wheeler, Rob Withagen, Mark Wrathall, Jeff Yoshimi, Julian Young, and Corinne Zimmerman.

We taught seminars on this material at Franklin & Marshall College, Carleton College, and at the University of Cincinnati. We are grateful to students in those seminars, and to Jenefer Robinson, for helping us to present the material more clearly.

We are grateful to Pascal Porcheron and the editorial team at Polity Press for all of their assistance and to Fiona Sewell for careful and thoughtful copyediting. Thanks also to Gui Sanches de Oliveira and Taraneh Wilkinson for their help with the page proofs and index.

Large portions of the first edition of this book were written during research leaves from Franklin & Marshall College and the University of Cincinnati. We are grateful to these institutions for their support.

Most of all, we are grateful for the love and support of our families.

Figures

Introduction

Phenomenology is a loosely grouped philosophical tradition that began with Edmund Husserl in the 1890s and is still practiced today, though some of its current instantiations no longer use the name. The tradition is old enough to have a history, and it includes claims that seem odd, quaint, or outdated. And yet it is recent enough that even the work of its founders is alive with ideas that still challenge us and hold great promise. Arguably philosophers are only now beginning to fully appreciate the core insights of phenomenology, as we learn to construct rigorous analyses of perception and cognition in a phenomenological framework.

This book covers what we believe an interested reader ought to know about phenomenology, its history, its most important authors and works, and its influence on branches of current philosophy, psychology, and cognitive science. We discuss the history of phenomenology through the work of Husserl, Heidegger, and Merleau-Ponty, their arguments against scientific psychology, and their critical examination of Gestalt psychology. As part of this history, we also include extended discussions of Gurwitsch, Sartre, and the history of psychology. We go on to discuss contemporary developments in critical phenomenology of gender and race, ecological psychology, critiques of cognitivist approaches to artificial intelligence, and embodied cognitive science. This mix of topics and level of detail make this a good textbook for undergraduates studying philosophy, psychology, or cognitive science, and a good starting point for graduate students and academics who are new to phenomenology.

What you will not find in this book

Here is one way to explain our focus and distinguish it from strains of phenomenology that we will not pursue in this book. One prominent concern of phenomenology has been to provide an account of the structures that make a shared, objective world intelligible. This account focuses on perception and cognition, and recognizes that bodies and skills are fundamental in making up this intelligibility. We consider this to be the central, most important, and most productive strain of phenomenology, and this book is intended to give a clear introduction to it.

Another strain of phenomenology, which we can only explore briefly in this book, is concerned to give a description of subjective experiences, especially of experiences that are unusual and hard to explain. So, for example, phenomenology might provide an analysis of what it is like to experience religious faith, overpowering sentiments such as love or anxiety, aesthetic highs, inescapable ambiguities and paradoxes, and so forth. This is an important task, and quite often it intermingles with the first task. In Heidegger's work, in particular, an understanding of anxiety and contingency is part and parcel of his explanation of the intelligibility of the world. In general, Husserl, Heidegger, and Merleau-Ponty were broad and innovative thinkers and their writings touch on art, religion, politics, aesthetics, and morality. Existentialism is largely an offshoot of phenomenology, and so is much critical theory in literary studies. Consequently, phenomenology has influenced many different fields, too many to cover in a single book. Browse the faculty pages of a university website, and you may find a large number of people in literature departments, film and theater studies, theology, art, and political science who identify their work as "phenomenology." We do not deny the importance of this phenomenology in these various fields. But a single book cannot presume to cover all this material. Our choice of topics and authors is motivated primarily by our conviction that contemporary work on embodied cognitive science is a particularly clear and relevant continuation of the most central concerns that Husserl, Heidegger, and Merleau-Ponty were pursuing.

A further preliminary distinction might be helpful. As is well known, English-speaking philosophy has for over half a century perceived a division between so-called "analytic" and "continental" approaches. Some philosophers on either side of the divide want to identify phenomenology with the "continental" approach, either to acclaim or to disparage the entire tradition wholesale. Those who prefer a "continental" approach would probably choose a sequence of authors that leads from Heidegger and Merleau-Ponty to Sartre, Derrida, and Levinas, and perhaps more current authors such as Badiou. That is a fine sequence of authors to study, and such overviews are available in many other books. But that is not our approach. We do not think the distinction is helpful or accurate at all, even aside from the obvious incongruity that "continental" is a geographic term while "analytic" is a stylistic or methodological one. Much analytic philosophy is done on the continent, and much good work in English-language philosophy consists of using analytic methods to explain the work of European philosophers. That is what we aim to do in this book. The goal of all philosophy, we think, is to give as clear an account as possible of the best available view on the big questions that motivate philosophy in the first place. We think that Husserl, Heidegger, and Merleau-Ponty articulate hard-won insights into the nature of the human ability to make sense of the world. Their writing is sometimes obscure, because they address very fundamental questions, make unexpected proposals that fly in the face of centuries of philosophical tradition, and often invent new language to render their ideas. Our job is to use what scholars have learned over the past decades to try to make it easier for today's students to appreciate the insights of phenomenology.

Phenomenology now

A broad range of researchers in philosophy and psychology departments are empirically and conceptually investigating affordances, or the role of our bodies in perception and cognition, or action as a condition for maintaining a sense of the self. We claim that such work is not merely *influenced* by phenomenology, something that most of these people would readily accede to whether they have read Heidegger or not. We think that they are *doing* phenomenology, insofar as they are pursuing the basic ideas and insights this tradition was founded on. Still, some readers may be surprised that ecological psychology and embodied cognitive science belong among the proper successors of Heidegger and Merleau-Ponty. This is understandable, because the chain of influence that leads from Heidegger to, say, Gibson, dynamical systems theory, or enactivism is not clear or well known. It is easier and more common to point out more obvious threads, such as that Merleau-Ponty and Sartre were friends and collaborators for a while, and that Sartre was a giant in post-war French philosophy, from which Levinas, Derrida, and Deleuze emerged as important figures.

We hope that the narrative of this book vindicates our claim in detail, but here are two quick reminders that should make it plausible from the start. Merleau-Ponty's work is obviously indebted to Husserl, and even more deeply to Heidegger. The third big source of his thought is his sustained critical examination of Gestalt psychology. This also had a major impact on Gibson, who was Kurt Koffka's colleague at Smith College for several years in the 1930s, just as Gibson was beginning to develop the first ideas of ecological psychology. Beyond this parallel influence of Gestalt psychology on Merleau-Ponty and Gibson, there was possibly a direct influence of the former on the latter. Though Gibson himself would deny it, some of his students recall that later he would often compare his work to Merleau-Ponty's *Phenomenology of Perception*, to the point of trying to ward off prospective graduate students by telling them they should read this impenetrable book first, and only come back when they had understood it.

More crucial than a common ancestry in Gestalt psychology is the work of Hubert Dreyfus, who brought the views of Heidegger and Merleau-Ponty into current philosophy and cognitive science. In the 1960s and 1970s Dreyfus used his unusually insightful understanding of Heidegger's work to formulate sharp criticisms of the then burgeoning research projects in artificial intelligence. The following three decades of artificial intelligence research tell the history of the many ways in which Dreyfus' original critique transformed the field's understanding of human intelligence. It has led to many attempts to explain intelligent behavior in terms of the coupling of agent, body, and environment.

Why study phenomenology?

The simplest reason why you should study phenomenology is because everyone should. Even a fairly superficial study of Husserl, Heidegger, or Merleau-Ponty and those influenced by them can have a profound positive impact on your understanding of a host of issues relating to perception, cognition, and the general meaningfulness of human lives. Phenomenological approaches to a broad spectrum of issues are interesting, accurate, and promising. Any serious study of philosophy or psychology ought to include at least some exposure to phenomenology.

At the more ponderous end of the spectrum, phenomenology is an ontology of human existence. Heidegger is most explicit about this, but Merleau-Ponty and Gibson also think of their work in these terms. So their work may lead you to think that people in general, and you specifically, are a different kind of entity than you might have thought. In particular, you might think that you experience the world by passively and reflectively cognizing objects; the phenomenologist, however, argues that you experience it through competent, unreflective action. At the more lively end, the authors and theories we discuss here provide a host of thought-provoking examples to make you question some basic assumptions about what we perceive. We do not see the shapes and sizes of objects, but the possible actions they afford us, invitations to act shaped by our own bodily capabilities. Such examples make reading about phenomenology both rewarding and entertaining.

If phenomenology is an important and influential school of thought, this is because the main phenomenologists think and write with remarkable insight and creativity. So another good reason to study phenomenology is to become familiar with Husserl, Heidegger, and Merleau-Ponty as authors. Though their writing can sometimes be unclear and frustrating, it is ultimately exhilarating.

Overview

This book proceeds in roughly chronological order and most chapters cover one main figure or movement. The chapters stand on their own, so if you are short on time or more interested in some topics than others, you can pick and choose. However, the overall narrative is richer than a collection of individual portraits.

We have aimed to make this book easy to read without sacrificing accuracy or detail. We avoid jargon. While we use and define key technical terms proffered by the various authors, we think their insights are independent of any particular way of expressing them. In fact, you can only appreciate that phenomenology is alive and ongoing insofar as you can recognize that the same approach and the same basic views animate the different styles of the authors you will encounter in this book. We provide a glossary of key technical terms at the end of each chapter for reference.

Notes on the second edition

For the second edition, we have revised, reorganized, and expanded substantially. A list of the most important changes follows.

Chapter 2 "The Rise of Experimental Psychology" is a new chapter, collecting material that was spread across several chapters in the first edition, and with an additional section on the structuralism–functionalism debate in psychology. In its current form, it is better in keeping with the chronological structure employed in most of the rest of the book.

Chapter 3 "Edmund Husserl and Transcendental Phenomenology" has a new section on Husserl's writings on the body (section 3.5), the purpose of which is to draw closer connections between Husserl and Merleau-Ponty.

Chapter 5 "Gestalt Psychology" collects material that was distributed across several chapters in the first edition.

Chapter 6 "Aron Gurwitsch: Merging Gestalt Psychology and Phenomenology" is entirely new. Gurwitsch is a key figure in the history of phenomenology, and was a major influence on Merleau-Ponty.

Chapter 7 "Jean-Paul Sartre: Phenomenological Existentialism" is significantly expanded from the first edition. It now includes in-depth discussion of three more of Sartre's major works, *The Transcendence of the Ego*, *The Imagination*, and *The Imaginary*.

Chapter 9 "Critical Phenomenology" is new to this edition. It collects and expands upon the discussions of the phenomenology of gender and race from the first edition, and includes new discussions of Frantz Fanon and trans phenomenology.

Chapter 12 "Enactivism and the Embodied Mind" is also new to this edition. It includes an expanded version of the basic discussion of enactivism from the first edition. It also includes new sections on 4E cognitive science and enactivist approaches to social cognition and language.

All citations give the date of the first edition listed in the references. Where English translations of foreign works are listed, they are the source of our quotations. Where no English translations are listed, the translations are our own.

1

Immanuel Kant: Eighteenth- and Nineteenth-Century Background

Husserl thinks phenomenology is a new beginning in philosophy, a budding new science. At the same time he acknowledges the deep influence of the philosophical tradition. For most of his career he thinks of his work as "transcendental phenomenology," thus locating it within Kant's broad philosophical project. Heidegger similarly thinks he is making a new start, reawakening questions whose meaning, he claims, has been lost since antiquity. But he, too, knows that his work owes much to the tradition. Much of the first part of his most important book, *Being and Time*, has its origins in his earlier lectures on Aristotle. And in a lecture course in 1927 – the year *Being and Time* was published – he describes his deep involvement in Kant's work: "When, a few years ago, I studied the *Critique of Pure Reason* again and read it against the background of Husserl's phenomenology, it was as if the scales fell from my eyes, and Kant became for me an essential confirmation of the correctness of the path on which I was seeking" (Heidegger 1927/1928, p. 431). Merleau-Ponty's *Phenomenology of Perception* is no less ambitious than the books of his two predecessors, although he is more modest in characterizing its revolutionary nature. He cites and refers to a vast literature of nineteenth- and twentieth-century philosophy and psychology and develops his ideas in an active dialog with his contemporaries. At several points he, too, singles out the importance of Kant's transcendental framework.

It would be an endless exercise to attempt to explicate all the historical influences that shaped phenomenology. But we think it is important to spend a few pages reviewing central concepts from Kant's critical philosophy, because many of Kant's ideas have a very direct influence on Husserl, Heidegger, Sartre, and Merleau-Ponty. While, for the most part, these authors toil within Kant's overall framework, they are not Kantians in a strict sense. Kant comes in for some trenchant criticism. Heidegger sharply rejects Kant's focus on cognition through representations, and Merleau-Ponty similarly condemns Kant for ignoring the importance of the body and the indeterminateness of things in our experience. Gibson rails stridently against Kant's distinction between concepts and intuitions. Still, some of Kant's key arguments have clear successors in the work of the phenomenologists, and a quick overview of these arguments will prove helpful. For readers with some background in the history of eighteenth- and nineteenth-century philosophy, most of this will be familiar.

1.1 Kant's critical philosophy

Kant is fond of astronomy. He thinks of it as an example of a discipline that struggled for a long time to produce theories and predictions with certainty, until Copernicus' revision of its foundation put it on what Kant calls "the secure path of a science." Kant likes to compare the main insight of his *Critique of Pure Reason* to this Copernican revolution. In the preface to the B edition (published in 1787), he writes:

> Up to now it has been assumed that all our cognition must conform to the objects; but all attempts to find out something about them *a priori* through concepts that would extend our cognition have, on this presupposition, come to nothing. Hence let us once try whether we do not get farther with the problems of metaphysics by assuming that the objects must conform to our cognition. (Bxvi)

Copernicus enabled progress in astronomy by presupposing that the earth revolves around the sun, despite the intuitive evidence to the contrary. Kant sees himself as enabling progress in metaphysics. By metaphysics Kant means an account of non-empirical truths, that is, propositions that are necessarily true and whose truth we can establish without recourse to particular experiences of the world. He claims that we can only give such an account by presupposing, counter-intuitively, that objects conform to our *a priori* cognition of them, rather than the other way around. This claim is more readily expressed by saying that the structures of cognition *constitute* general features of objects or, as Kant himself puts it, that "we can cognize of things *a priori* only what we ourselves have put into them" (Bxviii). Besides constituting the objects of our experience, the same basic structures also constitute ourselves. So, although he is not consistently clear about this, Kant ends up with the view that subject and object are two interdependent poles in a single structure that constitutes the origin of meaningful experience. The task of philosophy is to analyze and spell out this underlying origin.

1.2 Intuitions and concepts

Cognition, says Kant, has two stems. On the one hand, we are receptive to sense data. Objects affect our sensory surfaces and give rise to a mostly unstructured "manifold" of sense impressions that means nothing by itself, but is a necessary element of any experience of an object. Kant calls our capacity to be affected by objects our "sensibility," and he calls this mental content "intuitions." A book on the desk or a familiar face, for example, affect our sense surfaces and give us a manifold of visual or tactile sense data including colors, lines, lighting, smoothness, and so on. This manifold resembles what William James called a "blooming, buzzing confusion" in his *Principles of Psychology*. It is mostly unstructured, but not entirely, for the sense data present themselves in a temporal sequence and in a spatial arrangement. The spatial and temporal order may be vague at first, but at least we have a sense that the orange patch is distinct from the brown patch and both are distinct from myself, because we intuit them at different moments and as located in different places. Kant argues that all intuitions must come in some temporal sequence, and all intuitions of objects distinct from us – that is, objects in the world, as opposed to our own thoughts – must present themselves in some spatial arrangement. A rough intuition of space and time, then, underlies all our sense data.

On the other hand our mind also actively structures experiences. We do this by organizing mental content according to concepts. A concept is a rule for recognizing a given intuition or a set of already cognized objects as an instance of a general type. Kant calls our capacity for spontaneously ordering a manifold and recognizing it under a general type the "understanding." The understanding organizes the orange and brown patches and lines given in intuition as edges of a compact, colored object on a smooth surface, and recognizes it as a book on a desk. Just as space and time underlie all intuition, the understanding has some basic concepts that are required for all active structuring of mental content.

Kant thinks, for example, that without basic notions of quantity (such as "one" or "many"), of negation, existence, or substance (a thing can persist as the same while some of its properties change), our understanding could never get off the ground. Kant produces a table of such basic concepts, which he calls the "categories." The details of this table and Kant's method for producing it may be challenged. But the overall point is well taken. A cognizer can certainly have experiences without *some* of our concepts. We can imagine a cognizer who lacks the concept of a book, of food, money, or whatever. But the categories are so fundamental to our cognition that without them no object-recognition, cognition, or experience is possible.

Obviously an unstructured manifold of intuitions is not yet an experience of anything. Less obviously, using concepts by themselves without applying them to intuitions also does not amount to an experience of anything. Cognition requires both stems. Kant puts this eloquently in a famous passage:

> Thoughts without content are empty, intuitions without concepts are blind. . . . The understanding is not capable of intuiting anything, and the senses are not capable of thinking anything. Only from their unification can cognition arise. (A51)

This two-stem feature of Kant's theory of cognition is fairly radical. Most philosophers prior to Kant think that a sense impression of a book and the concept of a book are the same kind of mental content. Hume, for example, thinks that they differ only insofar as the sense impression is more vivid than the concept, which is an attenuated and modified copy of the original impression. Leibniz, by contrast, thinks that the concept is clearer and more distinct, while sense impressions are vague and imprecise instances of conceptually determined experience. Kant's reasons for claiming that intuitions and concepts cannot be reduced to one another derive mostly from his older argument about "incongruent counterparts," which are pairs of objects that are conceptually equivalent, but differ perceptually. Regardless, in his *Critique* he focuses much of his analysis on explaining how intuitions and concepts are brought together in consciousness to produce objective experience. And that is where his view becomes truly groundbreaking.

We saw above that metaphysics, for Kant, consists of non-empirical knowledge, which he also calls *a priori* knowledge, and that Kant is trying to explain how and to what extent such knowledge is possible. According to the two-stem view of cognition, Kant is committed to saying that metaphysical knowledge must consist of *a priori* intuitions and *a priori* concepts. Kant believes that there are such intuitions and concepts. In fact, they are precisely the important basic structures we just outlined – space and time for intuitions and the categories for concepts. This *a priori* mental content ultimately grounds all possible metaphysical knowledge.

Kant's argument that space, time, and the categories are *a priori* is fairly straightforward. All sense data are given as spatial and temporal (except for sense data that the mind gives to itself, which are only temporal). Since we need to have a representation of space and time in order to be given any sense data at all, we cannot derive our representation of space and time from what is given to us. Space and time are thus *a priori* intuitions. They cannot be *concepts*, because, as quoted above, Kant states explicitly that the understanding, that is, the faculty of concepts, "is not capable of intuiting anything."

Moreover, space and time display some crucial hallmarks of intuitions. For example, unlike concepts they are not general terms that have a lot of instances falling under them. Different spaces or times are all parts of the same single space and time, not exemplars or instances of it. Kant's argument that the categories are *a priori* is similar. Since they are necessary preconditions for having any experience at all, we cannot derive them from experience. I cannot get my concepts of existence or unity from my visual and tactile experience of a book, because I must be able to conceive of single, existing things in order to have an experience of the book in the first place. But if the categories cannot be derived from experience, they are not empirical ("empirical" just means "derived from experience") and must be *a priori*.

If space, time, and the categories are not derived from experience, they must come from somewhere else. Kant thinks that they are innate in the human cognitive apparatus (and non-humans as well, if any of them are cognizers like us). Kant recognizes clearly that as subjective structures space, time, and the categories are specific to our experience. Space, he writes:

> is nothing other than the subjective condition of sensibility, under which alone outer intuition is possible *for us*. . . . We can accordingly speak of space, extended beings, and so on, only from the human standpoint. If we depart from the subjective condition under which alone we can acquire outer intuition . . . then the representation of space signifies nothing at all. (A26, emphasis added)

He makes analogous claims about time (A34–5). And Kant also acknowledges that there could be an altogether different kind of cognizer, whose mind would not require concepts at all. He envisions, for example, a "divine understanding, through whose representation the objects would themselves at the same time be given, or produced" and notes that for such an understanding "the categories would have no significance at all" (B145).

Kant's view that objects are intelligible to us only from the human standpoint is called his "transcendental idealism." Idealism is the view that objects depend on our minds. Kant's idealism is "transcendental," because on his view this dependence only shows itself insofar as we consider the basic constitutive structures of the human standpoint. This is a specific, limited philosophical perspective that we only adopt when we are doing transcendental philosophy, that is, a philosophical analysis of the constitution of experience. For all ordinary and scientific purposes, we necessarily remain within the human standpoint, and must therefore be realists about objects. In fact the main lesson from transcendental philosophy is that the objects of experience have a lot of universal and necessary features that we can know about. Kant therefore pairs his transcendental idealism with a clear commitment to empirical realism. For example, he insists on:

> the reality (i.e., objective validity) of space in regard to everything that can come before us externally as an object, but at the same time the ideality of space in regard to things when they are considered in themselves through reason. (A28)

In this respect, Kant's transcendental idealism differs from the views of Descartes or Berkeley, who doubted the reality of external objects from within the human standpoint.

1.3 The transcendental deduction

With this we have come to the crux of Kant's critical philosophy, and also to the beginning of his most important and most difficult argument, the "transcendental deduction." Obviously space, time, and the categories constitute experience for us. We cannot have experience any other way. But why should we think that the forms of *our* sensibility and the basic concepts that *we* must rely on as a matter of the finitude of our minds are an appropriate fit for the way things really are? What rational justification can we have for taking our so-constituted experience to be objective? The purpose of Kant's transcendental deduction is to explain how these subjective conditions can constitute *objective* experience. Kant actually produces two versions of this long and complicated argument, one for each edition of the *Critique of Pure Reason*, accordingly known as the A-deduction and the B-deduction. They differ in the details, but have the same overall strategy. Like the table of categories (and much else in the *Critique*), some of the detailed claims Kant makes in the deduction can be challenged, and it is debatable whether the overall argument works. Scholars even debate what the structure of the deduction is, whether it consists of a single argument or two independent ones, what the premises are, and so on. However, all agree that the basic insights that drive the deduction are groundbreaking and define the development of post-Kantian philosophy for well over a century.

The deduction hinges on the notion of the unity of our consciousness. As is clear from the two-stem view, any cognition or experience of objects requires that the mind bring together given intuitions and concepts. This can only occur if the mind itself is unified. If one person has the sense data of the orange patch in her mind, while another has the concept of a book in hers, neither of the two perceives the book. All relevant mental content must be held and processed in the same, single mind. This much is obvious. Kant's genius lies in his realization that the requisite unity of consciousness is more complex and structured than others had realized, and he gives a stunningly subtle analysis of this complexity.

The unity of consciousness is not a passive state. The mind is not a receptacle, like a bowl in which we mix several ingredients to make a cake. Rather, Kant argues that the unity of consciousness is an active mental process of unifying. He calls this process *synthesis*, and he claims that the unity of consciousness that makes cognition possible is a *synthetic* unity. Synthesis is required even for the elementary task of intuiting a manifold of sense data. To have such a manifold, the mind needs to be aware of each element of the manifold, and it needs to be aware of them (or at least to represent them at a pre-cognitive level) as distinct from one another. To intuit an orange patch *and* a brown patch requires that I can represent the orange and the brown as well as their difference. The representation of their difference, and hence the representation of their "two-ness," or manifold, is more than the sum of two distinct representations. It requires the mind to apprehend one datum and keep it present, or reproduce it, while it apprehends the second. To further recognize these sense data as a book on a desk, or even just as a manifold of colored objects, the mind runs through this manifold of intuitions and organizes them according to a rule that constitutes the concept of that object. Kant therefore speaks of a "threefold synthesis" of apprehension, reproduction, and recognition. The A-deduction goes through this threefold synthesis in great detail. The B-deduction goes through it quickly and focuses on trying to spell out the important philosophical claims that follow from the recognition of this fundamental synthetic process.

The first consequence relates to the object side of the synthesis, and addresses the central question of the deduction. Since consciousness of anything is an achievement of synthesis, the structures implicit in this synthesis must be basic determinations of anything that we could encounter as an object of consciousness. That is to say that the very notion of "object" has the structures that accrue to it in synthesis. Kant goes on to claim, more or less plausibly, that these structures are precisely the categories whose objectivity is in question, and that therefore the categories are objectively valid. Note that this conclusion is substantially stronger than the previously established claim that the categories are *a priori* concepts. One could think that concepts are *a priori*, that is, not derived from experience, and that we cannot help but use them in experiencing, but still doubt that they characterize intrinsic features of objects. This is what Hume thought about causation, for example. According to Hume, we cannot get the concept of causation from experience, so it is non-empirical, and we use it all the time in judging matters of fact. But we cannot rationally justify this use. One of Kant's big goals in the *Critique* is to find a solution to Hume's skepticism about the rational legitimacy of our *a priori* concepts. Kant therefore mentions Hume as one of his targets as he introduces the deduction (B128). In the deduction Kant concludes from the necessity of synthesis that we cannot even make sense of the notion of an object aside from categorical determinations. We cannot rationally entertain Hume's skeptical worry about *objects*, because the fully understood notion of an object already answers the skepticism.

A second consequence has to do with self-consciousness. Just as a synthesis is required to represent a manifold, a synthesis is also a necessary condition for self-consciousness. In particular, Kant focuses on a kind of self-consciousness that he calls "apperception." Apperception is my consciousness that a particular thought or cognition is mine. When I see the book on the table, I am conscious that *I* am perceiving it, or at least I can become conscious of this. In general, I can apperceive any act of my consciousness, for otherwise it would not count as an act of *my* consciousness. To apperceive distinct conscious acts is to be conscious of myself as the same consciousness in each apperception, and this *apperception of the sameness of the self* across different self-conscious acts is a further apperceptive act beyond the particular ones. Kant calls this background awareness of the unity of consciousness the "synthetic unity of apperception," because it presupposes a synthesis. In fact Kant thinks that this is the same synthesis that makes consciousness of objects possible. The same necessary conditions apply to object-consciousness and self-consciousness. Kant's argument in the transcendental deduction, therefore, establishes an essential connection between objective features of the world and self-consciousness.

In more general terms, Kant's deduction undermines the starting point of both Humean empiricism and Cartesian skepticism. On the empiricist side, Hume thought that all mental content derives from original impressions. Kant shows that we cannot presume that the mind is simply given discrete impressions of the world. By the time the mind can represent even simple impressions from given objects, it has already engaged in extensive conceptual processes that introduce a robust *a priori* structure into the world of possible experience. Descartes thought that his famous cogito, that is, subjective self-consciousness, is intelligible in complete isolation from any possible object of thought. Kant undermines this claim as well. Self-consciousness involves a synthesis that constitutes general features of objects, so it depends essentially on some relation to objects. One can tease this claim out of Kant's argument in the deduction, and he makes it explicitly in a short argument that he adds to the second edition of the *Critique*, called the "Refutation of Idealism." Here he argues that the mind can only be conscious of itself insofar as it manages to unify the sequence of its own thoughts, experiences, representations, and so on. Unifying a sequence of different states requires that the mind can contrast the flow of the sequence to something persistent and unchanging that is distinct from it. Therefore the fact that we are self-conscious implies awareness of the existence of something permanent outside of us. We can only have a Cartesian cogito if we also have basic background knowledge of objects.

1.4 Kantian themes in phenomenology

Kant's influence on the development of philosophy and psychology throughout the nineteenth and early twentieth century is enormous, and this sketch only scratches the surface of the main ideas from his critical philosophy. But it suffices to highlight several key aspects in which phenomenology from Husserl to Merleau-Ponty is a Kantian enterprise: the idea of constitution, the temporal structure of synthesis, and the idea of subject–object identity.

The first of these is the idea that subjective structures somehow *constitute* the objects of experience. In most of his writings, especially early on, Husserl takes his work to be concerned with spelling out constitutive structures of experience. He maintains much of Kant's cognitivist approach, that is, the idea that the constitutive structures derive from the mental processes that make up conscious experience. But he thinks that these structures are more prevalent and varied than Kant's comparatively austere list of twelve categories. In some of his later work, Husserl develops other approaches in his phenomenology that are closer to the views of Heidegger and Merleau-Ponty.

Both Heidegger and Merleau-Ponty sharply reject the cognitivism of Kant's philosophy. They do not think that the basic structures that enable us to experience an objective world are conceptual, or even primarily mental. They do not think of object-constitution in Kantian or Husserlian terms. Nevertheless they, too, argue that a hidden, pre-personal structure makes experience possible and that it is the job of philosophy to uncover and describe this structure. Rather than concepts, they argue that pre-personal conditions of intelligibility consist of our bodily habits and skills, developed and deployed in a specific cultural setting.

Kant's analysis of the threefold synthesis has a direct impact on the work of both Husserl and Heidegger. It is the basis for Husserl's theory of time consciousness. Inspired by his mentor Franz Brentano (who, in turn, is influenced by Kant), Husserl develops an account according to which we are always conscious of temporally thick objects. A present intention is always coupled with conscious retention of the immediate past and a forward-looking "protention." We discuss this account in Chapter 3. Like Kant, Husserl also uses his analysis of the temporal structure of consciousness to give an account of the nature of the conscious self, analogous to Kant's analysis of apperception.

Heidegger writes and lectures extensively on Kant's analysis of the threefold synthesis (Heidegger 1927/1928, 1929). Since Heidegger rejects Kant's cognitivism, though, his interpretation forces a substantial transformation onto Kant's core insight. The synthesis, for Heidegger, is not an activity of the mind in which it brings distinct conscious representations together. Instead it is a pre-cognitive unifying activity of the whole person, in which your purposive abilities reveal things as already mattering and inviting you to act. Like Kant, Heidegger locates the structure of the self in this unifying structure, and like Husserl he thinks the structure is fundamentally temporal. But both the notion of time and the notion of the self undergo a deep transformation. We discuss Heidegger's account of temporality and the self in Chapter 4.

A final theme from Kant that becomes a fundamental tenet of phenomenology is the idea of subject–object identity. As we saw, Kant argues in the deduction – and more explicitly in the refutation of idealism – that the cognizing subject can only exist as such in relation to some object. This becomes one of the dominant themes in German idealism. In this movement the generation of philosophers after Kant, led by Reinhold, Fichte, Schelling, and Hegel, sets to work on adapting and changing Kant's critical philosophy in order to overcome some of the tensions they perceive in it. In particular, they think that a more detailed account of the identity of the knowing subject and its object can obviate the need for the awkward and unpopular aspect of transcendental idealism that claims that we cannot know objects as they are in themselves. The basic idea is that any perceived limitation on our ability to know things as they are in themselves is due to an incomplete understanding of ourselves as knowing subjects. Hegel drives this thought to its full logical conclusion in his *Phenomenology of Spirit*, in which he argues that we achieve absolute knowledge of the world of objects at the same time, and by virtue of the same conceptual transformation, as we achieve complete self-consciousness.

Hegel's system is a breathtaking and daring revision of Kant's critical philosophy. But Hegel still maintains Kant's overall focus on consciousness. Absolute knowing, for Hegel, is the province of a conscious, conceptually mediated relation to objects. Even though he recognizes the crucial role of desire, the body, physical work, and the fear of death as constitutive processes in a gradual, historical process of achieving self-consciousness, their contribution to his analysis is always conceptual. Heidegger and Merleau-Ponty, on the other hand, think that the essential connection between subject and object consists of non-conceptual interaction. The subject, they argue, only exists and can only find itself "out there" among the entities it is at grips with in the course of pursuing some purposive way of being.

Key terms

a priori – non-empirical. Intuitions, concepts, and cognitions are *a priori* if we do not derive them from, or justify them on the basis of, sensory experience.

apperception – Kant's term for self-consciousness.

cogito – the "I think" that, according to Descartes, constitutes our identities as thinking things. Kant claims that the "I think" must be able to accompany all our representations.

cognition – human knowledge about, or experience of objects. Cognizing objects requires the unification of intuitions and concepts.

cognitivism – Kant's focus on mental cognition as the basic way in which objects are intelligible to us.

intuitions – the given data yielded by our senses. They are spatially and temporally structured, but not yet cognized.

metaphysics – propositions about the world that are necessarily true and whose truth we can establish without recourse to particular experiences of the world.

refutation of idealism – Kant's argument that some external, persisting object distinct from us must exist.

representation – mental content, such as intuitions, concepts, ideas, or judgments. We cognize objects by representing them in our minds.

representationalism – the broad philosophical view that objects are intelligible to us only insofar as we have mental representations of them. This view is a commonplace for Kant and eighteenth-century philosophy, but is rejected by phenomenologists from Heidegger onwards.

sensibility – our capacity to be affected by objects. Sensibility yields a manifold of given sense data called intuitions.

synthesis – a cognitive process of combining a manifold of representations by subsuming them under a concept. Synthesis is the precondition for our ability to cognize objects.

synthetic unity of apperception – the role of self-consciousness in making a synthesis of a manifold of representations possible.

threefold synthesis – a basic form of synthesis that makes up the background processing through which we can acquire representations. It consists of three processes that condition one another: apprehending a manifold, distinguishing individual elements of the manifold, and recognizing them according to a concept.

transcendental deduction – a key argument in Kant's *Critique of Pure Reason*. Kant argues that the processes that enable self-consciousness also make cognition of empirical objects possible according to general rules.

transcendental idealism – Kant's claim that the objects of experience are empirically real, yet transcendentally ideal. This means that anything we can experience as an object is structured by a general lawfulness. However, we cannot know anything about the nature of things considered beyond the human standpoint.

transcendental philosophy – Kant's philosophical stance in the *Critique* *of Pure Reason.* Transcendental philosophy aims to uncover the hidden background conditions that make experience possible and structure experience according to general rules.

understanding (*Verstand*) – Kant's term for our capacity to use concepts.

Further reading

Allison, H. (2004). *Kant's Transcendental Idealism: An Interpretation and Defense.* New Haven: Yale University Press.

Henrich, D. (1994). *The Unity of Reason: Essays on Kant's Philosophy*, ed. R. Velkley. Cambridge, MA: Harvard University Press.

Longuenesse, B. (2005). *Kant on the Human Standpoint.* Cambridge: Cambridge University Press.

2

The Rise of Experimental Psychology

Kant's critical philosophy is the most important philosophical precursor of phenomenology. Another important piece of the background to phenomenology is the rise of psychology as a scientific discipline in the nineteenth century. Wilhelm Wundt draws on work in psychophysics by Gustav Fechner to rebut traditional arguments that a scientific psychology is impossible because its subject matter cannot be observed and measured with precision. Kant holds this traditional view, and it is therefore part of the philosophical orthodoxy of the nineteenth century. Wundt's energetic pursuit of scientific psychology, consequently, brings about a rift and establishes psychology as a separate field, rather than a sub-discipline of philosophy. The relevance to phenomenology is twofold. First, in its beginnings, phenomenology thinks of itself as a type of psychology. Husserl calls it "descriptive psychology." Its self-conception is bound up with a reconfiguration of the field, which is rooted in basic questions about the nature of the mind. The emergence of scientific psychology contributes to these basic questions. Second, Wundt's scientific psychology is an important foil for Gestalt psychology (Chapter 5) and ecological psychology (Chapter 10). Both of these approaches interact closely with phenomenology's conception of the mind and argue against the dominant views of perception and cognition of Wundt's school.

2.1 Wilhelm Wundt and the rise of scientific psychology

Besides his decisive impact on phenomenology, Kant also deeply influenced the development of scientific psychology, albeit in a more indirect way. While the phenomenologists pursued an openly Kantian project at the margins of the mainstream neo-Kantian philosophy of the late nineteenth century, the rise of scientific psychology as an academic discipline separate from philosophy took a more tortuous path. For Kant argued against the very possibility of scientific psychology, both in his *Critique of Pure Reason* and in his *Metaphysical Foundations of Natural Sciences* (*MFNS*). Given Kant's stature in the German academy of the nineteenth century, his arguments needed to be addressed by anyone who wished to engage in scientific psychology.

Thus Wilhelm Wundt, the founder of the world's first experimental psychology lab in 1879 at Leipzig and widely known as the "founding father of psychology," addresses Kant's arguments in the early pages of his textbook *Principles of Physiological Psychology* (1874/1902/1904). He begins with a summary of Kant's arguments from *MFNS*:

> Kant once declared that psychology was incapable of ever raising itself to the rank of an exact natural science. The reasons that he gives for this opinion have often been repeated in later times. In the first place, Kant says, psychology cannot become an exact science because mathematics is inapplicable to the phenomenon of the internal sense; the pure internal perception, in which mental phenomena must be constructed – time – has but one dimension. In the second place, however, it cannot even become an experimental science, because in it the manifold of internal observation cannot be arbitrarily varied – still less, another thinking subject be submitted to one's experiments, conformably to the end in view; moreover, the very fact of observation means alteration of the observed object. The first of these objections is erroneous; the second is, at the least, one-sided. (1874, p. 6)

Wundt responds to these objections to the possibility of scientific psychology by drawing on nineteenth-century advances in sensory physiology.

For most of the nineteenth century, our current understanding of the division between the sciences and humanities was not yet in place. Hermann Helmholtz, for example, made crucial contributions in geometry, physics, physiology, and philosophy. In the 1840s, Helmholtz was a member of the Berlin Physical Society, whose members signed an oath to explain life and consciousness in terms of only known physical and chemical principles. Consciousness, that is, is made of the same stuff, obeying the same laws, as everything else in the universe. Helmholtz invented the ophthalmoscope (1850), making it possible to study vision in greater detail than ever before. He also was the first to measure the velocity of neural conduction, which he estimated as 25–40 meters per second. Combined with his views that perceptual experience was nothing other than the activity of neurons, this implies that our experience is not of what is happening right now, but of the very recent past. These and many other findings lead Helmholtz to a detailed theory of perception as unconscious inference that is equally physiological and philosophical and that continues to inform twenty-first-century views of perception.

Along with Helmholtz's work, members of the Berlin Physical Society and their fellow travelers produced innovations in *psychophysics*, seeking correlations between changes to the material world and changes in the mind that experiences it. Gustav Fechner's *Elemente der Psychophysik* (1860; *Elements of Psychophysics*) describes decades of work by Ernst Weber and Fechner himself, among others, from the middle 1800s. Research in this period by Weber, for example, focused on *just noticeable differences* (*jnd*), differences in physical magnitudes (mass, brightness, intensity of sound) that are sufficient for an experimental participant to notice. For example, participants are given a standard object and asked to wield test objects each of which is slightly heavier (or lighter) than the standard object and to report when they get to a heavier (or lighter) one. The jnd is the mass difference (measured by a non-human device) that leads to a difference in human-experienced mass. Studying this in multiple sensory modalities led to what is now known as Weber's law: the ratio of the change that leads to a jnd to the standard object is a constant. So, if I is the magnitude of the standard object and DI is the size of the jnd,

$$\frac{\Delta I}{I} = constant$$

For example, suppose that for a 20-gram standard mass, participants do not notice that an object is heavier until it weighs at least 22 grams and do not notice that it is lighter until it weighs less than 18 grams (these numbers are for illustration only). Then $DI = 2$, and $DI/I = 2/20 = 0.1$. According to Weber's law, the jnd for a 60-gram standard object should be 60 grams * 0.1 = 6 grams, so participants should not notice a difference in weight between the standard object and a test object until the test object weighs 54 grams or less, or 66 grams or more. Similarly, there should be no noticeable differences between masses between 90 and 110 grams for a 100-gram standard object (100 grams * 0.1 = 10 grams), or between masses of 900 and 1,100 grams if the standard object weighs one kilogram (1,000 grams * 0.1 = 100 grams), and so on.

These findings provide Wundt with a reply to Kant's first objection, that mathematical methods cannot be applied to perception. Wundt points out that time is not the only variable in experience: there is also the quality of the sensation, which is proportional to the stimulus. "But, as a matter of fact, our sensations and feelings are intensive magnitudes, which form temporal series. The course of mental events has, therefore, at any rate two dimensions; and with this fact is given the general possibility of its presentation in mathematical form" (1874, p. 6).

This takes care of Kant's first objection to scientific psychology. Wundt also relies on psychophysics to rebut Kant's claim that one cannot get knowledge of the mind from introspection. First, Wundt agrees with Kant that *ordinary* introspection is unreliable. Psychophysics, though, shows that one can nonetheless measure experience. It is worth quoting Wundt at length on this:

The arguments that Kant adduces in support of his second objection, that the inner experience is inaccessible to experimental investigation, are all derived from purely internal sources, from the subjective flow of processes; and there, of course, we cannot challenge its validity. Our psychical experiences are, primarily, indeterminate magnitudes; they are incapable of exact treatment until they have been referred to determinate units of measurement, which in turn may be brought into constant causal relations with other given magnitudes. But we have, in the experimental modification of consciousness by external stimuli, a means to this very end – to the discovery of the units of measurement and the relations required. Modification from without enables us to subject our mental processes to arbitrarily determined conditions, over which we have complete control and which we may keep constant or vary as we will. Hence the objection urged against experimental psychology, that it seeks to do away with introspection, which is the sine qua non of any psychology, is based upon a misunderstanding. The only form of introspection which experimental psychology seeks to banish from the science is that professing self-observation which thinks it can arrive directly, without further assistance, at an exact characterization of mental facts, and which is therefore inevitably exposed to the grossest self-deception. The aim of the experimental procedure is to substitute for this subjective method, whose sole resource is an inaccurate inner perception, a true and reliable introspection, and to this end it brings consciousness under accurately adjustable objective conditions. (1874, p. 7)

Here, Wundt not only gives a (partial) response to Kant, but also lays out the plan for the whole of his psychology. First, Wundt makes a distinction between inner and outer experience, acknowledging that inner experience is indeed inaccessible to experimental methods. Indeed, what is generally known as Wundtian psychology, the kind that was undertaken in his laboratory at Leipzig and in which he trained nearly every member of the first generation of scientific psychologists, is his science of outer experience. Wundt's psychology of inner experience, called *Völkerpsychologie*, had virtually no influence on later psychology (Leahey 2000). *Völkerpsychologie* (Wundt 1912) applies historical and anthropological methods of the kind Kant recommended in his *Anthropology from a Pragmatic Point of View* (1798). So Wundt accepts Kant's arguments about inner experience, but argues that it is possible to experimentally access outer experience using the method of psychophysics. Psychophysics does not do away with introspection, but uses trained introspectors in highly controlled circumstances to experiment upon the basic elements of conscious experience. Subjects, for example, are presented with a series of tones that are increasingly high in pitch and are asked to report when they experience a pitch difference; or they are asked to press a key when a light appears on a screen; or they are asked to press when a blue light (but not a red light) appears on a screen. Experiments such as these are used to examine the variety of sensations humans are capable of having, and the temporal duration of sensory processes.

Using psychophysics to study outer experience places strict limits on the scope of experimental psychology. According to Wundt, psychology is the study of the elements of immediate conscious experience:

> Psychological analysis leaves us with two such elements [of conscious experience], of specifically different character: with sensations, which as the ultimate and irreducible elements of ideas we may term the objective elements of the mental life, and with feelings, which accompany these objective elements as their subjective complements, and are referred not to external things but to the state of consciousness itself. In this sense, therefore, we call blue, yellow, warm, cold, etc., sensations; pleasantness, unpleasantness, excitement, depression, etc., feelings. (1874, p. 12)

Sensations and feelings are the atoms of conscious experience. They are combined by unconscious processes to form the molecules: sensations combine to form ideas; feelings combine to form complex feelings. Wundt's experimental psychology was reductionist in that it focused on the smallest possible bits of conscious experience. It was also atomistic in that it thought that the elements maintained their identities in whatever context they appeared. ("As conscious contents, blue is and remains blue, and the idea of an object is always a thing ideated in the outside world, whether the external stimulus or the thing outside of us be really present or not" [1874, pp. 13–14].)

Wundt's pioneering scientific psychology was, thus, a reductionist, atomistic science of outer experience. It was a successful science, and Wundt was very influential. He published more than 60,000 pages during his lifetime, and educated thousands of students in his methods (Fancher 1995). One of these students was William James, the "founding father" of American psychology. James later became an opponent of Wundt's methods, which he mocked as "brass instrument psychology." Another was E. B. Titchener, a proponent of Wundt's methods who founded the psychology department at Cornell. In his 1898 textbook Titchener claimed to have identified more than 30,000 elementary visual sensations (1898b, p. 40). Most importantly for current purposes, Wundt's was the scientific psychology that was in place when Husserl began his work as a phenomenologist. Husserl criticized Wundt specifically in establishing his phenomenological methods. Moreover, the psychological theories of the first half of the twentieth century that we will discuss later in the book defined themselves explicitly in opposition to Wundt's views. The Gestalt psychologists, who were profoundly influential on Merleau-Ponty and on Gibson, rejected Wundt's atomism (see Chapter 5). The functionalists and pragmatists, who were profoundly influential on Gibson, also rejected Wundt's narrow focus on conscious experience (see Chapter 10).

2.2 William James and functionalism

At the same time that Wundt developed his scientific psychology, William James was teaching a very different version of the science, one whose primary influence was Darwin. For Wundt, scientific psychology was the use of the methods of psychophysics to study simple sensations. As he wrote in his 1890 textbook *The Principles of Psychology*, James doubted that there even were simple sensations, and thought that Wundt's focus on them was harmful to the science.

> Most books start with sensations, as the simplest mental facts, and pro-
> ceed synthetically, constructing each higher stage from those below it.
> But this is abandoning the empirical method of investigation. No one
> ever had a simple sensation by itself. Consciousness, from our natal
> day, is of a teeming multiplicity of objects and relations, and what we
> call simple sensations are results of discriminative attention, pushed
> often to a very high degree. It is astonishing what havoc is wrought

in psychology by admitting at the outset apparently innocent suppositions, that nevertheless contain a flaw. The bad consequences develop
themselves later on, and are irremediable, being woven through the
whole texture of the work. The notion that sensations, being the simplest things, are the first things to take up in psychology is one of these
suppositions. (1890, p. 225)

Focusing exclusively on simple sensations, James argued, missed most of
what a science of the mind should be about:

Psychology is the Science of Mental Life, both of its phenomena and
of their conditions. The phenomena are such things as we call feelings,
desires, cognitions, reasonings, decisions, and the like; and, superficially considered, their variety and complexity is such as to leave a
chaotic impression on the observer. (1890, p. 1)

The science imagined by James was thus much broader in scope than the
studies of sensations being undertaken at Wundt's institute in Leipzig.
Although not mentioned in this quotation, habits, emotions, consciousness, instinct, perception, imagination, and memory receive explicit
attention in the text, along with the mental lives of infants and non-
human animals. Of course, James thought we should study sensations
– he devotes a chapter to them – but not as the sole or foundational
subject matter as Wundt did.

Because James was explicitly Darwinist in approach, he argued for
understanding each of these aspects of the mind as an *adaptation* to the
environment. Just as your lungs are a lifelong adaptation to our oxygen-
rich atmosphere, your belief that you are holding a book is a temporary
adaptation to your current situation. Aspects of our mental life, in other
words, were to be understood in terms of what they are for. Because of
this, Titchener (1898a) mockingly called the Jamesian approach "functionalism," a name that stuck. Understanding the mind as a collection of
adaptations makes the contrast with Wundtian psychology even starker.
Particular adaptations must be understood in the context of the environment, and in the context of the whole animal. Lungs have their functions
only in oxygen-rich environments, and only when paired with hearts
and circulatory systems. Moreover, adaptations can only be understood
historically, over developmental and evolutionary time. Understanding
how lungs came to have the functions that they do requires understanding how our lungs develop and how they functioned in our evolutionary
ancestors. While Wundt and his followers focused narrowly on instantaneous simple sensations, functionalist psychologists studied aspects of

the mind in the context of the environment, over developmental and evolutionary timescales.

James published his textbook at the time when psychology began to become a discipline separate from philosophy. He stayed with philosophy, and his own work became increasingly philosophical. He called his later philosophical views "radical empiricism." He characterizes radical empiricism as consisting "first of a postulate, next of a fact, and finally of a generalized conclusion" (1909 p. xii). His postulate is that all and only things that are experienced exist. His fact is that relations are experienced. It follows, of course, that relations exist. His generalized conclusion is that the world is experienced directly. This last point is an explicit rejection of the Kantian distinction between the empirical world that we experience and the world-in-itself. James is claiming that there is only the world of what he calls "pure experience." His view amounts to a sort of neutral monism – there is only one world, and it is neither material nor mental. The world experienced and the experiences themselves are the very same thing:

> As "subjective" we say that the experience represents; as "objective" it is represented. What represents and what is represented is here numerically the same; but we must remember that no dualism of being represented and representing resides in the experience *per se*. In its pure state, or when isolated, there is no self-splitting of it into consciousness and what the consciousness is "of." Its subjectivity and objectivity are functional attributes solely, realized only when the experience is "taken," i.e., talked-of, twice, considered along with its two differing contexts respectively, by a new retrospective experience, of which that whole past complication now forms the fresh content. The instant field of the present is at all times what I call the "pure" experience. It is only virtually or potentially either object or subject as yet. For the time being, it is plain, unqualified actuality, or existence, a simple *that*. (1904, p. 484)

This passage is from "Does consciousness exist?" (1904). James' answer to the question is that it does not exist, if what you mean by consciousness is something inside your mind and representing the external world. This view becomes very influential on the work of James Gibson (Chapter 10).

2.3 The structuralism–functionalism debate

At the end of the nineteenth century, psychology was growing quickly as a discipline, as more and more universities opened new departments and research institutes. Because there were two importantly different versions of scientific psychology at the time, each university had to decide whether its psychology faculty would be Wundtian structuralists or Jamesian functionalists. This led to a fierce and often impolite debate between structuralists and functionalists in the 1890s and the first decade of the twentieth century. Because psychology was a new discipline at the time, much of the debate was published in what we now think of as philosophy journals (such as *Mind* and *The Philosophical Review*). Here we will consider three key entries in the debate: E. B. Titchener's "Simple reactions" (1895) and "The postulates of a structural psychology" (1898a) and John Dewey's "The reflex arc concept in psychology" (1896).

The names "structuralism" and "functionalism" appear for the first time in Titchener's "The postulates of a structural psychology" (1898a). Titchener uses these names to make a straightforward argument by analogy with research in biology. In biology, one must first do anatomy, to see what the parts of the organism are; then one does physiology, to see how those anatomical parts behave. Only after these two steps is it appropriate to speculate about the function of these parts and processes. Structural psychology, Titchener's new name for Wundtian atomistic psychology, respects this ordering; functional psychology, Titchener's new name for Jamesian descriptive psychology, does not – it starts by speculating about what psychological entities are for, before knowing what psychological entities exist.

The debate between these two positions precedes the invention of their names, however. In "Simple reactions" (1895), Titchener recounts and defends the experimental results of Ludwig Lange, a researcher in Wundt's lab. Lange had gathered evidence that experimental participants have slower reaction times if they attend as much as they can to the sensory stimulus (e.g., a flashing light), rather than attending as much as they can to their behavioral response to it (e.g., pushing a button). Several of the later attempts to replicate the finding failed to do so. On its face, this does not seem to be the sort of claim that would attract criticism, or the need for defense from that criticism. In fact, however, the experiments stand in for the whole of the structuralist research program. "The simple reaction-time is the interval elapsing between the mental 'receiving' of a sense-impression and the execution of a movement in response to that impression" (1895, p. 74). In structuralist psychology, all of the basic

atoms of conscious experiences, as well as all of the unconscious infer-
ences that are involved in perception and thought, exist in that interval.
In Lange's findings, for example, the atoms required for the two tasks
are the same, except for the object of attention. Therefore, any differences in timing that occurs is because of differences in temporal duration
between attention to stimulus and attention to response. So experiments
like Lange's are investigations of the temporal properties of the atoms of
conscious experience, in this case two different forms of attention. This
kind of experiment is the foundation of the structuralist approach. "The
reaction method has been extensively employed for the determination of
the duration and for the analysis of certain complex mental 'acts': cognition, discrimination, association, choice, etc." (1895, pp. 77–8).

According to structuralists like Titchener, not just simple reactions but
all mental activities have the following structure: first, there is a stimulus,
caused by physical stimulation of receptors; then there is a linear series
of mental acts; then there is a behavioral response. Suppose that there are
two simple reactions, A and B, which differ only in that A requires the
series of mental acts one, two, three, and four whereas B requires only
mental acts one, two, and three. Then one can determine the duration of
mental act four by subtracting the time it takes to perform simple reaction B from the time it takes to perform simple reaction A.

Although he mentions neither Lange nor Titchener, Dewey is directly
responding to them in his "The reflex arc concept in psychology" (1896).
Dewey describes the structuralist view of simple reactions as a "reflex
arc." (It is an arc because it begins in the body, ascends to the mind,
and returns to the body.) He argues that the structuralist understanding
of the reflex arc commits "the empiricist fallacy," the assumption that
the parts of something are prior to the whole. The empiricist fallacy, in
other words, is nothing other than the Wundtian and structuralist claim
that whole mental acts, like the reflex arc, are molecules composed of
more elementary atomic sensations and feelings. In rejecting this, Dewey
argues that all actions, from simple reactions to the most complex intelligent behavior, are *organic circuits* that cannot be understood by breaking
them into parts. Out of context, a part of an action is devoid of meaning
of any kind, a "series of jerks." Furthermore, the division of a simple
reflex into parts can only be done after the fact. Something can only be
identified as a stimulus *after* one identifies the response. In other words,
in an organic circuit, what the response is determines the nature of the
stimulus. That is, a visual stimulus never results in mere seeing; rather it
leads to seeing-in-order-to-grasp or seeing-in-order-to-identify or seeing-
in-order-to-touch. So, the Wundtian and structuralist idea that different
simple reactions are composed of the same parts, mixed and matched,

is fallacious. This view is an important precursor of James Gibson's ecological psychology (Chapter 10)

The back-and-forth between structuralists and functionalists did not end with a decisive victory, but simply fizzled out. Most American psychologists of the first ten years of the twentieth century considered themselves functionalists. In Europe, and especially Germany, function-alism found essentially no footing. The debate was effectively ended by the rise of behaviorism, a version of psychology that led the discipline into closer alliance with the natural sciences, and away from the humani-ties permanently.

Key terms

feelings – in Wilhelm Wundt's psychology, the irreducible, affective ele-ments of experience. Feelings are atoms from which experiences are built.

functionalism – an early twentieth-century psychological movement, inspired by the work of William James. Functionalists studied the mind, emotions, habits, and so on as temporary adaptations to the environment.

inner experiences – in Wilhelm Wundt's psychology, complex thoughts, emotions, and attitudes. Inner experience is inaccessible by scientific psychology.

outer experiences – in Wilhelm Wundt's psychology, simple sensations and feelings. Outer experience can be studied scientifically using the methods of psychophysics.

sensations – in Wilhelm Wundt's psychology, the irreducible, qualitative elements of experience. Sensations are atoms from which experiences are built.

structuralism – an early twentieth-century psychological movement, inspired by the work of Wilhelm Wundt. Structuralists study the mind by identifying the elements of conscious experience.

Further reading

Many of the works discussed in this chapter are available online at the Psych Classics website, ed. C. Green. http://psychclassics.yorku.ca

James, W. (1890). *The Principles of Psychology*. Boston: Henry Holt.

– (1904). "Does consciousness exist?" *Journal of Philosophy, Psychology, and Scientific Methods*, 1: 477–91.

Wundt, W. M. (1874/1902/1904). *Principles of Physiological Psychology*, trans. E. B. Titchener from the 5th German edn., published 1902. (Original German edn. published 1874.)

3

Edmund Husserl and Transcendental Phenomenology

3.1 Transcendental phenomenology

Husserl's phenomenology is a systematic study of the *essential* content of our experiences. By "essential" Husserl means the content that makes experiences into experiences of a certain kind. For example, to *see* a tree, as opposed to imagining or hallucinating one, means to see it as robust and permanent. The tree did not just appear and will not suddenly disappear. If we did not experience the tree as temporally robust, then our experience would not count as really *seeing* a tree. Importantly, some essential content of experiences goes beyond what is immediately presented to the senses. For example, we see the tree as having a back side, even though that other side is not visible to us. Features such as the tree's back side and persistence in the near future are not directly given to the senses, but they are nevertheless essential to the experience. Husserl thinks they are contributed by the mind. He claims that we can systematically spell out essential features of the entire range of different mental acts that make up our experiences of objects.

This idea of phenomenology resembles Kant's idea of transcendental philosophy. Both rest on the central claim that some important features of our experience are subjectively constituted. Indeed, for much of his career Husserl calls his project "transcendental" phenomenology, and many Kantian arguments appear in Husserl's work. But there are some basic differences. One difference concerns the focus of the analysis. Kant focuses on *a priori* contributions of the mind and tries to spell out universal and necessary features of experience. Husserl's notion of an essence is broader than Kant's notion of the *a priori*. The essences Husserl identifies can change over time, or in different cultural contexts. Husserl also does not focus primarily on concepts. Some of his "essences" are nonconceptual features of an act of consciousness. Another key difference lies in the method of analysis. While Kant's distinctive method lies in his analysis of background conditions that must obtain in order to explain familiar experiences, Husserl proceeds by describing experiences in great detail. Indeed, Husserl sometimes calls his phenomenology "descriptive psychology." He is convinced that careful, elaborate description of our experience can reveal essential features that have been overlooked by previous philosophers. While Kant's constitutive conditions are hidden in the background and only revealed through transcendental arguments, Husserl's essences are evident in the experiences themselves once we know how to look for them.

Husserl is often called the "founder" of phenomenology. Between 1890 and 1900 he started using this term to denote his specific approach to philosophy, and in his 1913 *Ideas* (the full title is *Ideas Pertaining to a Pure Phenomenology and a Phenomenological Philosophy* – succinctness was not one of Husserl's virtues) he defined the method and basic concepts of phenomenology. He hoped that this would lay the groundwork for a collaborative research project, or a phenomenological "school," in which his followers would use the method he had defined to complete phenomenological research in various domains. That did not happen. Even though Husserl had important followers – notably Heidegger, Aron Gurwitsch, Max Scheler, and Edith Stein – for the most part they deviated from his method and his choice of topics. Husserlian transcendental phenomenology differs in important ways from the approaches of Heidegger and Merleau-Ponty (and, to a lesser extent, Sartre), which are usually called "existential phenomenology." Instead of a rigorous research project, phenomenology became a loosely defined movement.

3.2 Franz Brentano

Husserl's phenomenology draws on his interests and background in mathematics, psychology (such as it was at the time of his studies in the 1870s and 1880s), and Kantian philosophy. He started out studying physics and mathematics in Leipzig, where he also attended Wundt's lectures on psychology. After completing a doctorate in mathematics, Husserl went to

Vienna to study philosophy with Franz Brentano. Brentano was an unusually original thinker and fascinating teacher. He attempted to lay a new foundation for a philosophical analysis of the mind, combining insights from his study of Kant, Aristotle, and the scholastics with a descriptive, common-sense approach to mental experiences inspired by Hume. It is noteworthy that two important pioneers of Gestalt psychology were among Brentano's many students. Carl Stumpf, who did foundational work on the psychology of harmony and dissonance, was one of Brentano's earliest students. Husserl went on to write his philosophical dissertation under Stumpf. Later, Stumpf became professor of philosophy and director of the Institute of Psychology at the University of Berlin, where he trained Max Wertheimer, Kurt Koffka, Wolfgang Köhler, Adhemar Gelb, and Kurt Lewin. Another student of Brentano was Christian von Ehrenfels, who introduced the concept of a *Gestalt* to psychology. We will see later that phenomenology and Gestalt psychology converge. Gurwitsch makes their commonalities explicit. Both Sartre and Merleau-Ponty engaged deeply with Gestalt psychology, and so did Gibson.

Husserl takes three important basic ideas from Brentano. The first is the emphasis on description in the study of the mind. In his main book, *Psychologie vom Empirischen Standpunkte* ("Psychology from an Empirical Standpoint"), Brentano sought to develop an analysis of mental content from the ground up in a scientific way. His psychology rests on the "empirical" point of view, not insofar as it uses the methods of "empirical" psychology – this was Wundt's proposal, and Brentano thought it was misguided. Rather, Brentano thought that psychology ought to derive its basic grasp of its subject matter from careful observation, analogous to the observation of nature that lies at the heart of the natural sciences. So for Brentano psychology must begin with careful observation and classification of the mental. The term "descriptive psychology" derives from Brentano's work, and Husserl still uses it to refer to phenomenology in the introduction to his first main book, the *Logical Investigations*.

Brentano's first move is to delimit mental entities as such. Since Descartes, it is common to define the difference between mental and physical entities in terms of spatial extension. All physical entities are extended, while mental entities are not. Brentano does not think this criterion describes mental phenomena well. The sensation of a tingling in my leg, for example, may appear to me as extended. Instead of extension Brentano turns to a notion from scholastic philosophy, intentionality, as a positive feature of the mental. Intentionality means "directedness" or "aboutness," and Brentano claims that all mental content has this feature. In other words, all mental experiences are directed at an object that is part of the content of that experience. Brentano describes it as follows:

> Every psychical phenomenon contains something within itself as an object. . . . In representation something is represented; in a judgment something is accepted or rejected; in love loved, in hatred hated, in desire desired, etc. (1874, p. 115)

Husserl takes over this idea that intentionality is the basic characteristic of mental phenomena.

Note that in Brentano's characterization the intentional object of a mental experience is internal to that experience itself. In the case of judging, imagining, or hallucinating this seems clear enough. But it is somewhat counter-intuitive in other cases. For example, it seems more natural to say that when I see a tree, that tree is the intentional object of the experience, and the tree is "out there" in the real world, rather than in my mind. Similarly the object of my love, hatred, or desire is typically something in the world. However, Brentano thinks that this objection mistakes the nature of intentionality. The tree may be the intended object of the perception, but the fact that the perceptual experience is an experience *of* a tree is a structural feature of the experience, and as such has nothing to do with the actual tree in the world. Brentano here makes a presumption that dominates philosophy in the early modern period through Kant. The mind is directly aware of representations of objects, not of those objects themselves. And the representational object is the intentional object of the mental act.

This leads to a third basic point that Husserl takes from Brentano. Following Kant, Brentano distinguishes between inner and outer sense, where inner sense is our capacity for perceiving or intuiting mental phenomena. For Brentano, a second distinguishing mark of mental phenomena is that they "can only be perceived in inner consciousness" (1874, p. 118). This has an important consequence, for inner consciousness is distinguished by its "immediate, infallible evidence" (1874, p. 119). If I see a tree, I am conscious that I am having that experience, and I cannot possibly be wrong about that. I can, of course, be wrong about the tree. Maybe I am merely imagining one, or I am looking at a mural painting of a tree, or I am fooled by a cleverly disguised cell phone tower. But I have "infallible evidence" that I am having the experience of seeing a tree. Husserl similarly thinks that intentional acts are immanent, that is, mind-internal, and that they are given to us completely and with a special, infallible evidence. This contrasts with transcendent features of the objects themselves. Objects are transcendent insofar as there is always more to them than we can become conscious of.

Heidegger and Merleau-Ponty disagree with Husserl's view that phenomenology must focus on immanent content. Husserl focuses on cognitive structures in the mind. Heidegger and Merleau-Ponty instead focus on structures involving bodily skills at grips with the world. For them, the features that constitute the intelligibility of our objective experiences are in the world itself.

3.3 Between logic and psychology

Husserl combines mathematics, psychology, and philosophy in his first book, the 1891 *Philosophy of Arithmetic*. The subtitle of this book is "Psychological and Logical Investigations." The book's main concern is to give an account of the nature of mathematical entities, especially the concepts of multitude and unity that constitute the concept of number. Rather than trying to define multitudes, Husserl aims to give a "psychological characterization of the phenomena on which the abstraction of this concept rests" (1891, p. 21). He argues that these phenomena are "reflections on the psychic act" in which we unify a collection of parts. His suggestion is that our ideas of numbers and addition derive from our mental experiences of putting distinct parts together.

Gottlob Frege wrote a devastating critical review of this book. Frege's review argues that Husserl makes a basic mistake by trying to explain logical and mathematical objects in terms of psychological processes. There is a fundamental difference between a number, a mathematical law, or an equation on the one hand, and the way we experience, discover, or come to construct these things on the other. Mathematics and logic are precise and universally valid, while our psychological processes are often vague and changeable. Frege calls this basic mistake "psychologism." His critique affected Husserl deeply. In his later writings Husserl rejects this early work. He begins his next book, the *Logical Investigations*, with an extensive volume of *Prolegomena* in which he develops a wide range of arguments against psychologism (Husserl 1900).

Nevertheless, by focusing on the shared ground of logic and psychology, the *Philosophy of Arithmetic* shows the beginnings of the basic idea that led Husserl to phenomenology. Our experience contains elements that go beyond what is given to us. Such elements appear to originate in our minds. And yet they do not have the character of individual, subjective mental events. In one especially interesting section of the *Philosophy of Arithmetic*, Husserl points out that certain mathematical entities resemble our experience of collective terms, such as swarms, groups, heaps, and so forth. In such things, Husserl writes, we encounter a "figure" that cannot be reduced to, or constructed from, the individual members that make them up. A heap of apples consists of nothing but apples, but nevertheless it presents a "figure" that shines forth immediately and that we perceive as a unity distinct from a mere aggregate sum of apples (1891, p. 204). Husserl himself compares this section of the book to work by von Ehrenfels. And while Husserl does not pursue this line of thought further in the direction of psychology, it informs his conception of phenomenology. The mental structures that constitute experiences of an objective world, and which phenomenology aims to study, are closely related to the original notion of a Gestalt. (Gestalt psychology later develops this notion in much greater detail. One big difference from Husserl's proto-phenomenological notion of a figure is that a Gestalt is an object in the world. In other words, Gestalt psychologists claim that the heap, just like the apples, is an object in the world that we can perceive. See Chapter 5.)

By the time of the *Logical Investigations*, Husserl has developed this basic idea into a more robust conception of phenomenology. Armed with the detailed criticism of psychologism in the *Prolegomena*, he sets out to analyze immanent structures that determine the content of various experiences. In contrast to his earlier approach, he now explicitly denies that "reflection on psychic acts" can be the source of logical categories such as unity, multitude, or number (1901b, p. 668). In other words, psychology is not the right science for explaining the origin and meaning of the elements of mathematics and logic. Mathematical and logical objects – such as number, multitude, unity, being, negation, or consequence – are given as the objects of our acts, that is, we experience them as objective. The question instead becomes what the immanent structure of such acts is, so that they can be properly directed at logical or mathematical entities. This question characterizes the central aim of Husserlian phenomenology.

3.4 *Ideas*

The most systematic exposition of Husserl's central view is his 1913 book *Ideas Pertaining to a Pure Phenomenology and a Phenomenological Philosophy*. One of Husserl's main tasks in this book is to make his conception of phenomenology clear and methodologically rigorous. He points out that phenomenology resembles and is inspired by Descartes' skepticism and Kant's transcendental idealism. However, Husserl also insists on crucial differences. He claims the type of reflection demanded by phenomenology is brand-new in the history of philosophy. It requires a shift in attitude toward the content of our mental states that is quite unusual and probably was impossible to discern prior to the increased attention devoted to psychology in the latter half of the nineteenth century.

Husserl makes two important decisions to help capture the novelty and subtlety of phenomenology. First, he introduces a phenomenological *method*. This method consists of several steps, called *reductions*, that each reader needs to perform and constantly remind herself of, in order to remain focused on the proper object of phenomenology (see below for more on reductions). This method is designed to prevent confusions of the kind that led Husserl himself to commit the errors of psychologism in his earlier work, failing to distinguish between subjective and objective structures. Husserl's intention was that his readers and followers would learn to perform the reductions and then proceed to do phenomenology from within the standpoint reached through this method. In other words, he did not expect his explanation of the method itself to become a topic of contention among philosophers. As it turned out, however, that is precisely what happened. Heidegger thought that a central aspect of Husserl's method was incoherent and undermined much of Husserl's phenomenology.

Husserl's second decision is to introduce, as far as feasible, an original vocabulary for the basic concepts of phenomenology. So, for example, he wants to avoid the words "*a priori*," "ideas" (in the technical sense), "sense," and "intuition," because he worries that the traditional meaning of these terms would mislead his readers and obscure the proper topic of phenomenology.

Above, we said that phenomenology studies the essential content of experiences that is not given to our senses from objects. In other words, phenomenology focuses on non-arbitrary contributions that we, the experiencers, make in constituting our experience. Consequently, Husserl's phenomenological method consists of two distinct reductions. He calls one the *eidetic reduction*. It is supposed to shift our focus from accidental or non-essential features of an experience to essential ones. The other is called the *transcendental reduction*. It aims to shift our focus from the object of experience to the way that object is constituted. Taken together they add up to the *phenomenological reduction*. We will discuss it below, after a quick survey of some basic terms.

3.4.1 Intentionality

Phenomenology wants to explain the meaning of our experiences. Husserl thinks that all experiences that bear some kind of meaning are conscious, and phenomenology therefore focuses on conscious events. Consciousness is a steady, uninterrupted stream, which shifts and vacillates between manifold objects and attitudes. Husserl divides the conscious stream into individual acts. An *act* of consciousness is any portion of the stream that has a single object as its content and consists of a single attitude toward that object. For example, seeing a tree is an act, admiring the majesty of that same tree is a distinct act, remembering the tree is another one, and reflecting on one's perception of the tree is yet another act. Acts can be instantaneous, or they can go on for some time. Several acts can occur simultaneously, and there can be stretches in which the stream of consciousness is interrupted and no acts take place. So we cannot individuate acts in terms of the chronological flow of the stream of consciousness. Instead we individuate acts by their content.

Strictly speaking, phenomenology does not investigate the structures of consciousness as such, but the structures of specific acts of consciousness. All meaningful experiences occur in acts. An experience is only meaningful if it has some content, and that means that it takes place in an act, even if that act is obscure and confused and misapprehends its object. A vague memory of an impossible object is still an act.

Husserl, following Brentano, thinks that all conscious acts are *unified* and *transparent*. The unity of conscious events allows us to divide an amorphous stream into distinct acts: one act per attitude and object. Transparency means that besides experiencing our acts, we can also be self-consciously aware that we are experiencing them and we can reflect on every structural aspect of the act. The transparency of mental acts therefore has important implications for Husserl's method of phenomenology. Since all content of our mental acts is available to self-conscious reflection, phenomenology can spell out the essential structures of acts by reflecting. (On an interesting side note, Sigmund Freud also heard Brentano's lectures in Vienna. Freud, of course, rejected the claim to transparency, arguing that many meaningful experiences exert their significance precisely because they are not transparent to us.)

For Husserl the most important of the features of consciousness is its *intentionality*. We can often use the intentional object to individuate acts, though different acts can share an object. For instance, the same tree may be the object of the distinct acts of seeing the tree, remembering it, or admiring it. Some intentional objects are more elusive. Consider my act of wondering whether the world has a beginning in time, or vaguely recalling a proof for the existence of the largest prime number. These examples show that there is an important difference between actual objects and intentional objects. We can intend objects that do not actually exist, and our intentional objects may have features that actual objects do not have. To the extent that the two diverge, phenomenology focuses on the structures that are necessary for intending an object, and does not concern itself with properties of the actual object.

We can compare Husserl's analysis of conscious acts to the way we look at paintings. A painting, say of a landscape or a fruit basket, is a picture *of* something. We can take two distinct attitudes to it. Normally we will look through the image and focus on the represented object, that is, we will see the landscape with its hills, valleys, and other features. However, we can also look at the painting as such. In this case we pay attention to the colors, brushstrokes, and so forth, and we can ask how these features of the painting itself manage to represent the landscape. Consciousness similarly has its own internal features that enable it to be about objects. Ordinarily our conscious acts go through the features of the acts themselves to the object. So, if I am seeing a tree I ordinarily focus on the tree, not the internal features of this act of perception. But, Husserl argues, we can also focus on the internal features themselves, and that is what phenomenology aims to do.

3.4.2 Transcendental reduction

What Husserl calls "reductions" are methodological moves that serve to focus on the kind of thing that phenomenology aims to study. The main idea can best be captured in two separate stages.

First, there is the *transcendental reduction*. Phenomenology is a science of consciousness. It concerns itself not with physical objects, but with our conscious experiences of physical and other objects. This requires a somewhat counter-intuitive shift of standpoint that is not easy to maintain. We have to abandon the "natural attitude," which says that for the most part things are as they appear to us. In the natural attitude the contents of our conscious experiences are the objects that we have experience of. The objects of my perception are the books and papers I see in front of me, and the sounds I hear all around me.

Prior to Husserl, several movements in philosophy already question the natural attitude. Stoicism, for example, aims to teach its followers that the objects of the real world are of no real significance. Various versions of skepticism teach that these objects do not really exist at all. Descartes' epistemological skepticism fosters an attitude of doubting the existence of ordinary objects, only to resurrect them within the framework of a rationalist account of knowledge. These movements share a general structure: they suspend the natural attitude toward objects and then replace it with another, philosophically motivated attitude toward the same objects. Husserl's transcendental reduction asks us to take only the first of these steps, to suspend ordinary beliefs in ordinary objects. He does not want to substitute some other attitude toward them. In fact, phenomenology accepts that the natural attitude is exactly the right attitude for a scientific worldview. Husserlian phenomenology simply takes itself to be concerned with other objects, with things that are immanent in consciousness, rather than with the ordinary objects that are outside of consciousness. Husserl calls this step "bracketing" or "*epoche*," which is Greek for suspending belief. We bracket questions about physical objects, not because we think we ordinarily are wrong about them, but because we do not want to mistake the focus of phenomenology. We remain agnostic, and for phenomenological purposes uninterested in ordinary objects.

Bracketing the natural world does not empty the content of experience. If I see a piece of paper and bracket any presumption that there really is a piece of paper, I nevertheless have an experience of seeing the paper or, better, an experience that is *as if* I were seeing a piece of paper. The content of this experience is not the actual paper, but the immanent consciousness of the paper with everything that belongs to it. This conscious experience includes expectations about what the back side of the paper looks like, what it might feel or sound like, how it relates to other indistinct objects surrounding it, that it endures through time, and so on. Phenomenology studies these aspects of the conscious experience. Husserl claims that such consciousness of background, surrounding, and temporality is essential to any act of perception. In a specific sense they constitute the original act as an act of perception. We can therefore say that phenomenology studies the act-constituting features of consciousness. This, in Husserl's terminology, is what he means by transcendental phenomenology. The transcendental reduction is the shift of focus from the object of experience to the structures that constitute the act in which that object can be experienced.

3.4.3 Eidetic reduction

Seeing a piece of paper is very different from seeing an elephant in the wild. And yet, as acts of perception they share some general constituting features. In both cases, the consciousness has a certain temporal structure typical of visual perception, the object is experienced against the background of its surroundings, and so on. Husserl calls these general features "essences" or *eidos*, which is Greek for "form" or "idea." Phenomenology is an *eidetic* science, because it studies these essences. The eidetic reduction is a preparatory step that shifts our focus to the essential features of an act.

We can compare the eidetic reduction to the stance we take toward illustrations in geometry. What is interesting about *this* right triangle is that it illustrates the general properties of right triangles. Similarly, Husserl uses the example of seeing a white piece of paper, and at some point he actually looks at a piece of paper. From the standpoint of phenomenology, that particular act of actually looking is only relevant insofar as it illuminates general, essential features of acts of perception. Like phenomenology, geometry and arithmetic are eidetic sciences and require the eidetic reduction. Unlike phenomenology, though, they are not transcendental sciences. Geometry is very much about figures and planes, not about our experience of them. We can also illustrate the eidetic reduction by an analogy with the meaning of words. Words can express the content of a particular experience, but the meaning of the words is general and goes beyond the specific case. Similarly the eidetic structures that make each conscious experience meaningful are more general than their use in specific cases. Because phenomenology is an eidetic science, it differs sharply from scientific psychology. Psychology is concerned with actual objects, whereas phenomenology is concerned with essences.

Husserl introduces the terms *noesis* and *noema* to capture the relevant notion of generality. A noesis is a specific act of consciousness. The noema is the general meaning or content of that act, which it shares with other acts that have the same meaning. Every noesis is particular, it comes and goes. The same noema, however, can be experienced many times. If you look at the clock tower every morning, you have a new noesis every time, but the same noema. The noema of this act is similar to the sense of the phrase "that clock tower." However, it is more fine-grained and detailed than that linguistic sense, because it also includes figurative information for organizing the perceptual data. So, besides intending the linguistic sense, through its noema the act also intends the "look" of the clock tower, and similar perceptual features.

3.4.4 Hyle, fulfillment, and adumbrations

Conscious acts are directed at an object by way of the intentional content. This content is spelled out in the noema of the act. While the noema constitutes the meaning of the intentional object, the object is also experienced as given to us. Husserl uses the term *hyle* to characterize this givenness. The hyle are the sensory data, or the appearance of sense data, that *fulfill* the intended meaning and hence constrain the meaning of the act. Note that, given the transcendental reduction, the hyle are mind-internal structures, so it is not the actual object that fulfills the intention. Hallucinations, imaginings, and memories have hyle. Husserl points out that there are different degrees of givenness within consciousness itself. In perceiving or hallucinating, for example, the object is given as it were "in the flesh," while in imagining the object is given in a more attenuated, variable way. Acts of seeing a tree and imagining a tree share much of the intended meaning, but the fulfillment of the intention is different. In perception, the tree is given more completely, so the intention is fulfilled more completely. The hyle are richer and more detailed. By the same token, the act of perception is more constrained than the act of imagination. The perceived tree is relatively stable and unchanging, while the imagined tree can very well grow, shrink, change color, go up in flames, and so on. Nevertheless, in acts of imagination the imagined object is present as given to us. In that respect imagining a tree differs from a mere, empty thought of a tree.

An intention can be empty, or it can be more or less fulfilled. An empty intention might be a non-sensical thought, or a merely formal thought. Perception is fulfilled more completely than imagination. Finally, Husserl says, there is also an ideal of perfect fulfillment, in which every part of the noema is entirely filled. This ideal constitutes the meaning of the notion of truth, but it does not apply to ordinary perception. Husserl argues that in ordinary perception there are many partial intentions in the noema that are not fulfilled, so that the noema itself is not completely filled. For example, the back side of the tree is part of the intended meaning of a tree-perception, but we have no hyle representing its presence. We see only aspects of the tree. Husserl calls these partial aspects or perspectives on the object *adumbrations (Abschattungen)*. The unfulfilled intentions make up what Husserl calls the *horizon* of the act. More precisely, he distinguishes the inner horizon from the outer horizon. The inner horizon includes intended aspects of the object that are not fulfilled, such as the back side of the tree, or our expectations about the temporal robustness of the tree, the smell of its resin, and so on. The outer horizon includes the broader context that forms the background against which the perception of the tree stands out as meaningful. Depending on the situation, the outer horizon might consist of our general knowledge of what one does in public parks, or how one safely maneuvers a car, and so forth.

In most cases of perception we are given only some perspectives, and there are sides of the object that we do not see at all. Husserl thinks that we experience adumbrations even if we do see all sides of the object. Say, for example, that we see the entire surface of a table. Looking at the table, our gaze moves from edge to edge and all around as we walk around it. In doing so, we take in many different patches in different lighting conditions and from different angles. However, we experience them as a unity, as a single "color" of the table. This single color is part of the noema, or the meaning of the experience. It stands out as such precisely through the range of adumbrations that are given in the variation of the gaze. Even though we see the entire colored surface, the color itself is only given as adumbrations that fulfill partial intentions.

Husserl's analysis of perception, therefore, argues that we never perceive an object completely, but only through adumbrations. At the same time, however, he can claim that we see complete objects. We see complete objects, but we do not see them completely. We have to be careful about the distinction between these two statements. When you look at a tree, you see the complete tree. This is because your noema intends a complete, three-dimensional, temporally robust, fully colored tree. This is the meaning of the act. However, you do not see the tree completely, insofar as not all parts of that noema are fulfilled by hyle. The back side, the recent past, the smell, and so forth are intended, but you experience no rich, detailed givenness of those aspects of the tree. Like all perceptual objects, the tree is *transcendent*. This means that there is more to the object that you can explore. You can get closer and scratch the bark, take in the resinous odor, and so on. The experience is very different if you look at a fake tree, a mock-up, or an image. The hyle might be roughly identical to the ones that make up our perception of a real tree, but the noema is different. Of course sometimes we may start out thinking that we are looking at a real tree and then discover that it is a cardboard cutout. In such a case, says Husserl, the noema "explodes" and is replaced by another. This phrase indicates that the perceptual switch happens quickly, completely, and involves a moment of confusion and disorientation, during which we have no grasp of the perceived object at all. The perceptual noema is then replaced with the noema of a cardboard cutout, which does not include partial intentions of three-dimensionality, odor, and so forth.

3.5 The body

The method Husserl outlines in the *Ideas* focuses on the immanent content of consciousness insofar as it constitutes the meaning of an act. This is the method Husserl adopts for the majority of his work, and because of it, his approach is called "transcendental phenomenology." Heidegger and Merleau-Ponty also analyze transcendental constitution, but they focus more on the constituting role of practical skills, the body, and one's embeddedness in one's surrounding. Their approach is commonly called "existential phenomenology," in contrast to Husserl's. Nevertheless, many commentators maintain that the distinction between Husserl's transcendental phenomenology and the existential phenomenology of Heidegger and Merleau-Ponty is not as sharp as may appear. Merleau-Ponty himself suggests this in the preface to his *Phenomenology of Perception*, where he presents his own approach as Husserlian and claims that Heidegger's phenomenology is already suggested in Husserl's work.

In fact, Husserl analyzes the role of the body in perception throughout the period in which he develops his transcendental phenomenology. He recognizes early on that we can only be conscious of perceptual objects insofar as we are also conscious of ourselves as having bodies. The first detailed analyses of this essential connection between perception and the body come in lecture courses Husserl gave in 1907, which are now known as *Thing and Space* (*Ding und Raum*). The material on the body from these lecture courses is also included and elaborated in more detail in drafts for a second volume of the *Ideas*. However, Husserl published neither the *Thing and Space* lectures, nor the second volume of the *Ideas*. He continued to work on this material, and on several occasions asked his research assistants Edith Stein and Ludwig Landgrebe to transcribe and edit various manuscripts, without ever being satisfied with the final product. Heidegger would have been familiar with the material through discussions with Husserl, Stein, and Landgrebe. Merleau-Ponty visited the newly established Husserl Archives in Louvain in 1939, specifically to consult the draft manuscripts of *Ideas II* as he was beginning his work on the *Phenomenology of Perception*. The phenomenology of embodiment begins with Husserl.

3.5.1 The role of the body in perception

When we see an object in space, we see it as located at a certain point in space, as having a shape and an orientation. These spatial and dimensional features of visual objects are constitutive aspects of the perceptual experience, that is, they are part of what it means to see a thing. Obviously, the way in which these spatial features of objective things are presented to us will differ between cases in which we stay perfectly still and cases in which we ourselves are moving. If we remain still, the presentations of a stationary thing are themselves motionless. If we are moving our eyes, head, or bodies, we will perceive the stationary thing in a changing stream of visual presentations. In such cases, Husserl asks, "how do multiplicity and continuously changing appearances bring it about that they present to our eyes something completely unchanging?" (1907, p. 159). The answer, he points out, must be that the constitution of the consciousness of the visual object must account for, and hence include an awareness of, the movement of the point of view of the observer. This awareness turns out to be complex. It aims at the perception of the thing in space. At the same time, however, it constitutes an awareness of space and the spatial position of the observer.

Finally, it also constitutes an awareness of the body of the observer, both as the point of view of the thing-perception and as a peculiar thing of its own.

This awareness of the body is given through "kinesthetic sensations," such as sensations that arise in moving one's eyes, head, or body. These sensations contribute to visual perception, even though they themselves do not present visual images of the object. If I move my body or eyes, or accommodate my eyes to focus on a near or far object, there is a kind of sensation that I am moving. My bodily movements form a system that corresponds to specific sequences of visual presentations. For example, if I stand in a room and turn in a circle, the same series of images will repeat itself with every turn. I will see the desk, the door, the bookcase, and the window in this sequence, again and again. If, on the other hand, I walk away without turning around, I will see an unending sequence of new images without repetition (1907, p. 205f.). If I move or tilt my head I will see that certain portions of the visual field stretch out or narrow, or move toward the margins. These sequences of images are linked by necessity to certain types of movement, and our consciousness of objects in our visual field partly depends on being conscious of the systematic correlation formed by this link. The sequence of images makes sense so long as we are aware of the sequence as accompanying the corresponding bodily movements. As Husserl puts it, kinesthetic sensations "make representation [of visual objects] possible, without themselves representing" (1907, p. 161). As opposed to visual or tactile sensations, they have their "own specific peculiarity." We must know how we are moving in order to know what we are seeing.

One of Husserl's crucial insights about the role of the body in perception is that our awareness of the systematic correspondence is not the result of a kind of psychological association between muscular sensations and visual images, as if two kinds of conscious contents that are external to each other are then subsequently connected to each other. Muscular sensations can be impossible to notice in cases such as eye accommodation and it is unlikely that they show up phenomenologically in many other types of movement. Moreover, muscular effort is not even necessary for the systematic link between the moving body and changing images. Husserl considers the difference between walking alongside a carriage and mounting the carriage. When we hop on, the effort of walking is suspended, but the sequence of images remains the same, as does our ability to make sense of what we are seeing. In this case, Husserl says, "the carriage, with its moving state and the respective phenomenological changes, takes over the function of the kinesthetic sensations" (1907, p. 282). In other words, kinesthetic sensation is not muscular sensation, or the effort involved in walking and moving.

Rather than an association between two distinct types of sensation, Husserl argues that that necessary link between movement and sequence of images is phenomenologically detectable in the experience itself. "Everywhere we find the if–then, or because–therefore. . . . Thus, in vision, the ordered system of sensations of eye-movements, or the movements of the freely moveable head, gives rise to this or that series" (1952, p. 58). The experience of seeing has a phenomenologically twofold articulated structure (*Zweigliederung*). "On the one hand are the kinesthetic sensations, the motivating ones; on the other hand are the sensations of qualities, the motivated ones" (1952, p. 58). In kinesthetic sensations we are aware of the freely motivating nature of the bodily movement with respect to the resulting ordered sequences of images. The bodily movement has causal implications. A specific movement determines a specific series of images; for example, if I turn around, the sequence of images will unfold according to the pattern desk–door–bookcase–window. Moreover, kinesthetic sensations feel motivating because of the *freedom* of the movement. Husserl points out that the movement of the head is free or discretionary, and the "freedom in the consciousness of the course of kinesthetic sensations is an essential piece of the constitution of spatiality" (1952, p. 58).

Husserl drives the analysis of the motivating–motivated twofold structure of perception further. The free motivation of the kinesthetic sensation is not aimless. It aims at a normal or optimal grasp of the visual content. For example, "certain conditions turn out to be 'normal:' seeing by sunlight and clear skies. . . . The 'optimum' that is here reached counts as the color itself" (1952, p. 59). In such normal conditions, we have a "preferred givenness of the thing, in which its relative best is given. . . . It is especially intended; the 'interest' aims prevalently at it; the tendency of the experience terminates in it, is fulfilled in it, and other ways of givenness contain an intentional relation to this optimal one" (1952, p. 60). This means that the motivation in the bodily movement that produces a changing series of visual images tends toward an optimum. For sure, there is not much that the body can do to move out of a sunset into broad daylight. Often the optimum presentation of a given object is not attainable. But the interest of vision is to see the visual thing itself, and every adumbration, every givenness points to an optimal one. We can say that the system of kinesthetic sensations is motivated toward the optimal grasp of the visual object, and this motivation shows up in the intentional relations that each mode of givenness bears within itself. As perceivers we are moving our bodies in order to produce a series of images that reveals and tracks this tendency toward the norm.

Hence the body is implicated in visual perception not merely by the necessary correlation of movement and changing images, but by the normative tendency in the visual experience toward the preferred given-ness of the thing. While Husserl does not work out this structure in detail in the unpublished second volume of the *Ideas*, this kind of normative motor intentionality becomes one of the main themes of Merleau-Ponty's phenomenological analysis of perception.

3.5.2 Apperception of the body

The body, as the "sensory organ of the experiencing subject," is "always also there" (Husserl 1952, p. 144). As we see other things with the body, we are also conscious of the body itself. This consciousness of our bodies has its own constitutive structure. "The constitution of physical materiality is interwoven in a peculiar correlation with the constitution of a first-person body [*Ichleib*]" (1907, p. 162). Husserl considers this consciousness of the body in two distinct senses. First, we are conscious of our body as a physical, material thing. Second, we are conscious of our body as a spatial origin that centers and organizes spatial relations to things around us.

Like other things, our bodies are physical things located in space, and each of us is conscious of our body as it is given in sensations. Husserl points out that "this happens in a way that essentially distinguishes the body from all external things. On the one hand, the body is also a thing, a physical thing like any other. . . . On the other hand, this thing is body, bearer of the I; the I has sensations and these sensations are 'localized' in the body" (1907, p. 161f.). If I run my hand and fingers over the table surface or the paperweight, I have sensations of the smooth surface tex-ture or the cool metal of these external objects. At the same time, I can also focus on these sensations as located in my hand. This is very different from sensing an external object. The paperweight is cool and smooth, but the hand that feels these qualities is itself neither cool nor smooth. "These localized sensations are not properties of the body as a physical thing; and yet they are properties of this thing, the body" (1952, p. 146). The act of tactile sensations has a dual structure. On the one hand, there is the sensation of a quality or property of the physical object, such as the smoothness of the paperweight. On the other hand, there is the experi-ence of such sensations in the hand, the sensing organ. Husserl calls the latter an *Empfindnis* (a neologism, roughly equal to "sensedness") to distinguish the experience of the body from the *Empfindung* (sensation) of the object. *Empfindnisse* do not conform to the logic of sensations of external objects. For example, they are not given in adumbrations, insofar as they do not present themselves as partial aspects of a transcendent object. Unlike sensations, which cease when the hand stops touching the object, the *Empfindnis* of coolness or smoothness lingers in the hand. The smoothness of the paperweight is located in space on the surface of the paperweight. The *Empfindnisse* of this smoothness in the hand, however, are "fundamentally distinct from extension as the determination of all material things. To be sure, they spread out in space and in their own way they cover areas of space; but this spreading-out is essentially different from expansion in the sense of all characteristics of the *res extensa*" (1952, p. 149). In general, the "sensedness of touch [*Tastempfindnis*] is not a state of this material thing, the hand. It is, rather, the hand itself, which is more for us than a material thing" (1952, p. 150).

Hands and the sense of touch in general have a fundamental function in the constitution of our conscious apperception of the body. "The body as such can originarily only constitute itself in tactuality and in all that is localized with tactile sensations, such as heat, cold, pain, etc." (1952, p. 150). The sense of sight does not have the same dual structure of sensation and *Empfindnis*. If I see the smoothness or the glossy coloration of the paperweight, I do not at the same time have a smooth or glossy experience localized in the eye. In seeing, there is no direct experience of the eye itself as a sensing organ in visual sensation. The eye is localized in the sensing body not by sight, but indirectly through tactile sensations. When I touch my eye, if it is touched by another object like a branch or a cold breeze, or if I sense the movement of the eye muscles, the eye has an *Empfindnis*. It is "thus apperceived as necessarily belonging to the body" (1952, p. 148). This distinction between touching and seeing (or hearing, which Husserl finds analogous to sight) is evident when I touch or look at my own body. If one hand touches the other, for example, each hand has sensations of the other and *Empfindnisse* within itself. The touching hand thus reveals the touched, physical object as my sensitive body. On the other hand, when I see my hand, I have visual sensations of the hand as a physical object, but I do not see it as a seeing body, as a body that itself has visual sensations. "I see myself, my body, not in the same way as I touch myself. What I call my seen body is not a seen seer, as my touched body is a touched toucher" (1952, p. 148). The location of sensations within the body, not as a property or state assigned to it from the outside, but as the original experience of the body itself, is thus crucial for our consciousness of our bodies. Sight itself could not accomplish it. Husserl says that "a merely eye-like subject could not have an appearing body at all" (1952, p. 150).

Still, the visual experience of my own body differs from the visual experience of an external object. While the "merely eye-like subject" cannot have a body constituted through localized *Empfindnisse*, it nevertheless has a body constituted through its location and relations to things in space. "The multiplicity of images belonging to the body has a distinctive kinesthetic motivation as opposed to other things" (1907, p. 280). If I turn around or walk away, visual images of things in space change according to a sequence that corresponds to the specific movements of the body. What I see of my own body, however, does not change according to the same sequence. "We cannot walk around our hand or our body, we cannot choose to come closer to it or remove ourselves from it" (1907, p. 280). The way the body looks close to us is not the way an object can look close to us. Our body always spills over the edge of our visual field and it is not possible to follow it visually beyond this edge. Some parts of our bodies can only be seen according to a "peculiar perspectival foreshortening" and some parts we cannot see at all. "The same body that is my means for perception gets in the way of my perception of itself and is a peculiar, incompletely constituted thing" (1952, p. 159).

The body shows up as the "center of orientation." While we move around from place to place, "at every moment the subject is in the center, in the 'here,' from where it sees all things and gazes into the world" (1952, p. 159). The body is the center of orientation because every thing shows up as being near to me or far from me, above or below, to my right or to my left. There is a spatial center that is located where the body is, inside the body, and it is "a here that has no other outside itself relative to which it could be a 'there'" (1952, p. 158). The system of orientation is not an objective spatial system with a fixed origin that could be alternately occupied by different objects. Orientation and distance are implied in the body and inseparable from the body. They are constituted by the system of changes in sensation of spatial things in relation to movements of the body.

Husserl's phenomenology of the body shapes much of the work of Heidegger and Merleau-Ponty. Yet, from the perspective of later phenomenologists Husserl's work on the body is limited. For the most part, Husserl analyzes the body of a solipsistic subject. This body is mostly generic rather than the body of a culturally and bodily situated individual. Husserl's body is also a passive perceiver, rather than constituting perceptual objects by actively and skillfully engaging with them. Husserl himself is aware of these limitations of his analysis, and this may help explain why he was reluctant to publish this material.

Though he does not connect it to his analysis of the body, in *Ideas II* Husserl sketches the concept of *Umwelt* (environment), the shared, social, communicative world of practical, useful, and aesthetic objects. The conscious subject here is desiring and practically engaged. The environment is suffused with motivating objects that the conscious subject intends in terms of their purposes. This notion prefigures the concept of the environment that Heidegger develops in great detail. Husserl revisits it in his 1936 *The Crisis of European Sciences*, now under the title "life-world" (*Lebenswelt*). He still maintains that phenomenology requires a reduction, or a shift of focus. However, rather than the transcendental reduction to the object-constituting features of consciousness, Husserl here understands the reduction as the shift from understanding the world in physical or mechanical terms to focusing on the world as we experience it, with values and attractions, vagueness and indeterminacy.

3.6 Phenomenology of time consciousness

Our perception of enduring objects and our awareness of our bodies through motivated sequences of images require that our consciousness takes place over time. Husserl analyzed the phenomenology of our experience of time throughout his career and he repeatedly lectured on the topic. But he never developed his view in a book. We owe the publication of his view mostly to the work of Edith Stein, who carefully transcribed and organized various lecture notes on time and prompted Husserl to update and revise some of them. Though Husserl gave this project relatively little attention, he seems to have been motivated to finally publish the material when Heidegger's *Being and Time* came out. Heidegger's book came out in the *Yearbook for Philosophy and Phenomenological Research* in 1927, and Husserl's *Lectures on the Phenomenology of Internal Time Consciousness* were published in that same venue one year later. Husserl asked Heidegger to edit the lectures, but Heidegger made very few changes to Stein's substantial work.

3.6.1 The basic problem

The consciousness of time is part of almost all conscious acts. For example, we perceive objects as enduring through time. We are able to distinguish perception from memory, and so on. Besides consciousness of various objects, therefore, we are always also conscious of their temporal structure and ultimately of time itself. This consciousness of time poses a basic problem that Husserl tries to solve. It can be easily stated. On the one hand, it seems evident that consciousness is always consciousness of the present moment. Similarly, we always perceive what is given to us in the present. We cannot see or hear past or future stimuli. On the other hand, it seems equally evident that we often perceive objects that go beyond the present. We see objects as persisting, moving, changing, and so on. Together these seemingly obvious claims imply the paradoxical one that we perceive *in* the present moment objects that are not present.

Husserl, as always, is interested in the transcendental structure of conscious acts that are directed at objects, and he brackets the intentional object. This means that in the phenomenology of time consciousness Husserl is not seeking to address metaphysical questions about whether change and motion are real, whether the present is more real than the future, and so on. Instead he begins with attempts to describe the phenomena that appear to us and investigates the structures of consciousness that make it possible for us to be intentionally directed at moving, changing, and persisting things, irrespective of whether those things really exist.

To be precise, there are two distinct kinds of intentional objects that Husserl is concerned with in his phenomenology of time consciousness. First, we occasionally perceive or are conscious of some aspect of time itself. For example, we may be consciously directed at the length of an interval, or the fleetingness of an instant. In such acts, time itself is the intentional object of our consciousness, and so phenomenology investigates the transcendental structures that make it possible for acts to be directed at time. Second, there are many acts in which we are not specifically directed at time, but in which we perceive other objects that present themselves to us with certain temporal features. One good example of such acts – which Husserl takes over from Brentano – is the perception of a melody. The intentional object of such perception is obviously the melody, or a phrase of the melody, and not time itself. Nevertheless we could not perceive the melody unless we perceived tones in succession. So one very important transcendental structure of the consciousness of melodies is the constitution of temporal succession. In fact, the vast majority of our basic acts of consciousness – perception, memory, imagination, anticipation – involve temporal structuring, so time is more than merely one kind of intentional object among many. Our ability to be intentionally directed at time is fundamental for much, if not all, of our conscious experience.

3.6.2 Kant and Brentano

Husserl's view draws indirectly on Kant and directly on Brentano. Kant is important both for the way his transcendental philosophy frames questions about time, and for his specific views about time consciousness.

Regarding the general framework, recall that Kant claims that time is an *a priori*, subjective form of intuition. In other words, he claims that it is a feature of the human cognitive apparatus that objects necessarily appear in time-relations. Beyond the human standpoint, he famously writes, time signifies nothing. This general framework casts time as a transcendental structure of consciousness. Insofar as time is a transcendent feature of empirical objects, this feature derives from and can be explained in terms of the transcendental structure.

Beyond this general point, Kant develops several detailed accounts of the structure of our consciousness of temporal objects. He believes that all cognition of objects combines sense data given to us in intuition with concepts that are supplied by the understanding. As the form of intuition, time determines how intuitions, or sense data, are given to us. They are always given to us in a sequence, or as simultaneous. In order for us to cognize anything by means of these sense data, they need to be organized by a concept. This means that our minds must be able to fit concepts onto the temporal order in which the sense data are given to us. Kant thinks that this requires that our minds actively construct the apparent simultaneity or succession of objects. This construction happens as intuitions and concepts are combined in a pre-cognitive process that Kant calls the "threefold synthesis" (see Chapter 1).

Consider what happens when you read a word, or recognize a face. You take in a variety of sense data – a "sensory manifold." This is the first aspect of the threefold synthesis, which Kant calls the "apprehension in intuition." Depending on how complex the object is, it may take some time, maybe a tenth of a second or so, for your eyes to scan the shapes of the letters on the page, or the defining features of a face. We do not usually notice that there is a period during which we are only taking in sense data without knowing what they add up to. In consciousness we are always already directed at the object, the word or the face that we recognize. This is because the threefold synthesis happens pre-cognitively, and very quickly. By the time we notice anything, we have already constituted the object of cognition. The second aspect of the synthesis is the "reproduction in imagination." It enables the mind to take in the sensory manifold, rather than a single sense datum. As the eye scans the various marks that make up the letters of a word on a page, the mind reproduces or recollects the previous one. This is how the mind can attend to the manifold of sense data together. You would never see a word or face if you could only apprehend one sense datum at a time without holding on to the previous ones. Finally, apprehension and reproduction of sense data cannot remain a random process. Otherwise you would not be able to tell if you are reading the word "stop" or "pots," and a face would look like a jumble of facial features. At some point the mind structures the sensory manifold according to some regularity. Kant thinks that such regularity derives from concepts, so he calls this structuring "recognition in a concept."

This theory of the threefold synthesis does not provide much of an answer to the basic problem outlined above, since all the processing is pre-cognitive and happens in time spans too short for humans to notice. When we hear a melody, on the other hand, we fully cognize the first note (presumably through some process like the threefold synthesis). The question then becomes how this perception is united with the later perception of subsequent notes so that we hear a melody, rather than isolated single tones, or a chord of several tones. Nevertheless, Kant's analysis is an important precursor of later views, since it suggests that consciousness is not instantaneous, and that the background processing that structures our cognition of an object does so by means of sequencing the sense data in the course of combining them with the pertinent concept. In other words, it shifts the focus from the temporality of the object onto transcendental structures that determine the possibility of being intentionally directed at temporal objects.

Brentano confronts the basic problem directly. He argues that perception is instantaneous, and that the perception of succession or duration is the combination in the present instant of a present perception and a representation of past perceptions. In the case of a melody we hear the present tone and at the same time represent the past tones as past. So we perceive a melody, rather than a single tone, because we combine a present perception with a present memory. Brentano follows Kant and argues that this combination happens in a judgment in which the manifold of representations – perception plus memories – are subsumed under a single concept. However, he departs from Kant by claiming that since we only experience change or duration through the association of perceptions and memories, we only think that we perceive change, but do not really do so. Kant, by contrast, argues that our transcendental constitution gives us cognition of empirically real objects. Husserl, of course, brackets this question.

Husserl accepts the basic structure of Brentano's view and develops it further. Like Brentano, Husserl thinks that consciousness of temporally extended objects or events is instantaneous, and he defends this view against an alternative presented by William Stern. Stern argues that the consciousness of extended objects must itself be extended over time, so that my perception of a melody, for example, derives from a series of conscious states that unfold over the same time span as the melody itself. We combine these several states in a unifying act, which gives us the phenomenal experience of being conscious of the whole melody at once (Stern 1897). Husserl thinks that this view simply shifts the bump in the rug, since it still needs to explain the structure of the unifying act, so that in our consciousness of the melody, we are conscious of the past tones of the melody as past.

Husserl similarly thinks that Brentano fails to provide an account of the peculiar status of a present representation of a past tone, which differs phenomenologically from an ordinary memory. We cannot understand the "pastness" of the representation of the first tone in the melody as a transcendent feature of the actual tone itself, since this is not part of the content of the representation. Either we no longer hear the tone, or we do still hear it in a peculiar mode, which means that it is not past. Nor can we understand this pastness as an immanent feature of the representation, since that begs the question how this representation is a representation *of* a past tone (Husserl 1928, p. 382). Husserl thinks that Brentano cannot give a thorough explanation of this phenomenon, because he is not sufficiently clear on the basic distinctions between the intentional structure of the act and the transcendent object. The pastness is an aspect of the intentional structure, not the transcendent object.

3.6.3 Retention and protention

As usual, Husserl begins his analysis with a description of the phenomena. He focuses on the experience of a tone, given as a hyletic datum, while bracketing questions about the actual tone as a transcendent object. Husserl points out that the single tone is given as temporally extended, so the same problem that we encounter in explaining our conscious experience of a melody already applies to single tones. Where in the former case we talk of a melody consisting of a sequence of tones, the tone itself consists of a continuity of tone-phases. In fact, this basic temporal description applies to all ordinary cases of perception, since we typically perceive ordinary objects as going beyond the momentary instant, either as enduring or as changing. They are all given in consciousness in a sequence of phases.

The tone is given to us as an impression that immediately "recedes" or "sinks down" into the past, while the givenness of the present impression continues. The receding impression is still there, we "hold on" to it as a modification of the given impression. This modification is an essential feature of consciousness. In other words, a hyletic datum only counts as an impression if it conforms to this law of modification. "The tone-now changes into a tone-having-been; the impressional consciousness, continually flowing, passes over into an ever new retentional consciousness" (1928, p. 390).

Husserl fixes the structure that emerges from this description with some technical vocabulary. In perception we are given hyletic data in a *primal impression* (*Urimpression*). This impression recedes into a modified *retentional* consciousness, which accompanies new primal impressions. At the same time the impression is also accompanied by more or less definite expectations of impressions in the immediate future. These expectations can be specific, such as when we know exactly what the next note in the melody should be, or they can be vague or "empty" if they are merely the expectation that we will hear *something* next. Husserl calls this expectation that accompanies impressions a *protention*. The main focus of Husserl's phenomenological argument lies in spelling out the nature of retentional consciousness. His brief remarks on protention mostly mirror the analysis of retention.

Retentional consciousness is a present consciousness, not a past one. This crucial feature of retention is clearer in the phrase "primary memory," which Husserl uses to designate the same phenomenon. (Husserl comes to prefer the term "retention," presumably because it resembles "intention" and thus indicates that it is part of being directed at an object.) Remembering obviously takes place in the present, though the content of what we remember usually (but not always) is past, and this is the temporal structure of retention. It is a present consciousness of a just-past impression. Husserl uses the phrase "secondary memory" for our ordinary notion of memory or recollection. The object of our secondary memory is not usually related to our present perception (I remember the beach while I am sitting in my office), and we can produce it more or less at will. The object of primary memory, or retention, by contrast, is part of the present perception, and we have no volitional control over it.

Perception and retention are closely related. As we saw above, Husserl claims that there is a "law of modification," according to which all primal impression changes over into retentional consciousness. The converse relation also holds. It is an essential structure of retention that the retentional object has been perceived in a primary impression. The essential connection between primal impression and retention points to an ambiguity in the meaning of "perception." Husserl distinguishes a narrow from a wider sense of perception. In the narrow sense, perception refers to the primal impression of an object. In the wider sense, perception means the entire combination of primal impression, retention, and protention in a single act. Temporal objects can only be perceived in this wider sense. While a tone or a tone-phase can both be perceived immediately in a primal impression, a melody can only be perceived in an act that combines impressions with retention (1928, p. 398).

3.6.4 The temporal structure of the self

Husserl's account of time consciousness explains how we can be conscious of temporally extended objects by constituting their temporal features in intentionality. Beneath the temporal structure of objects, however, Husserl notices a deeper structure of the constitution of time itself. He calls this deeper structure an "absolute subjectivity."

Say we hear a melody. We first hear the tones in primal impressions. As they pass into retentional consciousness, we hear the next tone or tone-phases in primal impression. In doing so, we maintain consciousness of the present moment, while we are simultaneously conscious of the former present as now having-been. But by what intentional act can we be directed at the present now and the flow of the now into the retentional past? Obviously it cannot be the same act that is directed at the tones themselves, or the melody. The melody is only constitut*ed* as time flows, so it cannot account for the constitut*ing* now-ness of the present experience. Indeed, no object-directed intentional act can account for the consciousness of the present moment in the time-constituting acts. The consciousness *of* a now is not the same as the now-ness of that consciousness. Husserl describes it as follows:

> If we consider the constituting phenomena, we find a flow. . . . This flow is something we speak of in conformity with what is constituted, but it is not "something in objective time." It is absolute subjectivity and has the absolute properties of something we can designate with the image of a flow; of something that originates in a point of actuality, in a primal source-point, "the now," and so on. . . . For all this, we lack names. (1928, p. 429)

This absolute subjectivity is not itself experienced as an object. We experience objects as occurring in time, as changing, passing, accelerating, receding, and so forth. These temporal features of objects are determined with respect to an underlying fixed, uniform flow of time. The uniformity and unity of that flow itself, however, is not determined with respect to a further temporal benchmark; in that sense it is "absolute." And it is "subjectivity" insofar as it makes up the unity of consciousness in which we experience intentional objects. When I experience the tones of the melody, I am also conscious that I am the one experiencing them. The unity of the underlying temporal flow in which we experience objects is precisely the unity of the subjective consciousness of the experience of those objects. We do not experience ourselves as constituting subjects in the same way we encounter a constituted object, and we cannot get this subjectivity into our phenomenological sights by performing another reduction. And yet it is implied by Husserl's theory of time consciousness. At the limits of his transcendental reduction, therefore, Husserl is forced to abandon his usual reliance on phenomenological description and posit a time-constituting subject in his explanation of the conscious, temporal self.

Key terms

absolute subjectivity – the temporal flow that makes up the unity of our conscious experiences of temporal objects.

act – a unified conscious experience, directed at a single object in a single attitude.

adumbration – an aspect or perspective of a perceptual object.

bracketing – the way phenomenology addresses the natural world of objects. It studies consciousness *as if* it were of objects, and does not address questions about the actual features of actual objects, which it brackets.

eidetic reduction – the methodological step that leads us to attend to general, essential features of an experience.

eidos – Greek for "idea." Husserl uses this word instead of "idea" or "*a priori* feature" to denote essential features of acts of consciousness. Phenomenology studies essences, that is, it is an eidetic science.

Empfindnis – the experience of tactile sensations as they are localized in the sensory organs of the body.

epoche – Greek for "suspension of belief." In Husserl's phenomenology this suspension is the bracketing of the natural objects.

fulfillment – the given content that corresponds to the intention of an act. In cases of straightforward perception, the intention is fulfilled by the presence of the intended object "in the flesh." In cases of imagination or memory, it is fulfilled by a representation. Husserl thinks that abstract logical intentions can be fulfilled just like sensory perceptions.

horizon – the background of meaning against which an object of perception stands out. Husserl distinguishes inner and outer horizons. The inner horizon consists of those aspects of the intentional object that are not directly given, but that nevertheless make up the object (such as the back side of a tree). The outer horizon consists of broader background knowledge that forms any given context in which an intentional object is meaningful.

hyle – the constraints that sense data place on noemata.

immanent – an intentional object is immanent if it belongs to the same stream of consciousness as the act that is directed at it. Such an act is an immanent act. Phenomenology studies what is immanent in consciousness.

intentionality – directedness, the defining characteristic of consciousness. All conscious experience is intentional, that is, it is directed at an intentional object.

kinesthetic sensation – sensations of the movement of the body that are linked to changes in perception of external things.

lifeworld – the background of cultural knowledge that members of a given culture take for granted.

natural attitude – the normal, pre-philosophical attitude in which we attend to objects and accept our experience as veridical. Certain phenomenological approaches require us to suspend the natural attitude.

noema – the meaning of an act. Noemata are general, that is, several distinct acts can have the same noema.

noesis – a specific intentional, conscious act.

phase – a brief temporal span that makes up a perceived moment.

phenomenological reduction – the eidetic and transcendental reductions together. For Husserl, this methodological preparation is necessary to do phenomenology.

primal impression – the "source point" of perception in which we experience an object as given to us in the present.

primary memory – the same as retention.

protention – also called "primary expectation." In protentional consciousness we are conscious of an object as future. The content of a protentional consciousness is often indeterminate or empty.

psychologism – the mistake of explaining mathematical or logical objects in terms of psychological processes.

retention – also called "primary memory." Retention is the modification of a primal impression. In retentional consciousness we are conscious of the object as past, not as present. Retention is part of present consciousness.

secondary memory – the ordinary notion of memory, as opposed to retention (primary memory). The content of secondary memory is not intended as present.

transcendent – an intentional object is transcendent if it does not belong to the same stream of consciousness as the act. Examples include any act directed at real objects, or at essences and categorial entities.

transcendental – transcendental consciousness is the pure consciousness that is left over after the phenomenological reductions. Phenomenology is transcendental philosophy, because it studies the structures of consciousness that constitute the meaning of acts.

transcendental reduction – the methodological step that leads us to attend to the structure of acts that directs them at their objects, rather than the object itself.

transparency – the thesis that we can be aware of and reflect on any mental act. Husserl claims that mental content is transparent.

Further reading

Dreyfus, H., ed. (1982). *Husserl, Intentionality, and Cognitive Science*. Cambridge, MA: MIT Press.

Drummond, J. (1990). *Husserlian Intentionality and Non-Foundational Realism: Noema and Object*. Dordrecht: Kluwer.

Woodruff-Smith, D. (2013). *Husserl*, 2nd edn. London: Routledge.

4

Martin Heidegger and Existential Phenomenology

Husserl's innovative approach to philosophy, his optimism that phenomenology could become a scientific philosophy, and his many insightful phenomenological descriptions inspired many followers, though few of them chose to follow Husserl's approach directly, or participate in what he conceived of as a disciplinary research project. Martin Heidegger is arguably the most innovative and influential among these followers. Heidegger first studied theology and some mathematics at the University of Freiburg, before dedicating himself fully to philosophy. His first philosophical writings were shaped by the dominant neo-Kantian schools of thought, but after his doctoral dissertation he developed a strong interest in Husserl's phenomenology. When Husserl took a professorship in philosophy at Freiburg, Heidegger became his research assistant and the two discussed philosophy intensively. During this period Husserl thought of Heidegger as his intellectual heir. Heidegger, however, disagreed with basic aspects of Husserl's phenomenology as much as he was inspired by it. When his monumental book *Being and Time* was published, Heidegger wrote in a letter to his friend Jaspers that "insofar as this treatise is written 'against' anybody, it is written against Husserl" (Heidegger and Jaspers 1992, p. 71). In other letters Heidegger expressed much stronger disdain for neo-Kantian philosophy, so a reasonable interpretation of this statement is that he considered Husserl's phenomenology to be the best current philosophical view, and that *Being and Time* aims to improve on it in ways that are incompatible with Husserl's basic orientation. The book is dedicated to Husserl "in admiration and friendship."

Being and Time is Heidegger's most important and influential work. In fact, it is one of the most influential books in twentieth-century philosophy and it plays a crucial role in every movement in philosophy, psychology, and cognitive science that we will discuss in the remaining chapters. Heidegger wrote *Being and Time* in a hurry in 1926 in order to qualify for the professorship in philosophy vacated by Husserl at the University of Freiburg. He had planned two volumes with three divisions each, but in the end he completed only the first two divisions of the first volume. A few years after publishing it, Heidegger abandoned the attempt to write the incomplete portions of the book.

The first of the two extant divisions provides a detailed descriptive analysis of everyday existence, also called the "analytic of Dasein." In the second division Heidegger analyzes what he calls "temporality." By this he means the hidden structure that makes human existence possible. The first division contains predominantly phenomenological analyses, while the second focuses on existentialist themes.

4.1 The intelligibility of the everyday world

4.1.1 Equipment

The easiest way into Heidegger's phenomenology of human existence is his analysis of the world, in the third chapter of Division One. Heidegger admired Husserl's willingness to jettison traditional philosophical vocabulary and take a fresh approach to old questions, grounded in careful descriptions of the relevant experiences. In this chapter, Heidegger does this by asking in novel ways about the familiar things that surround us in ordinary life.

Heidegger does not want his description to be skewed by prior theoretical commitments, so he avoids the word "object," which has traditionally been used to name objects of cognition. Even the word "thing" – Latin *res* – is tied to Descartes' ontology of substances. Heidegger therefore chooses the German word *Zeug* to talk about the entities that surround us. *Zeug* is an ordinary term, used colloquially like the English "stuff." It is used to form compound nouns such as *Spielzeug* or *Werkzeug*, "stuff for play" or "stuff for work," that is, toys and tools. Heidegger points to such nouns in claiming that for the most part the ordinary entities that surround us have specific purposes and uses. Common translations of Heidegger's *Zeug*, therefore, are "equipment," "paraphernalia," and "gear." We will use "equipment."

Most ordinary entities we deal with on an everyday basis are useful and tool-like. Some of Heidegger's examples are literally tools from the workshops of carpenters and shoemakers, like hammers or shoe-leather. Other daily environments resemble workshops, insofar as the entities they contain have specific uses. In your study you are surrounded by pens, paper, a computer, books, a stapler, a briefcase. In the cafeteria there are napkins, silverware, plates, credit-card readers. These things are there *to be used*. They are meaningful by virtue of what they are normally used for. In a straightforward sense their "being," that is, what they are, is understood in terms of what they are for. Something is a pen if we are meant to write with it. Even "purely decorative" things are wrapped up in purposive equipment. The picture is in a frame, which has an eyelet for hanging it on the nail on the wall. Beyond man-made contexts, too, we encounter mountains, rivers, and the wind in terms of uses to which we put them, or from which we exempt them. A forest can be a nature preserve, or a source of timber.

Every piece of equipment points to some others. Pens are for writing, so they involve ink, paper, or other surfaces for writing on. This is so, even if no paper happens to lie nearby. The reference to other equipment is not an observation of the actual or typical arrangement of things, but a structure inherent in what it means to be a pen. It is part of what we understand insofar as we encounter pens, paper, ink, and other equipment as such. Heidegger writes:

> Strictly speaking there never "is" *one* equipment. To the being of equipment there always belongs a wholeness of equipment, in which it can be the equipment that it is. (*SZ*, p. 68)

In this passage Heidegger draws attention to a "wholeness of equipment" (*Zeugganzheit*). This "wholeness of equipment" in which pens can "be what they are" does not consist of a sum total of many pens and pieces of paper and desks and chairs. By itself, such an aggregated list does not make sense of how the items of equipment in it refer to one another, and it does not explain what makes a pen be a pen. Heidegger says that the wholeness is constituted by the "various ways of 'in-order-to,' such as serviceability, relevance, applicability, and handiness" (*SZ*, p. 68). We encounter pens as equipment for writing in the context of putting them to use, that is, in this case, the familiar practice of writing, which involves all this equipment. Pieces of equipment make sense in the context of such practices. So we should understand "wholeness" as a background, a context or practice in which individual items of equipment make sense.

Heidegger thus highlights the usability of equipment as its basic feature. Obviously, the usability of equipment makes up the meaning of these things insofar as we are users of equipment. We encounter pens, hammers, and so on through our abilities to use them. Again, this is not an observation of what we actually or typically do. I can encounter a lot of pens even if I write very little, or not at all. Rather, it is a statement of what it means for us to encounter equipment at all. We encounter equipment insofar as we participate in purposive practices. For such participation, it is not enough to know, in some general way, the fact that pens are for writing. We need to know how writing works, in an actively engaged way. In other words, if usability is a basic feature of equipment, then the basic manner of encountering equipment is to be a practically engaged user.

Heidegger emphasizes the distinction between practical engagement and reflecting, detached knowing. He makes this point in a well-known passage about hammers. The hammer is a piece of equipment, and to encounter a hammer as a hammer means to use it, to be practically engaged with it. Such practical engagement does not require reflection, and usually it requires just the opposite. We are most genuinely engaged in hammering when we do not think about how our practical engagement brings out the meaning of the equipment:

> The act of hammering need not know about the equipment-character of the hammer, yet it takes up this equipment in the most pertinent way possible. In such use, our concern for the equipment is governed by the purpose that is constitutive for it. The less we just gawk at the hammer-thing, the more we grab it and use it, the more originary our relation to it becomes, and the more undisguisedly we encounter it as that which it is, as equipment. (SZ, p. 69)

Like hammers, computer keyboards provide a good illustration of the distinction between engaged and detached encounters of equipment. We spend a lot of time typing on our laptops. In doing so we encounter the keyboard, even though we rarely pay direct attention to it. We usually focus on the text of the paper or email we are composing. We are using the keyboard in order to do something else. This is the most common way to encounter keyboards. Heidegger says that it is also the *right* way to encounter them, insofar as it is the way to deal with keyboards on their own terms, as it were. We deal with keyboards appropriately, that is, we are using them the way they are to be used, precisely when they are not the focus of our attention.

We can, and sometimes do, look directly at a keyboard, count how many keys there are, note their colors and arrangement, or study their icons and lettering. It is possible, but fairly unusual, to focus on the keyboard "itself," so to speak. But in such an attitude we are not really dealing with it as a keyboard. We are not encountering it in the context in which it can "be the equipment that it is." Such theoretical contemplation, which Heidegger dismissively calls "gawking," does not approach the keyboard the right way. It does not grasp and express its specific character as equipment.

Of course we can find out a lot about keyboards by gawking at them. Many of the facts that we uncover and appreciate by just staring at equipment remain hidden or covered up in the engaged attitude of grabbing and using it. An extreme example might be the color of the keys. Even though you spend many hours typing on your computer, you may not know what color the keys of your keyboard are. Or, if that seems too obvious to miss, you still may not know the color, size, and location of the lettering labeling each key. When Heidegger claims that using equipment is more fundamental than staring at it and brings out its features in a more pertinent way, he of course does not deny that facts such as the color of the keys are true of the keyboard. They are true enough. But they are not relevant to this equipment being the kind of thing it is, and they do not constitute the meaning of things that surround us in ordinary life.

4.1.2 Zuhanden and vorhanden

In order to capture the specific nature of equipment Heidegger distinguishes two "ways of being," which he calls *zuhanden* and *vorhanden*. Equipment is *zuhanden* insofar as it shows up in our experience when we use it, or can use it. *Zuhanden* means "to hand" or "at hand," practical, reachable, handy and useful in the pursuit of some purpose. It is usually translated as "ready-to-hand" or "available." The hammer is available insofar as it fits our hand and is ready for us to grab and swing. The keyboard is available for typing insofar as we know how to type.

Things can also show up as mere objects, stripped of their practical contexts, as, for example, the keyboard does when we gawk at it. In this case Heidegger says they are *vorhanden*, or merely present, just plain there. This is usually translated as "present-at-hand" or "occurrent." The keyboard is occurrent when we stare at it as if it were an unfamiliar object, without drawing on our practical ability to put it to use. Things are occurrent to the extent that they fail to be available, and vice versa. Equipment shows up as available precisely when we do not gawk at it but put it to use, and we scrutinize things with a theoretical gaze precisely by disengaging from any applied use of them.

> The way of being of equipment, in which it manifests itself on its own terms, we call availability. . . . A mere "theoretical" scrutiny of things fails to understand availability. (*SZ*, p. 69)

Heidegger says that availability and occurrentness are two "ways of being" (*Seinsarten*). That is to say that this is an ontological distinction, and his description of the practical usability in terms of which we primarily encounter equipment is part of an ontology.

A puzzling aspect of Heidegger's distinction is that he claims that one and the same thing – the keyboard or hammer – can have two distinct modes of being. It seems that there should be only one account of what that single thing is, that is, that there should be only one ontology. We should then be able to explain the other "way of being" in terms of this more basic account of what the thing is. Traditionally philosophy has focused on the kinds of features that Heidegger calls occurrent to give a basic ontology of the things that surround us, with the implication that the availability of those things can be explained in terms of their occurrent features. The hammer, for example, is an extended thing with a certain shape, size, and weight, made of iron and wood. Traditional ontology then claims that these occurrent features ground and explain the uses to which we can put a hammer. It works for banging nails into the wall, because of the density, hardness, and weight of the iron that its head is made of. According to such an account, the hardness of the iron is ontologically basic, and the readiness for banging nails is derivative.

Heidegger rejects such traditional privileging of occurrent features for two reasons. First, he denies that we can give an adequate account of availability in terms of occurrent features. No amount of information about the materials that make up the hammer suffices for making sense of the way we put hammers to use. The problem is not one of complexity. It is not that we do not have enough occurrent information about equipment. Rather, occurrent facts are not the right kind for explaining availability. For example, physical distances do not capture what it means for something to be "near" to our concerns, and in general occurrent features do not tell us what it means for equipment to be "there" for us.

The second reason Heidegger rejects attempts to reduce availability to occurrence is that occurrent features are not immediately and unproblematically available to us. One common way of framing the reductive point is to say that extension and matter are "what there is," while attributes such as usability and relevance are "subjective valuations" that depend on human purposes and therefore are not ontologically basic. While Heidegger concedes the interconnection between usability and human purposes, he challenges the supposed simplicity of occurrent objects. We disclose the occurrent features of objects as detached subjects, turning a purely cognitive gaze on them. But such detachment and pure cognition, Heidegger argues, are grounded in involved, familiar dealing. In other words, we can make sense of the occurrent features of things only against the background of our basic familiarity with a world of available equipment. In terms of their intelligibility, then, Heidegger argues that the priority is the other way around: occurrence is grounded in familiar use of equipment.

4.2 Descartes and occurrentness

Like Husserl's description of the "natural attitude" in the *Ideas*, Heidegger's approach is reminiscent of the beginning of Descartes' *Meditations on First Philosophy*. Descartes, too, begins by surveying his relation to the familiar objects that surround us on an everyday basis. But while Descartes is interested in the certainty of our knowledge of these ordinary objects, Heidegger asks about the being of these objects, that is, what kind of things they are and what makes them intelligible as things in the first place. In other words, Descartes is interested in epistemology, while Heidegger is after an ontology of ordinary objects.

As we saw above, Heidegger argues that the attitude of a detached observer misses fundamental features of the objects around us. If we just look at a keyboard or a hammer, we are not interacting with it as the kind of thing it is. Descartes privileges the detached attitude in his epistemology. As he pursues his skeptical method, his cognizer becomes ever more detached, until it is reduced to a pure, body-less intellect. Descartes argues that we can justify our knowledge of the surrounding world only on the basis of the certainty of the cognitions of the isolated ego. Heidegger thinks this is the wrong approach to epistemology, because cognizing an object is a derivative way of relating to the world, grounded on our prior practical engagement.

Epistemology aside, Heidegger thinks that Cartesian skepticism leads to a bad ontology. Descartes makes a fundamental distinction between thinking and non-thinking things. The essence of the latter, he claims, lies in their corporeal, or bodily, extension. The extension of things explains their phenomenal appearance, that is, their shapes, colors, hardness, and odors. But these latter features are not essential to the objects. An object remains the same, even if its phenomenal appearance changes. Extension also explains the motion of objects and their interaction, according to the rules Descartes outlines in his *Principles* (1644).

Descartes' philosophical analysis of the world surrounding him, then, leads him to the conception of a detached observer cognizing occurrent things, where the features and possible interactions of these things are understood in terms of various modalities of occurring alongside one another. Consequently Heidegger refers interchangeably to Cartesian ontology and the "ontology of occurrentness." He thinks this approach is widespread and shapes the work of many later philosophers who do not consider themselves Cartesians. And it is fundamentally mistaken, because its basic concepts make it impossible to adequately capture the phenomena of availability.

4.3 Being-in-the-world

Gawking does not reveal entities as they really are. We encounter them appropriately and fully only when we put them to use. Just as Heidegger's phenomenological analysis of entities challenges basic Cartesian conceptions of ordinary objects as extended things with properties, it also undermines the conception of us as detached thinkers and cognizers. Heidegger argues that the fundamental way we have and encounter our world is pre-cognitive and consists of skillful, familiar, disposed, purposive caring. This is what he calls "Dasein," and also "being-in" the world. The difference between being directed at objects in consciousness and being at grips with equipment in a purposive engagement is the most salient respect in which Heidegger may have intended to claim that *Being and Time* was written "against" Husserl.

4.3.1 Skills

Let us return to the keyboard example. If you know how to touch-type, then you know that the "i" is to the left of the "o." You can also come to know this by staring at the keyboard and determining the relative locations of keys in a detached way. These two ways of "knowing" this fact are quite different from one another. If you ask a competent typist about the location of the keys, she will first express and articulate her knowledge through a slight twitch of the middle and ring fingers of her right hand. Without such an effort at typing, she may not be able to say where the letters are. Merleau-Ponty discusses this example in his *Phenomenology of Perception*:

> One can know how to type without knowing how to indicate where on the keyboard the letters that compose the words are located. Knowing how to type, then, is not the same as knowing the location of each

letter on the keyboard, nor even having acquired a conditioned reflex for each letter that is triggered upon seeing it. ... It is a question of a knowledge in our hands, which is only given through a bodily effort and cannot be translated by an objective designation. The subject knows where the letters are on the keyboard just as we know where one of our limbs is – a knowledge of familiarity. (*PP*, p. 145)

This example illustrates the two different ways in which we can relate to equipment, as engaged users and detached cognizers. Above, we noted that we properly encounter equipment only when we deal with it as engaged users. To be an engaged user means to have relevant competences or skills. Such skills disclose the world.

The most obvious examples of world-disclosing skills are practical abilities of wielding equipment, such as typing or hammering. A host of more basic skills are tied up with these practical skills. Typing and hammering involve basic motor skills, such as balancing, standing, walking, reaching, or grasping, as well as a host of basic perceptual skills such as focusing our eyesight, tilting our heads in order to get better purchase on a sound or a clearer view of an object. These skills are nested and interconnected, and like equipment they form a holistic context. It is impossible to delineate where one skill ends and another begins, and no skill comes alone. Like equipment, skills are purposive. In Heidegger's language they have the structure of the "in order to," though the specific purposes may be vague, multi-layered, or hidden from us.

Our skills are culturally inflected. The equipment we deal with and the activities we engage in vary across time and cultures. Merleau-Ponty's typist, for example, was exercising her skill on a very different keyboard from the ones we handle today. The typing skill on mechanical typewriters involved modulating finger strength to depress the levers, and a regular cadence to allow the typebars to return and prevent jamming. Some skills have a passing relevance. For a few years everyone could skillfully take a CD out of its case, wind a watch, or dial a rotary phone. To some extent such inflections affect basic motor skills, too. We walk in different ways depending on whether we are walking indoors or out, through a crowd or into a church. Without having to think about it, we have a refined sense for how close we should stand to others, or how loud we should be. We whisper in movie theaters and shout in bars.

Just as Heidegger claims that the things we encounter first and foremost have the character of available equipment rather than occurrent objects, he also maintains that we encounter them through using them skillfully rather than through some detached stance. We do not first encounter objects and then separately bring our skills to bear on them.

The first encounter is already skillful. The example of typing on a keyboard illustrates this fundamental role of skills. The typist *knows* the position of the keys, but not in an explicit or reflective way. She knows it insofar as she can type, that is, by knowing how to deal with a keyboard. Explicit knowledge is no part of this skillful know-how. In fact, Heidegger points out that unless something goes wrong, our skillful know-how usually is entirely inexplicit. The typist knows the positions of the keys, but does not think of it. Her focus is not on the keyboard at all, but on the text she is composing.

The primary way we experience the world, then, is as skillful users. In such experience, the equipment we deal with usually does not stand out. As long as our know-how proceeds smoothly, the equipment remains transparent, that is, invisible to us. Merleau-Ponty, once again, gives us a telling example:

> The blind man's cane has ceased to be an object for him, it is no longer perceived for itself; rather, the cane's furthest point is transformed into a sensitive zone, it increases the scope and the radius of the act of touching. . . . The blind man knows its length by the position of the objects, rather than the position of the objects through the cane's length. (*PP*, p. 144)

This invisibility of the cane, the keyboard, or the hammer when we are skillfully using them does not imply that we are going about our business blindly. Heidegger refers to the specific kind of sight that guides skillful use as "circumspection" (*Umsicht*). A competent carpenter has a clear and detailed grasp of his surroundings in the workshop. He is intimately familiar with it. This grasp does not require him to focus explicitly on any part of it, but if something were out of place, the circumspect carpenter would notice.

In such cases – when something is amiss, broken, or out of place – the structure of circumspect use of available equipment shows up clearly. In such breakdown situations, we continue to encounter equipment, but it loses its readiness for use and so becomes *un*available. Heidegger says that the occurrent features of the equipment "announce themselves" and that "the character of occurrence is brought out in the available equipment" (*SZ*, p. 74). Unavailability does not usually reduce us to mere gawking; we still find ourselves surrounded by a world of equipment. But because our skillful coping is interrupted, we find that the transparency of equipment is partially lifted as our circumspection attends to what is amiss. "The nexus of equipment lights up, not as something never seen before, but as a whole that was always already sighted in circumspection" (*SZ*, p. 75).

4.3.2 Disclosedness

As we noted above, Heidegger for the most part eschews the terminology of traditional philosophy, so that his descriptions are not unduly influenced by the theoretical commitments of those views. He is careful to point out that first and foremost our experiences of the world are not explicitly cognitive or mental and he distances his phenomenology from Cartesian views. One aspect of such views is that our primary connection to the world is through consciousness. Heidegger, unlike Husserl, does not think that consciousness plays a fundamental role in our experience of the world. We are certainly conscious of many things while we are going about our business, but our most common and appropriate way to deal with equipment is not to attend to it explicitly. Heidegger instead uses the word "disclosedness" (*Erschlossenheit*) to describe the manner in which the world is "there" for us, that is, available for us as the setting in which we competently engage in projects. For the most part the world is disclosed without our being conscious of it. Heidegger says that the world is "always already disclosed." Unlike thinking or perceiving, disclosure is not an act that reveals its object in the moment. It is a familiarity with the context or setting of our concernful dealings that operates in the background.

Disclosedness differs from circumspection. Circumspection guides a skill. The skilled typist knows where the keys are in using them. If the keyboard misbehaves (the shift lock is on, or a key is stuck), the typist notices this. That we can *now* circumspectly notice the broken key shows that the wholeness of equipment in which the keyboard functions was already disclosed.

Consider a simpler, more ubiquitous skill, such as walking. On your way across campus you may walk up and down stairs, on carpeted and hard surfaces, up various inclines, over a curb, around other people, and so on. You circumspectly make proper adjustments (lengthen your stride, incline your torso, raise your knees, and so on) in response to changes in the setting. Your circumspection guides your skillful walking out the building, down the walkway, across the lawn, and up to the classroom in the next building. Much of this does not require you to pay explicit attention, while some of it (a puddle in the middle of the walkway, fallen branches, a golf cart executing a U-turn) shows up as unavailable. Circumspection thus is the "sight" that guides your skillful walking on the usual paths and is occasionally prompted to attend to features of things on your way.

Many features of our surroundings are not relevant to our walking skills and therefore we do not "sight" them circumspectly at all.

The fact that we do not attempt to walk up a wall is not a matter of our circumspectly exercising a skill. We do not need a skill to keep us from attempting this, because the world simply does not present walls, chasms, and thin air as walkable. We are open to our surroundings as a space in which we can move and manipulate equipment. Our bodies and basic motor and perceptual skills, our size, forward and upward orientation, the range of our reach, the aperture and strength of our grip, all serve to prefigure more or less definite possibilities and resistances in the world. This openness toward the world as a context or setting in which we can meaningfully deploy certain skills is what Heidegger calls disclosedness.

4.3.3 Disposedness

Heidegger analyzes two aspects of our skillful comportment. On the one hand, we actively navigate through space, or handle a familiar piece of equipment. At the same time, however, we experience our skillful activity as being drawn out by the equipment around us. In other words, we are simultaneously actively engaged and responsive to solicitations. The first of these two aspects consists of our skills. Heidegger calls it our "know-how" or "understanding" (*Verstehen*). He calls the second one "disposedness" (*Befindlichkeit*). Know-how and disposedness are not distinct in the phenomenology of our actual experiences. Heidegger calls them "equi-originary," pointing out that know-how is always disposed and disposedness always has its know-how. An empty chair in a crowded room shows up as inviting, that is, affects us and draws us in, only because we have the skills for sitting and navigating crowded spaces. Conversely, to be skilled at moving around crowds, for example, consists partly in being sensitive to empty spaces as inviting.

Disposedness shows up in ordinary contexts as familiar moods, such as joy, boredom, or fear. Heidegger notes that we are always in some mood, even if it is subdued neutrality, or disinterested indifference. Moods are pervasive and color a situation as a whole. If I am bored, the entire surrounding world, with its whole nexus of equipment, shows up as boring. Further, we cannot reconstruct or discover the specific content of the mood in any other way. The mood of apprehension or fear, for example, reveals the world as threatening. But "a pure examination, even if it penetrates into the innermost veins of an occurrent thing, would never be able to discover anything like a threat" (*SZ*, p. 138). This resembles the claim Heidegger makes about skills: they are a way of encountering the surrounding world that cannot be reduced to theoretical contemplation. "The possibilities of disclosure through cognition fall short of the originary disclosure in moods" (SZ, p. 134). Just as we are fundamentally engaged users, we are also fundamentally moody.

The familiar experience of being in moods leads Heidegger to the stronger claim that we must be affected by the world in order to have experience at all. Beyond specific experiences, such as threats or joys, moods are necessary for any kind of encounter of entities. They do not contribute piecemeal to a few experiences here and there, but enable all experience as such. "Mood first makes it possible for us to direct ourselves to entities" (SZ, p. 137). In this more fundamental, ontological role, disposedness names our ability to be affected by the world, through which we always find things mattering to us one way or another. Of course there are a lot of specific things in the world that do not particularly matter to us. But the structure of encountering a world of equipment at all requires some ways in which things matter to us and draw us to engage with the world. Unless something matters, nothing shows up, so disposedness is a fundamental, constitutive aspect of existence. As Heidegger puts it, "Mood has always already disclosed being-in-the-world as a whole," and "the disclosedness of the world is co-constituted by disposedness" (SZ, p. 137).

Moods such as joy, fear, and boredom have an obvious evaluative component. In disclosedness, however, there is no such obvious evaluation. The role of disposedness is to open up a world of possibilities and resistances, making equipmental roles manifest. To reveal lawns and not walls as "walkable" does not require an approbation in any obvious sense. Accordingly, the central point in Heidegger's analysis of disposedness is not that a good or bad mood psychologically colors our experience of the general situation, but that such moods point back to our basic openness to the world. Heidegger writes that "on the basis of disposedness we can see clearly that circumspect, concernful encountering has the character of being affected. Affectedness . . . is only possible insofar as we can be solicited (angegangen) by entities within the world. Such solicitation is grounded in disposedness" (SZ, p. 137).

4.4 Being-with others and the anyone

We experience the world as an interwoven texture of equipment and purposes. This nexus also involves other people, so our world is always also a "with-world" (Mitwelt). Heidegger's discussion of how people – both yourself and others – show up in the world of ordinary experience is relatively brief. The reason for this is that for the most part we do not show up at all, at least not in any special way. Other people are disclosed in the same disposed competences as equipment. There is no special kind of intelligibility that gives us access to other people. In particular, Heidegger argues that we do not have to *infer* that there are other people through some kind of "empathy" or similar transfer of our own experience to other bodies. Philosophical problems of solipsism and other minds are pseudo-problems that only come up if we ignore the basic ways in which we already "know" that others are there. If we understand the world, we understand it as a world full of others. The buildings and walkways on campus, the chairs in the lecture hall, and all the equipment of everyday concerns point to and involve others. Our skills for making sense of equipment are, in part, also "social" skills, both in the usual sense of having to deal with other people in appropriate and acceptable ways, and in a literal sense. For example, we adjust our gait and walking speed if the hallway is crowded, we maintain a certain distance from others, and so on. Being-in-the-world is being-with others.

Just as we fail to understand the being of equipment if we treat it as occurrent, we also cannot understand the presence of other people as an occurrent event. Heidegger points out that feeling part of a group or a community, as well as feeling lonely, is not a matter of being physically located among other bodies. Sometimes we feel lonely precisely when we are in a room full of people. What matters much more is whether we share a mood, a common mode of disposedness, with others, and whether our purposive engagement is tied to others. We can miss people, long for them in their absence, or rejoice in their presence because the meaningfulness of our engagement in the world is tied to them.

The same point, Heidegger claims, also holds for our own self. It does not stand out or show up in any particular way during our everyday engaged dealings. When we are skillfully dealing with equipment, we are fully absorbed in the activity. We have to interrupt or alter the experience if we want to reflect on ourselves as the "doer" of the activity. Indeed, Heidegger argues that the usual notions of the "subject" miss the point of who we are. They tend to focus on a mental state, a power of self-conscious reflection, or a conscious point of view in trying to identify who we are. In so doing, these traditional notions of the self assume a contrast or a distance between the subject and its activities or the objects of its experience. Heidegger says that the phenomenology of everyday existence shows precisely the opposite: there is no distinction in our experience between being the subject and engaging with equipment. He therefore devotes much of Division Two of *Being and Time* to a novel, non-traditional conception of the existing self.

The analysis of everydayness brings out one further crucial aspect of the everyday self. Heidegger writes that "in its absorption in the world of concernful dealings, which is at the same time being-with others, Dasein is not itself" (*SZ*, p. 125). This is a stronger claim than merely saying that in absorbed activity our own self does not stand out to us. Heidegger here claims that we are not ourselves at all, but that something else takes over the role of the "subject." This subject of everyday existence is "the anyone" (*das Man*). The anyone is the vague, elusive mass of everyone, yet nobody in particular, which holds sway over the norms that govern the meaningfulness of the world. The being of a hammer is determined by its usability, and this usability is delimited by how *anyone* uses it. Of course different individuals may deviate from or creatively reinterpret how the anyone understands equipment, but such deviant understanding itself only derives its meaning from a vague, publicly circulating understanding.

Heidegger attributes an essential positive, productive role to the anyone, but he also criticizes its limiting effects. On the productive side, the anyone makes skillful, disposed being-in-the-world possible. Most of the fundamental skills we need to have in order to disclose the world are essentially public. This is obviously true of our explicitly linguistic and communicative skills; these cannot be private or personal if they are to be meaningful. But our bodily skills, postures, expressions, and movements are also communicative in that they are imbued with an expressive power. We can stand or walk proudly, aggressively, meekly, hesitatingly, and so on. And our skills for dealing with particular equipment similarly depend on a social understanding of that equipment. If you are drawn to different comportment in a church as opposed to a bar, and yet another in a lecture hall, this is because you understand these spaces as *one* understands them. Trying to give a lecture in a bar does not change the public meaning of the space, and it will typically come out as something quite different. Indeed we learn our skills mostly by imitation, and thus from the very beginning we enter into an already existing, communally shared disclosedness, rather than constructing our own from the ground up. There is no Dasein, no disposed competences, without the anyone.

At the same time, however, Heidegger claims that the anyone has the effect of "leveling down" the possible ways to be. Anything that might be daring or new becomes commonplace, "everything exceptional is silently suppressed, ... every secret loses its power" (*SZ*, p. 127). So while the anyone makes understanding possible, it also restrains extraordinary modes of understanding. This is disturbing, because the public understanding of the anyone cannot distinguish between genuine and superficial insights. Heidegger says that first and foremost the construal of the world by the anyone always holds sway, even though it is "not receptive to differences between levels and genuineness" (*SZ*, p. 127). In the dominant public understanding, a rumor or a fad is not distinguishable from genuine insight or mastery.

Insofar as Heidegger's goal is to analyze human existence, the most problematic aspect of the leveled-down public understanding is its self-construal. It makes it difficult to gain a genuine self-understanding, and instead promotes and suggests self-understandings that are not genuine, and do not reveal what it means to exist. Heidegger calls the common idea of what it means to exist as a person the "anyone-self," and he distinguishes it from a genuine, or "authentic" (*eigentliches*) self. The anyone-self is the self-construal that says that to be a person is to be a "subject," a conscious mind, a substance that persists through various experiences and events that are merely contingent to its being. Genuine self-construal must be gained by existing authentically in the face of this misunderstanding propagated by the anyone. Authentic existence and the ontologically genuine interpretation of the self are the chief topics of the second half of *Being and Time*.

4.5 The existential conception of the self

4.5.1 The self of being-in-the-world

Husserl gives an ontology of the self on the basis of his phenomenology of time consciousness. The self, he argues, consists of acts that constitute the continuous temporal stream in which we are conscious of intentional objects and also conscious of our own consciousness. Heidegger also gives an ontology of the self, and it has some superficial similarities with Husserl's account. Like Husserl, Heidegger argues that we have to make sense of the self in terms of an account based on the transcendental role of time. In other words, time is a constitutive condition of the possibility of experiencing the world, and if we explain how time comes to play this constituting role, we thereby also explain what it means to be a self, or an I.

But this similarity is qualified by deep and important differences. Heidegger, unlike Husserl, does not think that consciousness is typical of, or essential to, our meaningful experiences. We experience the world in disclosedness, which consists of disposed competence, not of a conscious or self-conscious intentional act. Moods and skills need not be conscious to open up the world for us. Heidegger also does not think that time makes experience possible by structuring the stream of consciousness. Time is a necessary condition for meaningful experience, but it does not work through structuring consciousness. Instead Heidegger wants to claim that time structures disclosedness, that is, our disposedness and competences.

Similarly, Heidegger does not think that self-consciousness is a crucial or typical element of being a self. Husserl arrives at his notion of the self by analyzing the "double intentionality" of acts that are directed both at the intentional content of consciousness and at the consciousness itself (e.g., that I see a tree and am conscious of myself seeing a tree). Heidegger instead wants to claim that our relation to our selves lies precisely in our relation to the intentional object. In one of his lecture courses Heidegger puts this point very clearly:

> In existing we do not find ourselves by reflecting or turning back to ourselves, as if we were standing behind our own backs, rigidly facing things; rather we find ourselves precisely in the things themselves, in those that surround us on a daily basis. You are what you do and deal with. (1927/1975, p. 226)

He illustrates this point with the example of a shoemaker, who finds himself in the things that surround him and that he works with. Of course the shoemaker is not literally the needles, leather, and glue that he finds on his workbench. But Heidegger does not think of these tools as occurrent items. They are equipment whose being is constituted in the familiar nexus of possibilities, and what the shoemaker is cannot be separated from the disclosedness of these things.

This conception of the self as the invisible background structure of our ongoing dealings with equipment in the world, rather than an entity that can be explained in isolation from such involvement, is what Heidegger calls the *existential* conception of the self. He calls the structure of dealing with equipment the "care-structure." The self, he writes, is "implicit in the structure of care" (*SZ*, p. 323). To underscore the novelty of this view he says that we explain the self in terms of structural moments he calls "existentialia," as opposed to categories or occurrent properties.

4.5.2 Temporality and the self

Like Husserl, Heidegger claims that temporality is the basic structure of the self. Without temporality, there can be no existentiality and no self. Heidegger's notion of temporality, however, is not equivalent to the ordinary notion of objective time, which, he says, derives from an originary temporality. This originary temporality is the basis for the existential account of the self, and it has an unusual structure. Heidegger says, for example, that originary temporality is finite, and that the originary future precedes the past and the present.

Heidegger's emphasis on the future differs from the customary priority of the present. Husserl, for example, focuses his phenomenology of time consciousness on the present, explaining how a horizon of the past and an indeterminate horizon of the future can be intended in present consciousness. Retentions of the past are modifications of primary impressions of the present. For Heidegger, the present derives from a primary orientation toward the future and an orientation toward the past. In his terminology, the originary future and past "release" the present. "Beenness arises from the future, in such a way that the having-been future releases the present" (*SZ*, p. 326).

Similarly, on Husserl's account self-consciousness is consciousness of the present consciousness, and consequently the self-relation at the core of his account of the self is a relation that takes place in the present. Heidegger instead outlines a relation to the self that centers on the future. He says that we "come towards ourselves" in terms of the future. The German word for future is *Zukunft*, which literally means "coming towards," and Heidegger uses this literal meaning in outlining the temporal structure of the self (*SZ*, p. 325).

4.5.3 Existential possibilities

To understand Heidegger's existential notion of the self, we first need to focus on his notion of abilities. We have already seen that know-how and competences are crucial in our disclosure of the world. You encounter a surrounding world of equipment and meaningful possibilities because you know how to deal with equipment to get around in this world and because you are affected by it and always find yourself disposed one way or another. We have also seen that the world you disclose through your competences is structured as a holistic network, in which all equipment points to other equipment. The holistic background against which a given thing can show up as usable or meaningful is structured by purposes. So, for example, we can best explain the relation between chalk, blackboards, chairs, and tables by pointing to the multiple, nested purposes in terms of which the setting of a classroom is encountered. You use chalk in order to write on blackboards, in order to lead a discussion, in order to teach a course, and so on. Like equipment, your competences are also interconnected holistically, and here too the connections are purposive. So you reach for and grasp the chalk in order to write with it, in order to give the lecture, and so on.

Heidegger argues that the nested connections between the various purposes that structure our experience of the world reveal a single, more basic purpose that seems to organize them all, which he calls the "for-the-sake-of-which" (*Umwillen*). While there are many skills and a lot of different pieces of equipment at play in your experience of the classroom, they all fit together and make sense in terms of the more basic purpose of, say, "being a professor" or "being a student." We can characterize these basic purposes by pointing out that they are something you can *be*, rather than merely something you can do. Heidegger calls them existential possibilities. He also points out that the "for-the-sake-of-which" is a self-understanding. Understanding, here, also means a kind of competence. Just as you understand how to use equipment, you also understand how to be a student. In other words, to exist for the sake of being a student means that you competently and skillfully go about being one.

Recall that competences and disposedness constitute disclosedness. You cannot encounter things and experience a world without them. The same point holds for existential possibilities. Without them, there is no disclosedness. This means that you do not independently discover the classroom with all its equipment and then separately come to adopt a possible stance toward it in pursuing one purpose or another. You discover on the basis of disclosedness, and you disclose by already comporting yourself purposefully. Existential possibilities are fundamental to encountering meaningful situations.

Heidegger writes that we *are* being-possible, not that we *have* possibilities. This is a crucial point. Just as existential possibilities are a basic feature of disclosure, they are a basic feature of existence. As he puts it, existential possibilities are "the most originary and most basic positive determination of Dasein" (*SZ*, pp. 143f.). We cannot exist, except by being for the sake of some existential possibility. Heidegger denies that we can make sense of the notion of a "core" self or a substrate that somehow underlies our existential involvement in the world and can be analytically identified without such involvement. The Cartesian cogito would be an example of such a substrate. According to Descartes we are an "I that thinks" independent of any particular thought or object of thought. Heidegger argues that similar positions can be found in Husserl and Kant (*SZ*, p. 320). In general, Heidegger thinks that this view is characteristic of the tradition that approaches the self along the lines of the ontology of occurrent objects. We tend to think that there is an underlying substance that has properties. This may be the right approach for discussing the ontology of objects, but Heidegger claims that it only confuses us when we are trying to explain the being of the self.

4.5.4 Thrown projection

Possibilities, generally speaking, are basic purposes that can organize one's existence and that accordingly structure the meaningfulness of the world. Taken in such general terms, many possibilities can make sense of a given context of equipment. You may exist for the sake of being a professor, an educator, or as a builder, an anarchist, a parent, and so on. Depending on which of these possibilities structures your existence, you will encounter the world with a different set of emphases. If you exist for the sake of being a professor, the classroom shows up with certain saliencies and solicits you in certain ways. If you exist for the sake of being a student, different things are salient and solicit you. If you come into the classroom as a painter or electrician, it is different still.

Possibilities are ways of being that make sense. They have to be available in the world, and it must make sense to disclose the world in that way. The world allows for many possibilities, and in some cases we can even be creative and bring about new ways of being. However, our possibilities are also constrained by our culture, our historical situation, and so on. In William James' term, they have to be "live options." For example, it is no longer a live option in this century to be a court jester or knight errant. And it is not a live option in our culture to be a shaman. You can dress like one and pretend to be one, but your actions and declarations will not count as those of a shaman, despite your best efforts. Our culture is not receptive to it and the meaning for those actions is not available.

A second, more important issue is how we own or identify with our possibilities. Recall that Heidegger says that we *are* our possibilities. We are not something (an ego, or a substance, or a soul) that has possibilities, so who we are cannot be specified independently of our identification with a possibility. How does a specific possibility (being a professor) become *your* possibility? Heidegger explains this by describing the structure he calls *projection*. This has to be distinguished from a "project" in the sense of a plan. "Projecting has nothing to do with comporting yourself towards a contrived plan, according to which you arrange your being; but as existence you have always already projected yourself, and you project as long as you are" (SZ, p. 145). Projecting is not a deliberate act or stance, and it is not optional in the sense that you could get along without projecting. It is what you already find yourself doing and continue to do. If you exist for the sake of being a professor, or *project* yourself as a professor, at bottom this does not consist of your planning your day and year according to the typical activities of a professor. Projecting is more basic than such planning.

Take the example of your experience of the classroom. You encounter this setting as a student; that is, you experience the classroom by way of existing for the sake of being a student. (Of course this might not be your only "sake." In other contexts the relevant background purpose may be that you exist for the sake of being a sibling, and so on. In fact, no single, readily identifiable role or position may be sufficient to capture your self-understanding. It is more complex than "student and musician and sibling and . . . .") To encounter the classroom as a student means that you have a determinate, skillful grasp on the situation. You know how to comport yourself and how to cope with the environment. You experience the situation in terms of what is salient and what solicits you. You perceive the space as having an orientation. For example, you know where the "front" of the room is and what chairs are inviting you to sit in them. Your posture, focus, bodily stance, and so on come together in a mode of comportment that fits the space. There are many occurrent features of the space that do not draw you in and that you do not attend to, such as the color of the carpet. They are not immediately relevant to your skillful understanding of what you are up to.

In Heidegger's language, in this encounter you project entities onto their being. For example, you project the chair onto its being. This simply means that you treat the chair skillfully in such a way as to disclose its availability in the context of the meaningfulness of the situation as a whole. In other words, to project the chair onto its being is to sit on it, or at least to see it as a place for sitting. Similarly, you project the table, blackboard, floor, door, and so forth onto their being by using them appropriately. In all this, you also project yourself. Note that what counts as an "appropriate" use of the various items of equipment in this setting depends on what you are up to. For a student it is appropriate to sit on chairs, for a painter it is appropriate to cover them with plastic. So all the skillful coping with the setting is made coherent by a basic understanding of the purpose of the situation. This basic understanding is what Heidegger means by "projecting yourself." You project yourself as a student insofar as you disclose the situation in ways appropriate to being a student.

Projection, then, is the skillful deployment of a certain coherent set of disposed abilities. They cohere insofar as they point toward the same ultimate possibility "for the sake of which" you exist. Projecting a possibility is nothing else beyond these abilities. Say the possibility for whose sake you exist is being a student, that is, that you project yourself as a student. This means nothing other than that you are *able* to be a student. Existentially speaking, to be an X is to be able to be an X. Heidegger points out that we have "always already" projected. Your competent ability to be a student implies the corresponding disposedness to find yourself solicited as a student. Not only do you cope with classrooms as a student, you also find yourself drawn in and affected by them in the relevant ways. You already find the situation mattering in student-appropriate ways. For this reason Heidegger says that projection is "thrown projection."

4.5.5 Self-understanding vs. social roles

Many examples of possibilities we project, and for the sake of which we exist, resemble what we might call social roles. "Student," "athlete," "musician," "parent," and so on are all readily identifiable roles that we attribute to some people. There may also be institutional markers, milestones, or memberships that certify who belongs to such a group or fulfills such a role. But there are some crucial differences between social roles and the kind of self-understanding that Heidegger talks about.

A first difference is that one may occupy a social role, but not care about it and not comport oneself in terms of it. William Blattner uses the example of so-called "deadbeat dads" to illustrate this difference. A deadbeat dad is a father biologically and socially speaking. He may even be court-ordered to pay child support. But he does not care about being a father and does not experience the world in terms of the appropriate saliencies (Blattner 2006, p. 88f.). Child safety concerns, for example, do not matter to him. When he steps into a room, the choking hazards, sharp edges, and electrical extension cords do not show up as worrisome. Similarly, you can occupy the social role of a student; you have a student ID, wear a college sweatshirt, and somebody pays tuition on your behalf. But that is neither necessary nor sufficient for understanding yourself as a student. We saw above that projecting a self-understanding consists of finding things mattering and being competent in the appropriately coherent ways. Social roles need not imply such disposed abilities, although they often do.

A second difference is that social roles can be completely and safely attained, while an existential self-understanding is, in Blattner's phrase, "unattainable" (Blattner 1999, p. 81). Pass the bar and you are a lawyer; have a child, you are a parent. Once you have reached the relevant milestone, you have achieved that status and the corresponding role cannot fail to belong to you. Existential possibilities are not attainable in this sense. Heidegger says that we always exist "towards" the possibility, but existential possibilities are never realized or actualized. Heidegger makes this point by discussing various ways in which your comportment to your existential possibility can fall apart. You may understand yourself as a student, but you are never safely or essentially a student. This mode of disclosure can break down and you are then no longer able to be a student.

4.6 Death, guilt, and authenticity

Heidegger uses the themes of anxiety, guilt, and death to discuss possible breakdowns of self-understanding. Anxiety is a special mood, or a special mode of being affected. In anxiety, Heidegger claims, the ordinary solicitations are suspended and we fail to be drawn in by the world. There seems to be no point to the equipment around us. In anxiety nothing matters, there is no significance, no holistic context of relevant equipment, so in a sense the world is not there. Heidegger speaks of "the nothing of the world." However, being affected by the insignificance of entities as a whole is quite different from experiencing no entities at all. Insignificance is not absence. "The nothing of the world . . . does not mean that in anxiety we experience the absence of the innerworldly occurrent. It must be encountered, so that it can have no relevance at all and can show itself in its empty mercilessness" (SZ, p. 343). In their insignificance entities are very much there; they show themselves in their strangeness.

Heidegger thinks that the phenomenon of anxiety shows that with the dawning of such world-collapse, the self collapses as well. If you do not find anything mattering and lose your grip on a situation, you do not retreat to a "core" self. There is no such hidden essence that could remain after a complete world-collapse. In a sense, then, the phenomenological description of anxiety has a methodological role analogous to Cartesian or Husserlian introspection. It reveals what is left of the self once we strip the world away. While Descartes and Husserl find an essential self-contained self-consciousness, Heidegger finds that there is nothing left at all.

Anxiety announces a world-collapse, but does not bring it about completely. Even in bouts of anxiety, there are some basic competences that can help us get along and that constitute a minimal self-understanding, a stripped-down version of an existential possibility. Nevertheless, anxiety indicates the structural possibility of complete breakdown inherent in existence. Heidegger analyzes this inherent vulnerability in terms of the existential notions of guilt and death. He makes clear that these do not mean the same things that we ordinarily mean by these words. Guilt is not the state or feeling of having done wrong, and death is not the biological end of life. Instead Heidegger uses these terms to discuss the structural feature of existence that we can only have meaningful experiences by maintaining a grip on the world grounded in a self-understanding.

Existential guilt means that we must always find ourselves somehow affected by the world, but we cannot choose or explain this affectedness. "In existing we cannot get behind our thrownness" (*SZ*, p. 284). We experience the solicitations from the world as a "calling" and if we are properly attuned to this call, we take it upon ourselves to answer it. Somebody might experience a call to a certain kind of leadership or resistance and then take it up. Heidegger points out that the call really comes from ourselves, that is, from our own mode of being in the world, but we may not recognize it as such. By following the call we make our own what is already our own.

Death means that our entire commitment to a certain mode of being in the world is vulnerable and can dissolve at any moment. This can happen in many ways. On the side of disposedness, a priest can lose faith, a husband can fall out of love, a professor can lose interest. On the side of possibilities, your competences can cease to be relevant and your skills outdated when a type of living goes extinct, such as happened to court jesters and traveling salesmen. Or both can happen at the same time. This happens to Ophelia – the devoted daughter and presumed future queen – when her boyfriend kills her father. Ophelia goes on breathing and vegetating for a while, but existentially speaking she is dead. There is no longer any way for her to have a meaningful grip on her situation.

We hold on to our self-understanding in the face of its deep contingency. We make it our own by committing to it, in spite of the inescapable fact that it is not essentially or safely our own. Heidegger says that such contingent commitment is the best and only kind of self-identification that is possible for people. For the most part, we do not need to face up to this contingency. Heidegger claims that we usually flee any such recognition by throwing ourselves into our daily tasks. Therefore, if we stick to the phenomenology of ordinary daily existence, the basic contingency of our self-understanding does not show up in the phenomena. Ordinary daily existence covers up the basic structure of what it means to be a self. Heidegger calls it an inauthentic mode of existence. He contrasts it to the phenomenology of a rare and somewhat contrived mode of existence that presses into its own possibility by lucidly disclosing the world in light of the structures of guilt and death. Such an existence reveals the basic structure of existence. Heidegger calls it authentic. By embracing the fundamental contingency and vulnerability of its disclosedness, authentic existing owns its self-construal and genuinely expresses the ontological structure of existence.

Heidegger's existential phenomenology builds on Husserl's descriptive approach to the phenomena of intentionality, but introduces a fundamental change. Instead of the conscious subject, Heidegger draws our attention to the basic role of disposed, absorbed, competent activity. In doing so, Heidegger undermines a long tradition of cognitivism in philosophy, and he rejects many traditional philosophical problems as ill-formed. In their place he constructs the outlines of an entire ontology of existential phenomena. His work constitutes a new paradigm in philosophy.

Heidegger's big insights have been taken up in productive ways by philosophers interested in a broad range of disciplines. The overarching theme of such work is to challenge the distinction between subject and object, between consciousness and the environment. Most prominently, Hubert Dreyfus has shown how to sharpen and explain Heidegger's existential insights to criticize versions of cognitivism in current philosophy, especially the philosophy of artificial intelligence and the philosophy of mind (see Chapter 11). Other philosophers, inspired by a looser connection to Heidegger's work, apply his insights to the very question of cognition itself. Such "Heideggerian cognitive science" works from within the framework of an analysis of cognition to show that it consists of situated, bodily mastery of one's environment (see Chapter 13).

For all his analyses of skills and disclosedness, Heidegger is remarkably silent on two topics that are nevertheless central to his ontology: the body and perception. Skills and competences are bodily, but Heidegger does not discuss the role or structure of our bodies. Similarly, the disclosedness of the world explains many features of perception. Heidegger, however, does not draw out these implications. He thinks that the topic of perception (like consciousness, substances, subjectivity, and many more) is rife with philosophical misconstruals and confusions. On the few occasions that he mentions perception, it is usually to suggest that it misses the point. It is the great merit of Merleau-Ponty's work that he recovers these two topics and gives a detailed account of the body and perception, grounded in Heideggerian existential ontology.

Key terms

anxiety – the mood that discloses that the world can collapse, things can cease mattering, solicitations can lose their grip, and your abilities can be useless or inapplicable.

the anyone (*das Man*) – the shared, public sense of normalcy that guides most of our comportment most of the time.

available (*zuhanden*) – the mode of being of equipment. Sometimes translated as "ready-to-hand."

circumspection (*Umsicht*) – the sight that guides our skillful comportment. It allows us to remain absorbed in the situation while things progress smoothly, and leads us to attend to aspects of our activity that are not going smoothly.

death – Heidegger distinguishes an existential notion of death from the ordinary senses of the word (for which he uses "perishing" and "demise"). Existential death is the possibility of total world-collapse.

disclosedness (*Erschlossenheit*) – the way in which the broad background against which particular equipment makes sense is available for us. Disclosedness is broader than discoveredness. Heidegger says disclosedness constitutes our openness to the world.

discoveredness (*Entdecktheit*) – Heidegger's term for the way in which we reveal particular entities; engaged in the world, we discover entities.

disposedness (*Befindlichkeit*) – a basic constituent of disclosedness; we disclose the world insofar as it affects us, matters to us, and solicits us. Disposedness shows up in moods.

equipment (*Zeug*) – Heidegger's term for ordinary objects that we encounter first and foremost.

existentiality – Heidegger's claim that you are disposed ability (and not a substance, subject, ego that *is* disposed and *has* abilities).

for-the-sake-of-which (*Umwillen*) – the underlying purposive structure that organizes and makes sense of our engagement with equipment.

mood (*Stimmung*) – ways of being affected by a situation as a whole and finding things mattering to us. We are always in some mood or another.

occurrent (*vorhanden*) – an object is occurrent, as opposed to available, if it is detached from the context of its ordinary use. Sometimes translated as "present-at-hand."

resoluteness – being able to commit to a possibility (and hence disclose a world) even in the face of anxiety.

understanding (*Verstehen*) – skills, competences, and know-how. Understanding is one of two basic aspects of how we disclose the world, the other being disposedness.

with-world (*Mitwelt*) – the world, insofar as it always also involves other people.

world (*Welt*) – the holistic background that we disclose.

Further reading

Blattner, W. (2006). *Heidegger's* Being and Time: *A Reader's Guide*. London: Continuum.

Carman, T. (2003). *Heidegger's Analytic: Interpretation, Discourse, and Authenticity in* Being and Time. Cambridge: Cambridge University Press.

Dreyfus, H. (1990). *Being-in-the-World: A Commentary on Heidegger's* Being and Time, *Division I*. Cambridge, MA: MIT Press.

McManus, D., ed. (2014). *Heidegger, Authenticity and the Self: Themes from Division Two of* Being and Time. London: Routledge.

Wrathall, M. (2003). *How to Read Heidegger*. London: Granta.

– ed. (2013). *The Cambridge Companion to* Being and Time. Cambridge: Cambridge University Press.

5

Gestalt Psychology

At the same time that Husserl was working on his phenomenology, a group of psychologists in Berlin were developing what became known as Gestalt psychology. In fact, the origins of phenomenology and Gestalt psychology are intertwined. Von Ehrenfels and Carl Stumpf studied under Brentano in Vienna. Stumpf went on to supervise Husserl's philosophy dissertation and later directed the Institute of Psychology in Berlin, where Wertheimer, Köhler, and Koffka developed the foundations of Gestalt psychology. Like the psychological theories that were developed at the same time in the United States, Gestalt psychology explicitly rejected the views and methods of Wundt. Wundt's psychology is reductionist in that it focuses solely on the smallest elements of conscious experience, the atomistic sensations from which experiences are built. The Gestaltists, like the functionalists and behaviorists in the United States (see Chapters 2 and 10), oppose this focus on atomistic sensations and feelings. Unlike the functionalists and behaviorists, however, the Gestalt psychologists had limited impact on scientific psychology – more than a mere historical footnote, but less than contemporary movements in the United States. For current purposes their work is important because of the influence they had on Maurice Merleau-Ponty (Chapter 8) and James Gibson (Chapter 10).

At the same time that Wertheimer, Köhler, and Koffka were developing Gestalt ideas in Berlin, another group of psychologists developed a closely related approach under the supervision of Georg Müller in

Göttingen. Müller had founded his experimental psychology lab shortly after Wundt. While Müller's own stance was analytical, many psychology students at Göttingen were also influenced by Husserl and the circle of phenomenologists around him. Max Scheler spent some time lecturing in Göttingen, and Edith Stein studied and wrote her thesis here. Most notable among these young psychologists are Edgar Rubin, who did his experimental work on figure–ground perception here, and David Katz. Katz viewed phenomenology as a promising bridge between philosophy and psychology (Ash 1998, p. 78). He took seminars from Husserl, and in his work on color perception and the sense of touch he explicitly adopted a phenomenological attitude (Katz 1925, 1930). He understood this as bracketing existing theories of perception and producing extensive descriptions of the phenomena. In his habilitation thesis on color, Katz distinguished six different dimensions of color perception, including the novel distinction between surface colors and area colors. He also describes in detail the phenomenon of color constancy. Both of these are important for Merleau-Ponty's *Phenomenology of Perception* (see Chapter 8).

5.1 Gestalt criticisms of atomistic psychology

5.1.1 *Against the bundle and constancy hypotheses*

The specific points of Wundt's atomistic psychology that the Gestalt psychologists identify as faulty are called the "bundle hypothesis" (Wertheimer 1912) and the "constancy hypothesis" (Köhler 1913). These two hypotheses are described clearly in Koffka (1923), the first article in Gestalt psychology to have been published in English:

> All present or existential consciousness consists of a finite number of real, separable (though not necessarily separate) elements, each element corresponding to a definite stimulus or to a special memory-residuum (see below). Since a conscious unit is thus taken to be a bundle of such elements, Wertheimer, in a recent paper on the foundations of our new theory, has introduced the name "bundle-hypothesis" for this conception. These elements, or rather, some of them, are the sensations, and it is the first task of psychology to find out their number and their properties. (1923, p. 533)

In Wundt's psychology, outer experiences are molecular elements, composed of simple sensations. Each experience, that is, is a bundle of simple sensations.

Koffka goes on to describe the constancy hypothesis:

> In accordance with the method by which sensations have been investigated, it has been necessary to refer to the stimulus-side in defining the principle which underlies this concept. More explicitly, this relation of the sensation to its stimulus is expressed by a generally accepted rule, termed by Köhler the "constancy-hypothesis"; that the sensation is a direct and definite function of the stimulus. Given a certain stimulus and a normal sense-organ, we know what sensation the subject must have, or rather, we know its intensity and quality. (1923, p. 534)

According to the constancy hypothesis, the stimulus determines what bundle of simple sensations our experiences will be, and it does so in a point-by-point way. That is, to each atomic sensation will correspond some feature of the world. Imagine looking at a monitor displaying nothing but a red circle on a white background. The experience you have will be the bundle of simple sensations corresponding to, and only to, the pixels of the image on the monitor.

There was already good reason to doubt both the bundle and constancy hypotheses in the late nineteenth century, even before Wundt opened his institute in 1878. In 1870, the physiologist Ludimar Hermann published a paper describing what has come to be known as the Hermann grid. The grid (see Figure 5.1) is a light-colored or white lattice against a black background. Looking at the grid, most people see gray blobs at the intersections of the white lattice. Yet these blobs are not due to gray ink blobs on the page. The perceptual experience of the blobs is therefore inconsistent with the bundle and constancy hypotheses. This inconsist-

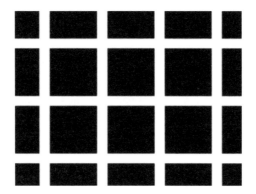

Figure 5.1 The Hermann grid
Source: Wikimedia Commons

Figure 5.2 Mach bands
Source: Wikimedia Commons

ency was discussed by Ernst Mach in his *The Analysis of Sensations* (1886), using the example of what are now known as Mach bands (Mach 1865; see Figure 5.2). The left and right extremes of Figure 5.2 are black and white, respectively. Starting near the middle of the figure, the black and white are separated by, from the left, successively brighter shades of gray, so that the black gradually shades into the white. Looking at the figure, most people see a band of extra dark black just to the left of the gradual shading and a band of extra bright white just to its right. These are Mach bands. There is no change to the ink on the page at either location. Mach suggested that these bands were instances of "spatial forms" (*Gestalten*), extra qualities that were bundled in with the more mundane sensations arising from the ink on the page. Spatial forms are inconsistent with the constancy hypothesis insofar as they are a simple sensation that does not correspond to any individual element in the world. Rather, this sensation derives from an arrangement of those elements. (Mach also discusses "tone forms" and makes analogous points.) Note that although spatial forms are inconsistent with the constancy hypothesis, they are consistent with the bundle hypothesis. In effect, the admission of spatial forms is sacrificing the constancy hypothesis, in order to maintain the bundle hypothesis.

5.1.2 Gestalt qualities

Mach's discussion of spatial and tone forms is the launch point for "On Gestalt qualities," the 1890 essay by Christian von Ehrenfels. Ehrenfels points out that by discussing spatial and tone forms as *sensations*, Mach's analysis implies that the forms are not the result of mental analysis or the application of concepts but are instead simply sensed. Given this, Ehrenfels asks about the nature of the sensation:

> Is a melody (i) a mere sum of elements, or (ii) something novel in relation to this sum, something that certainly goes hand in hand with but is distinguishable from the sum of elements? (1890, p. 83)

To answer this question, Ehrenfels considers transposing a melody from one key to another. Imagine, for example, "Happy Birthday" sung by a five-year-old and by an opera singer. These two different performances will share none of the same notes, but will still be the same melody. Indeed, it is the same melody if played on a guitar, a piano, or by an orchestra. However, suppose we take the notes that make up "Happy Birthday" in the key of C and play them in a different order. That would not be the same melody. You can change all the notes and maintain the same melody; and you can keep all the same notes and produce a different melody. So the melody must be something other than the notes that make it up. This something else is the Gestalt or form quality, which can remain constant despite changes in the parts. As we will see below, both Merleau-Ponty and Gibson inherit an interest in perceptual constancies from the Gestalt psychologists.

5.2 Perception and the environment

5.2.1 Perception and cognition

Wertheimer, who attended lectures by Ehrenfels (Smith 1988), published the first paper in Gestalt psychology in 1912. In it, he discusses the "phi phenomenon," which is the foundation of motion pictures. To produce the phi phenomenon, flash one light (A) on and off at a constant rate and another nearby light (B) at the same rate but set to be off when the first is on. That is, when A is on, B is off, and vice versa. If this is done at the right rate, people experience it not as two lights flashing, but as a single light moving back and forth from location A to location B. This apparent motion is the phi phenomenon. This is the principle behind movies and television: we see a series of static images in close succession as a single moving image. Phi (and the apparent motion in movies, of course) is a dynamic, Gestalt quality of the sort identified by Ehrenfels. Such qualities are ubiquitous in our experience, and our experience of elements is typically as components of forms. Crucially, what Wertheimer adds to Ehrenfels is the claim that not just any collection of elements can be a form. There are, Wertheimer argues, *laws* of form. This claim – that there are laws of form – contradicts the bundle hypothesis.

According to the bundle hypothesis, experiences are collections of simple sensations, combined by what Wertheimer calls "and-summation," the binding of elements into arbitrary wholes. "If I have a1, b1, and c1 and b2 and c2 are substituted for b1 and c1, I then have a1, b2, and c2" (1912, p. 289). But experiences are rarely like this. We cannot swap out parts of forms for arbitrary other parts, because only certain forms are possible. Wertheimer puts this clearly in a later paper (1923), which opens as follows:

> I stand at the window and see a house, trees, sky.
>
> Theoretically I might say there were 327 brightnesses and nuances of colour. Do I *have* "327"? No. I have sky, house, and trees. It is impossible to achieve "327" as such. And yet even though such droll calculation were possible and implied, say, for the house 120, the trees 90, the sky 117 – I should at least have *this* arrangement and division of the total, and not, say, 127 and 100 and 100; or 150 and 177.
>
> The concrete division which I *see* is not determined by some arbitrary mode of organization lying solely within my own pleasure; instead I see the arrangement and division which is given there before me. (1923, p. 71)

In short, we experience certain forms, and not others.

What is at issue here is the relationship between perception and cognition. The traditional idea is that perception or "outer experience" is of elements, and these elements are combined in cognition or "inner experience" into wholes. Wertheimer argues that forms are given to perception, not added in cognition. Outer experience is not of mere collections of elements; it is already the experience of wholes or forms. The composition of these forms is not arbitrary, but law-like. Wertheimer identifies a series of principles or laws of form as we experience it. There is *proximity*, which groups elements into wholes according to their location (Figure 5.3). In Figure 5.3(i), from Wertheimer 1923, we perceive the dots as collected into twos:

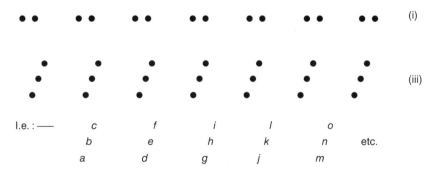

Figure 5.3 The Law of Proximity
Source: Wertheimer 1923

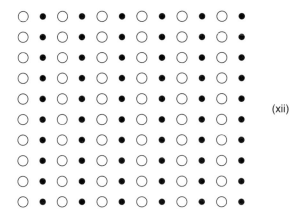

(xii)

Figure 5.4 The Law of Similarity
Source: Wertheimer 1923

ab /cd / ef / gh, etc.

and not as

a / bc / d / ef, etc.

Look also at Figure 5.3(iii). Wertheimer notes that "Quite obviously the arrangement *abc/def/ghi* is greatly superior to *ceg/fhj/ikm*." Wertheimer also identifies laws of *similarity*, which groups elements according to kind (Figure 5.4, from Wertheimer 1923) and *direction*, which groups lines according to direction (Figure 5.5, from Wertheimer 1923), and many others. Wertheimer's point in demonstrating all of these laws of form is that perception is not the bundling of simple elements into wholes according to "and-summation." The forms, the *Gestalten*, of perception are *given* in perception, not created in cognition. This implies that the bundle hypothesis is false. For Gestalt psychologists, the perceived whole is more than the sum of the parts.

Other Gestalt thinkers push this reasoning beyond simple perception of objects as wholes. In his famous studies on chimpanzees, Köhler shows that problem-solving insight, at least in non-human primates, is given in perception (1917). In the experiments, which Köhler carried out on Tenerife during World War I, chimpanzees were placed in a situation where their objective was in one way or another blocked, but indirect means for getting to the objective were available. In one example, the chimpanzees' usual fruit basket is hung out of reach from the roof of the play area by a rope. The rope passes through an iron hook on the roof,

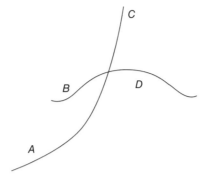

Figure 5.5 The Law of Direction
Source: Wertheimer 1923

and is looped over the limb of a tree in the play area. Köhler describes the male chimp Sultan's behavior when confronted with this situation as first displaying agitation, then looking to other chimpanzees (outside the play area) and the human handler for assistance, to no avail.

> After a time, Sultan suddenly makes for the tree, climbs quickly up to the loop, stops a moment, then, watching the basket, pulls the string till the basket bumps against the ring (and the roof), lets go again, pulls a second time more vigorously so that the basket turns over and a banana falls out. He comes down, takes the fruit, gets up again, and now pulls so violently that the string breaks, and the whole basket falls. He clambers down, takes the basket, and goes off to eat the fruit. (1917, p. 9)

Köhler reports many similar experiments, in which chimpanzees, faced with obstacles standing between themselves and their lunch, climb wooden boxes, use reaching tools, and construct stools by piling objects. In each case, there is initial agitation, followed by pleas for help, then, eventually, the solution to the problem.

These experiments are noteworthy for several reasons. First, they are a clear demonstration of animal intelligence and problem solving, and not mere trial and error, as Köhler's behaviorist contemporaries would have argued. It was clear that this was attempted problem solving and an eventual insight, because faced with similar situations in the following days, the chimps would skip the agitation and requests for assistance and immediately begin following the indirect route to the fruit. Second, it must be noted that the chimpanzees were not always able to solve the problems, and there were individual differences in that some of the chimpanzees were able to solve problems more regularly than others. Third, and most important for current purposes, the chimpanzees were only able to solve these problems when they could see the problem and the means of solving it all at once. For example, several chimpanzees were able to have the insight that stacked boxes are taller than a single box, and climbing something taller puts the basket of fruit within reach. But none were able to solve this problem unless they could see both the boxes and the hanging basket in one take; if the boxes were scattered away from the fruit basket, no insight occurred.

> In the field of experiments carried out here the insight of the chimpanzee shows itself to be principally determined by his optical apprehension of the situation; at times he even starts solving problems from a too visual point of view, and in many cases in which the chimpanzee *stops* acting with insight, it may have been simply that the structure of the situation was too much for his visual grasp (relative "weakness of form perception"). It is therefore difficult to give a satisfactory explanation of all his performances, so long as no detailed theory of form (Gestalt) has been laid as a foundation. The need for such a theory will be felt the more, when one remembers that, in this field of intelligence, *solutions* showing insight are necessarily of the same nature as the structure of the situations, in so far as they arise in dynamic processes *co-ordinated* with the situation. (1917, p. 268)

Problem-solving insight, that is, is a perceptual phenomenon, not a cognitive one. The chimpanzees do not think about what to do. Instead, to solve the problem, the chimpanzees explore the environment until the appropriate form is given in their perception. The insight occurs only when each of the necessary elements is literally in sight. As is the case with Wertheimer's laws of form, the solution to the problem is available to perception, and not added to perception by cognition

5.2.2 Lewin on motivation

Another Gestalt theorist, Kurt Lewin, expands on this point. In what became known as Lewin's equation, he argues that observed behavior is a function of a person in his or her environment (1936). Using this formulation, Lewin argues that many psychological phenomena that were thought to be traits of persons, such as personality traits and behavioral dispositions, are in fact complex relations between persons and situations. When we say that someone is outgoing, for example, we are not just saying something about her personality. We are saying something about how she relates to entire situations, including the people present as well as material, social, and cultural features. The situation is a Gestalt. Moreover, it is a Gestalt that is partly determined by the person perceiving it. To see this, consider Lewin's theory of motivation. Motivation was understood by behaviorists in Lewin's time as an internal force causing animals to act. Lewin reconceptualizes it as a vector (i.e., a *directed* force), the magnitude and direction of which are partly determined by the situation. Motivation, that is, does not just make animals act; it makes them respond in particular ways to particular features of a particular situation. The perceived situation is in part determined by the perceiver's motivations, and is perceived in terms of its valences or *Aufforderungscharaktere*. Valences are opportunities to engage in actions that structure a motivated person's perception of a situation and her subsequent actions. For a person who is motivated by hunger, a sandwich has valences that it does not have for a sated person, but only if it is reachable and does not belong to someone else. The key is that these valences appear in the environment as a function of the motivations of people, and vice versa. Valences are perceived forms that are a function of the person's state and the environment's characteristics.

This willingness to expand the forms given in perception from relations among elements, such as the circles in Figure 5.3, to relations among a person's motivations and environment made Lewin influential in social psychology. If these forms are not merely the sums of their parts, but wholes in their own rights, so too would be groups of persons. Lewin's work was also very influential on Gibson, who drew on both the concept and the name *Aufforderungscharaktere* for his theory of affordances.

5.3 Influence of Gestalt psychology

Throughout the first half of the twentieth century, Gestalt psychologists show repeatedly that abilities that seemed to be cognitive are in fact perceptual, a matter of finding the appropriate form or Gestalt given to perception. Despite the persuasiveness of many of their demonstrations, Gestalt psychology has had limited impact on mainstream thinking in psychology. There are many reasons for this, but perhaps the most important one is sociological. When Hitler came to power, Gestalt psychologists fled Germany for England and the United States. In the United States, the major Gestaltists, with the exception of Lewin, took jobs at institutions without Ph.D. programs: Wertheimer at the New School for Social Research, Koffka at Smith, Köhler at Swarthmore. Not having graduate students to run their laboratories and, then, to become a new generation of Gestalt psychologists certainly curtailed the influence of

Wertheimer, Koffka, and Köhler. Lewin is the exception in both cases. In the United States, he worked with graduate students at the University of Iowa, then at Cornell University, then as the founder of the Center for Group Dynamics at the Massachusetts Institute of Technology. Unlike that of the other Gestaltists, Lewin's work was extremely influential on subsequent psychology, especially social psychology.

As we will see in Chapter 10, Lewin's thinking was also very influential on James Gibson, who began his career as a colleague of Koffka's at Smith and whose concept of "affordance" is explicitly borrowed from Lewin's *Aufforderungscharakter*. Gibson argues that affordances are the primary objects of perception.

Despite the limited impact of the Gestalt psychologists on psychology, they are important to phenomenology and phenomenological cognitive science, via both the influence on Gibson just noted and also their influence on Merleau-Ponty at the beginning of his career. Lester Embree (1980) notes that Merleau-Ponty applied for a grant to study Gestalt psychology in 1933. He used the grant to complete his thesis, "The problem of perception in phenomenology and in Gestalt psychology," in 1934. Gestalt psychology is also foundational in Merleau-Ponty's first book, *The Structure of Behavior* (1942), in which he echoes Lewin's claims that behavior is itself a form:

> [B]ehavior is detached from the in-itself (en soi [physical]) and becomes the projection outside the organism of the *possibility* which is internal to it. The world, inasmuch as it harbors living beings, ceases to be a material plenum consisting of juxtaposed parts; it opens up as the place where behavior appears. (1942, p. 125)

and:

> [B]ehavior is not a thing, but neither is it an idea. It is not the envelope of pure consciousness and, as the witness of behavior, I am not a pure consciousness. It is precisely this which we wanted to say in stating that behavior is a form. (1942, p. 127)

In *The Structure of Behavior*, Merleau-Ponty grounds his phenomenology in the form of behavior. English "form" translates French *forme*, which translates German *Gestalt*. Behavior for Merleau-Ponty is a Gestalt. Behavior is neither material, nor mental. It is more than a series in time (i.e., more than the sum of its temporal parts). The world is the place where behavior occurs. Moreover, like the Gestaltists, Merleau-Ponty focuses on perception, not cognition. The world in which we behave is not the product of cognition; it is given in perception.

The important influence of Gestalt psychology on phenomenology depends, in part, on ambiguities about its own self-conception and methods. The Gestaltists for the most part conceived of their goal as a causal, naturalistic theory of perception and cognition. Beginning with Aron Gurwitsch, however, phenomenologists thought that this was ultimately incoherent and that Gestalt theory ought to be interpreted as phenomenology. The very phenomena that Gestalt theorists describe in such detail make a causal theory an inadequate framework for an account of perception. Instead, as Merleau-Ponty wrote, these phenomena require "an entire reformulation of the understanding" (*PP*, p. 50). In fact, Merleau-Ponty thought that at its best Gestalt theory should aim to be nothing other than "pure description" (*PP*, p. 17). Sartre similarly thought that the Gestalt descriptions of valences necessitate a reformulation of the ontology of human experience. Gibson's disagreements with the Gestaltists are of a different character. Like the Gestaltists, and unlike Merleau-Ponty and Sartre, Gibson was a scientific psychologist and, so, a naturalist. Gibson's naturalism, however, does not entail that his psychological theory is causal or mechanistic.

Key terms

behavioral field – Koffka's term for the set of valences that attract and repel a person to or from particular behaviors in an environment. The valences that make up the behavioral field are determined both by what the environment is like and by the person's motivations. Lewin called this set of valences the "life space."

bundle hypothesis – the assumption that experiences are made up of arbitrary combinations of sensations. The bundle hypothesis is an assumption of Wundt's psychology that is criticized by Wertheimer.

constancy hypothesis – the assumption that the same stimulus always produces the same elemental sensation. The constancy hypothesis is an assumption of Wundt's psychology that is criticized by Köhler.

Gestalt – German for "form." A Gestalt is a perceivable feature of a whole that is not identical to a mere summation of the parts.

laws of form – Gestalt psychologists claim that wholes are given in perception, not created in cognition. Wertheimer identified a series of laws that govern the way wholes are experienced.

life space – Lewin's name for the behavioral field.

valences (*Aufforderungscharaktere*) – Lewin's term for perceived opportunities for acting in a situation. Valences are partly determined by an animal's motivation and partly by the situation.

Further reading

Many of the works discussed in this chapter are available online at the Psych Classics website, ed. C Green. http://psychclassics.yorku.ca

Koffka, K. (1923). "Perception: An introduction to the *Gestalt-Theorie*." *Psychological Bulletin*, 19: 531–85.

Köhler, W. (1959). "Gestalt psychology today." *American Psychologist*, 14: 727–34.

Wertheimer, M. (1923/1938). "Laws of organization in perceptual forms," in W. Ellis (ed. and trans.), *A Source Book of Gestalt Psychology*. London: Routledge and Kegan Paul, 1938. (Original work published in 1923 as "Untersuchungen zur Lehre von der Gestalt II." *Psychologische Forschung*, 4: 301–50.)

6

Aron Gurwitsch: Merging Gestalt Psychology and Phenomenology

Phenomenology and Gestalt psychology have common origins. Both have direct roots in the philosophical work of Brentano and his student Carl Stumpf. Stumpf supervised Husserl's habilitation on "The concept of number" in 1887, and Husserl dedicated the *Logical Investigations* to him. In 1900 Stumpf founded the Institute of Psychology in Berlin, where Gestalt psychology effectively began. Both movements are critical of the naturalist foundations of experimental psychology in the late nineteenth century, arguing that the Wundtian approach misses basic structures of conscious experience. When Husserl spells out these criticisms in his 1911 essay "Philosophy as rigorous science," he exempts Stumpf, Theodor Lipps, and "people close to them" from the charges against "experimental fanaticism," because they "appreciate Brentano's epoch-making impetus and ... seek to continue his descriptive analysis of intentional experiences" (1911, p. 304). With his focus on the phenomenological reduction and eidetic structures, Husserl argues that properly capturing the basic structures of intentionality requires a holism that gives priority to the meaning or essence of conscious experience. The Gestalt psychologists make a similar point with their rejection of the constancy hypothesis.

Nevertheless, until the late 1920s phenomenology and Gestalt psychology develop mostly independently from each other. Husserl refers to von Ehrenfels in his *Philosophy of Arithmetic* and includes an extensive discussion of parts and wholes and "figural moments" in the *Logical*

Investigations. But his painstaking phenomenological analyses of the 1910s and 1920s do not draw on the emerging results of the Gestalt psychologists. In a 1935 lecture, Husserl briefly mentions Gestalt psychology – which he here tellingly calls *Ganzheitspsychologie* (holism psychology) – praising its rejection of atomistic psychology, but faulting its continued adherence to an "objectivism" that approaches consciousness in the natural attitude (1936, p. 297). Heidegger, who thoroughly emphasizes various holisms that make everyday experience meaningful, similarly does not refer to Gestalt psychology in his work, although he praises Gestaltist work in some remarks and letters (Radloff 2007, p. 22f.). This lack of close interaction can be explained by chronology and by the different methodological emphasis of the two schools. By the time Husserl publishes the *Ideas* in 1913, phenomenology has a well-articulated method as reflection on the constitutive structures of consciousness. The first papers on Gestalt psychology by Wertheimer and Köhler are published in 1912 and 1913, and they direct themselves toward fundamental issues in experimental work. Phenomenology understands itself as transcendental philosophy, while the Gestaltists propose a novel, internal critique of naturalistic, experimental psychology. Like Husserl, Heidegger understands phenomenology as a critical transformation of Kantian philosophy. He finds inspiration in the history of philosophy, not in the experimental results of his contemporaries. There is some mutual respect and appreciation, and there are occasional sparks of influence, but during the 1910s and 1920s – two extraordinarily productive decades for both fields – few people engage deeply in both.

This changes with the work of Aron Gurwitsch, who decisively influences Maurice Merleau-Ponty. The work of Gurwitsch and Merleau-Ponty combines Husserlian phenomenology with scientific work in psychology and neuroscience. In doing so, these authors open up the field of phenomenologically informed cognitive science that is such an important inheritance of phenomenology today.

Aron Gurwitsch studied philosophy, psychology, mathematics, and physics at the University of Berlin in 1919. Carl Stumpf noticed Gurwitsch's strong work in his philosophy seminar and advised him to take classes with Husserl in Freiburg. Gurwitsch was deeply impressed by Husserl's phenomenology and remained devoted to expounding and improving it for the duration of his career. After a year in Freiburg he once again followed Stumpf's recommendation and moved to Frankfurt to study with the Gestalt psychologist Adhemar Gelb. Gelb had written his doctoral thesis with Stumpf in 1910 and was now co-directing the Institute for Research on the Consequences of Brain Damage with Kurt Goldstein. Here Gurwitsch discovered deep connections between phenomenology and Gestalt psychology and became familiar with the clinical work Goldstein and Gelb were doing at the institute. In 1928 Gurwitsch attended the University Conference at Davos, where he was able to witness the debate between Ernst Cassirer and Heidegger regarding the latter's phenomenological interpretation of Kant. While at Frankfurt, Gurwitsch wrote his doctoral dissertation, which applied Gestalt insights to topics in Husserl's phenomenology. Gurwitsch submitted it under Moritz Geiger in Göttingen (Max Scheler had agreed to supervise this dissertation, but died before it was completed) and published it in 1929 in *Psychologische Forschung*, the main journal of Gestalt psychology. He also sent a copy to Husserl, who read it attentively and began a philosophical correspondence with Gurwitsch. Geiger and Husserl recommended Gurwitsch for a fellowship to work on his habilitation on the constitution of social relations. He completed a draft of this thesis in 1933, but was unable to submit it formally. Due to the Nazi takeover Gurwitsch, who was Jewish, was unable to assemble a committee and was barred from university appointments. Husserl read the draft and referred Gurwitsch to the work of the phenomenological sociologist Alfred Schütz, with whom Gurwitsch developed a deep and lasting correspondence and friendship.

In spring of 1933 Gurwitsch left Nazi-dominated Germany for Paris. In the next three years he gave lectures at the Sorbonne-affiliated Institute for the History of Sciences. Merleau-Ponty, who was already interested in Gestalt psychology and had read Gurwitsch's dissertation, attended these lectures and helped publish them in French. Over the following years Gurwitsch and Merleau-Ponty had frequent philosophical discussions. Gurwitsch pointed Merleau-Ponty to unpublished work by Husserl, including *Ideas II*, as well as unpublished details of Goldstein and Gelb's work with their patient Schneider. In 1940 Gurwitsch moved to America, where he held a series of temporary positions teaching mathematics and physics besides philosophy, until he obtained permanent positions at Brandeis University and, finally, at the New School for Social Research. (For details on Gurwitsch's biography see Embree 2009 and Robbins 2019.)

Against the background of his difficult and tortuous career path, Gurwitsch's work stands out for its clarity and consistency. He is an unusually perceptive interpreter of other people's work. His dissertation is a masterful reading of central topics of Husserl's *Ideas*, and his unpublished habilitation includes a detailed analysis of Heidegger's existential analytic. In 1941 Gurwitsch is the first to publish a discussion of Sartre's view of the pre-reflective ego in English. From his 1929 dissertation to his major publication *The Field of Consciousness*, published in French in 1957 and in English in 1964, Gurwitsch articulates a single vision of what he calls "constitutive phenomenology." This constitutive phenomenology brings about a thorough synthesis of phenomenology and experimental and clinical results from Gestalt psychology. Gurwitsch conceives of it as fundamentally Husserlian, although he disagrees with Husserl on several key points.

6.1 *Phenomenology of Thematics and of the Pure Ego*

The complete title of Gurwitsch's 1929 doctoral dissertation is *Phenomenology of Thematics and of the Pure Ego: Studies of the Relation between Gestalt Theory and Phenomenology*. It starts with a phenomenological analysis of what it means to be the theme of a conscious act and uses Gestalt ideas to modify and partly refute Husserl's view of hyle, noesis, noema, intentionality, and the ego.

6.1.1 *Theme and the field of consciousness*

The theme of an act is whatever you are thinking about. It is not necessarily the same as the intentional object, because the theme can span several acts and different objects. In the *Ideas* Husserl gives a brief analysis of the theme, saying that it belongs to an "important group of general modifications of acts" and makes up a specific kind of synthesis between acts (1913, §122). He gives the example of going through the steps of a mathematical proof. The intentional object of a specific thought might be a particular premise, but the theme goes beyond this premise to the proof as a whole. Consciousness engages in an ongoing modification of conscious acts and constructs a cumulative theme (*Gesamtthema*). Husserl also considers the example of a brief distraction. As you walk along the street engaged in thought, a whistle distracts you. You briefly look up and then return to your thoughts. You still have a conscious grasp of the sound, so it is an intentional object of thought, but it does not belong to the theme of consciousness. This structure of thematic objects also shows up in perception. You have a perceptual grasp of one object, and you hold on to this grasp as you look at other objects. Imagine, for example, looking at a shirt and then looking at various ties to see which one matches, or looking at an inkwell and then looking at various objects on the desk to find a pen.

Gurwitsch's dissertation argues that themes are a more fundamental concept for phenomenology than appears from Husserl's account. He captures the structure of themes through an analysis of what he calls the *field* of consciousness. His fundamental observation is that "we never deal with a theme *simpliciter*; instead we always confront a theme standing in a field" (1929, p. 203). Consciousness is centered on a theme that organizes objects in a field. This thematic field is surrounded by marginal consciousness of unthematic objects. For example, if the inkwell is the theme of a perceptual act, the desk, pencils, papers, books, and so on make up a thematic field of objects. They are oriented in the field in terms of their concrete relations to the inkwell. They are not the theme, but they are part of the overall orientation of the conscious experience in which the theme stands out. Beyond this thematic field you also see the wall and the façade of your neighbor's house through the window. These have no material connection to the thematic inkwell and relate to it merely negatively. They are in consciousness as possible objects of future thematic consciousness. Gurwitsch calls them the "marginal co-givens."

The theme of your conscious experience can change. Gurwitsch's theory of the field of consciousness lets him distinguish three types of modification of the theme. First, the thematic field can broaden as you discover or remember more objects with materially relevant relations to the central theme. You may recall more details of the mathematical proof you are reconstructing, or you remember that you put your favorite pen in the drawer. The theme stays the same, but its central position and orientation toward the field change. Second, there can be a transition in theme, as the former thematic object moves out of the center into the field, which is now reorganized around a different thematic object. For example, you finish thinking about the proof and now try to reconstruct a related one, or you give up on writing and instead decide to clean your desk. Or the former theme moves to the margin where it has no material relation to the new theme, as Husserl's distracting whistle does. Third, and most importantly for Gurwitsch, the entire field can be restructured wholesale, so that all the objects in the field and the relations between them appear differently. As an illustration of this kind of wholesale restructuring Gurwitsch points to Edgar Rubin's figure–ground structures, such as the well-known example that may be seen as a vase or two faces in profile. "We observe how the boundary between white and black changes its 'looks' and is totally transformed when we see it one time as the contour of the white vase and another time as that of the two black faces looking at each other" (1929, p. 238). In this case it is problematic to say whether the objects making up the thematic field are identical to what they were before. The vase is a different theme from the faces, but the faces have not moved from the center into the field, or into the margins. Nor have we turned our attention to a completely different object. Instead, the entire field of consciousness has been restructured.

Gurwitsch argues that the structure of theme and thematic field is the same as the relation between figure and ground. "The figure–ground relationship studied by [Rubin] is a special case of the general relation of theme to thematic field. . . . We can generalize the terms 'figure' and 'ground' beyond the visual realm in which they arose and identify them with the concepts of theme and thematic field" (1929, p. 204n). Gurwitsch applies the concept of a non-perceptual Gestalt to phenomenology and argues that the unifying theme of a conscious act is a Gestalt. In the example of grasping a mathematical proof, Gurwitsch writes, "suddenly an orientation comes into unordered trains of mathematical 'phantasies' and musings; what was still simply floating by acquires relatedness to a thought of which I am aware clearly and articulately as my theme and which dominates my field of consciousness, centralizing and directing it" (1929, p. 204). To grasp a proof is to be conscious of a theme that has the structure of a Gestalt. The objects in the field only show up as the objects they are in terms of the role they play in the structure of the whole. Consciousness of the whole precedes the consciousness of the parts. The field of consciousness in general has an orientation and a center that is given to it by the theme, that is, by a Gestalt.

6.1.2 Hyle and noema

This insight has far-reaching consequences for how Gurwitsch interprets the basic concepts of Husserl's phenomenology. Husserl ties the structure of themes to the concept of attention. You change themes by turning your attention to a different one. When a sudden whistle briefly distracts you from your thoughts, it is because it attracts your attention and then fails to hold it. Husserl characterizes this attention using the image of a spotlight. This spotlight, or "ego-ray" (*Ichstrahl*), emanates from the pure ego, illuminates some objects of consciousness and makes them stand out. Such spotlighting, says Husserl, does not change the meaning of what is spotlighted, but only its way of appearing (1913, §92). It is as if the attention of the ego picks out a theme from among an array of possibilities. Gurwitsch rejects this model of attention, because it does not fit his Gestalt-influenced phenomenology. Switching from the vase to the faces, for example, is not attending to one object lying in front of us and ignoring another. "It is not a matter of obscuring or brightening, but is one of organization" (1929, p. 205). The changeover in the theme affects the meaning of the objects in the field. We cannot even say that we are confronted by the same object.

If we are always conscious of a thematic field, and the theme is a Gestalt whose content consists of the organization of the entire field, then there is no room for hyle in phenomenology. Gurwitsch interprets hyle as raw data that are interpreted in a concrete act of consciousness, the noesis. On this account Husserl is committed to a "two-strata theory" of consciousness, where the hyle are immediately given sense data and the noesis is a higher function of consciousness that articulates them into a meaningful object. Gurwitsch argues that this two-strata view is not compatible with the phenomenological reduction. The lines on the paper that make up the ambiguous drawing of the vase and faces are never perceived as raw data, but always within the context of the vase or the face. If you see a vase and I see the faces, there is no single object that is immediately given to both our conscious acts. If you read Chinese and I do not, a Chinese character looks different to you than it does to me. "No hyletic datum is in any way independent, with regard to a 'higher stratum.' It is only at its place within an organized structure that a sensuous item becomes what it is in a given case" (1929, p. 256). The "organized structure" is already an interpreted Gestalt. Just as the Gestalt psychologists reject the idea that we directly perceive a stimulus, Gurwitsch argues that there are no hyle in our conscious experience.

This refutation of hyle depends on a particular reading of Husserl's texts. Other readings are possible. We can take Husserl's view to be that hyle are present in consciousness not as data, but as constraints. You can see the picture as a vase or as faces, but not as much else. The possibilities are constrained, we might say, by the lines on the page, and in this way the hyle are present in the conscious act even though there is no consciousness of raw data. Moreover, hyle mark the difference between an act of perception and one of imagination precisely by tying the conscious act to the immediacy of the perceptual given. Perceiving the picture of the vase differs from imagining it not because of the configuration of the Gestalt, but because of the constitutive feel that the image is immediately given. Considered this way, hyle are not raw stimuli external to the consciousness, but eidetic features of the conscious act.

Gurwitsch instead bundles these eidetic features into the noesis and noema. Without hyle, the noesis "can no longer denote an organizing and apprehending function [but] . . . extends to the experienced act of consciousness in its entirety . . . to which corresponds a noema as its intentional correlate" (1929, p. 257). For Gurwitsch the difference between perception and imagination is a matter of the noema. When you see rather than imagine a vase, your experienced act, the noesis, is intentionally directed at a noema that has the sense of a real perceptual presence. Noemata remain, for Gurwitsch, ideal and atemporal meanings. But they are not abstract meanings that impose structure on given hyle; instead they are meanings of what a perceptual object looks like or, more generally, how the object of consciousness can be experienced in a particular noesis as being the kind of object that it is. What it means to be a vase is, among other things, to have a certain look, to look *like that*. Hence what you experience in this noesis is a particular perceptual presentation of a kind of thing. This interpretation moves the noema out of the internal sphere of a meaning-giving consciousness and closer to the meaningful objects in the world. Both readings of the noema – that it is the sense or meaning imposed on external constraints, or that it is the real object as it can be understood in a concrete conscious experience – have some basis in Husserl's texts, and Husserl interpreters have debated the proper interpretation for decades.

6.1.3 The non-egological conception of consciousness

Gurwitsch also challenges the notion of the pure ego. As with the hyle and the noema, Husserl's writings are not univocally clear on this difficult topic. The pure ego is the ground of the unity of our conscious experiences. How do we explain that all the experiences that make up your stream of consciousness belong together in such a way that they all belong to you, and only to you? Gurwitsch finds that Husserl gave one account of this unity in his earlier *Logical Investigations* and a different account in the *Ideas*. According to the later account in the *Ideas*, the pure ego is "a transcendence in immanence" (1913, §57). It is a transcendence insofar as it appears as a separate entity that stands beyond the stream of consciousness. But it is in immanence insofar as it is not independent from the stream of consciousness. It is not constituted as an entity that can somehow exist apart from the stream of consciousness, unlike, say, a tree that is constituted by consciousness as a transcendent object and that we can very well strip away from consciousness without thereby affecting that consciousness. The pure ego is an identical thing that is invariably part of all the thoughts in the stream of consciousness. Because this single thing is part of all conscious experiences, it unifies them and explains why the entire stream of consciousness is mine. Husserl compares the pure ego to Kant's "I think" that must be able to accompany all my representations. Further, Husserl points out that we cannot bracket the pure ego in the phenomenological reduction, because that would essentially change the character of the experience. The pure ego is always there, even in the phenomenological reduction.

Gurwitsch's criticism of this view of the pure ego as "transcendence in immanence" parallels his refutation of hyle. Just as there are no raw givens in the phenomenologically reduced consciousness, Gurwitsch finds no ego that functions like a subject intentionally directed at an object. The entire structure of intentionality is an eidetic feature of consciousness itself, not a relation of ego to object, or a relation of the ego to its conscious acts. Gurwitsch bases this view of the ego on an earlier account that Husserl gives in the *Logical Investigations*. According to this account the ego is not an invariable ground that stands beyond the flow of experiences and confers unity on this flow; rather the ego is implicit in the flow itself (Husserl 1901a, p. 374). As Gurwitsch puts it, every stream of consciousness is a "thoroughgoing context in which every mental state is related to every other one" (1929, p. 279). This goes for present and past, marginal and central thoughts. How different mental states relate to each other varies widely, but they all belong to the same flow. Every conscious act has its specific content only in light of other acts that come before it, lie at the margins, can be remembered, and so on. This thoroughgoing context confers unity on the totality of mental states, and this unity by itself already makes up the pure ego. It explains how all conscious acts in a single stream belong together, and it also explains how they belong to you, to the ego.

Importantly, the fact that all the acts in a stream belong together and belong to you does not imply that you are aware of your ego in every conscious act. This is a crucial phenomenological motivation of this view. Gurwitsch writes, "as long as we live in straightforward experience, we are not aware of the ego, but we can, in principle, become aware of it at any moment. . . . The acts through which we are actually conscious of the phenomenological ego are acts of reflection" (1929, p. 280). In reflection we remember the noesis, rather than the noema. If you perceive a vase, you can then remember the vase (the noema) or that you were looking at the vase (the noesis). The latter act brings to the fore an awareness that it is you who saw the vase, whereas in the former act there is only the vase. Such reflection is always possible because a memory of the noesis is always a marginal co-given in the field of consciousness. Reflection makes this marginal consciousness thematic. Only in this case are we aware of the ego, which usually remains outside the thematic consciousness. Gurwitsch calls this view a "non-egological conception of consciousness." It is very similar to the view that Sartre develops a few years later in his *The Transcendence of the Ego*, which we discuss in the next chapter.

6.2 Others and the social world

Gurwitsch's doctoral dissertation on thematics works out the Gestalt-theory-inspired analysis of the field of consciousness and the resulting critical reinterpretation of basic concepts of phenomenology. Gurwitsch limits these analyses to acts of a single consciousness engaged in perception, theoretical contemplation, and reflection. His habilitation thesis, *Die mitmenschlichen Begegnungen in der Milieuwelt* ("Encountering others in the social world"), considers how we experience other people and how we experience the world of practical and useful objects. As before, Gurwitsch argues that Gestalt principles are the key to understanding these experiences.

The main project of the thesis is to develop a phenomenological account of our understanding of others. Gurwitsch considers the work of Theodor Lipps, Max Scheler, and Edith Stein, who each reject the idea that we cognize other people's mental states through an inference by analogy. Lipps leads the way by exploiting a similarity between aesthetic experience and our encounters with other people. Perceiving aesthetic objects triggers feelings of awe or pleasure beyond the perceptual content of colors and shapes. The nineteenth-century tradition of aesthetics coins the term *einfühlen* (feeling-into) for this type of aesthetic encounter. Lipps explains it by psychological processes in us that arise while we are perceptually directed at the object. If those processes are positive and life-affirming, then our "feeling-into" is positive and we see the object as beautiful. In the early 1900s Lipps begins to argue that our experience of other people works similarly. Perceiving others triggers psychological processes that enable us to see them not as mere objects, but as having mental experiences. These inner processes are a kind of simulation of the actions, gestures, and expressions we observe in others, and we understand the actions and emotions of others by experiencing our own simulations. Lipps thus originates the use of *Einfühlung* to name our understanding of the feelings of other people. In 1909 Titchener introduces the English neologism *empathy* as a translation of Lipps' term.

Lipps was sympathetic to Husserl's phenomenology and established a circle of phenomenologists at the University of Munich. Max Scheler was his junior colleague there. Later Scheler moved to Göttingen, where Husserl taught and Edith Stein was working on her doctoral thesis. Scheler and Stein both developed a phenomenology of empathy. They both follow Lipps in rejecting the account from analogy, but criticize Lipps for nevertheless interposing a psychological process between the perception and the recognition of the mentality of others. Stein argues that we perceive the mentality of others directly. In particular she focuses on the phenomenology of perceiving the bodies of others. The movement of lived bodies looks essentially different from the merely mechanical appearance of the movements of objects. Not only do bodies change location, but we see them as having a bearing and direction, as standing in tension, exerting pressure, having a spring in one's step, dragging and appearing fatigued, and so forth. These features of lived bodies are given along with other eidetic features of the perception of objects. Just as we see a tree or a vase as having volume, thickness, and a back side, so we see bodies as specifically alive. Empathy, for Stein, is the perceptual sensitivity to co-originary givens of living bodies, a sensitivity that allows us to trace and accompany the dynamics of the body. Gurwitsch agrees with much of this, but he rejects Stein's framework of perceiving others as if they were an external thing we perceive from an uninvolved third-person viewpoint. We usually experience others by finding ourselves in concrete situations with them. This is Scheler's main approach to empathy. Scheler argues that the experience of a shared world comes first and the distinction between others and the self is subsequently drawn against this basic understanding of the shared world. We never encounter others and then discover that they have mental and emotional states. Rather, we always encounter others within a context of shared emotions and affects, and then subsequently establish the distinction between other and self. Scheler calls this shared world the *Milieuwelt*.

While Gurwitsch largely agrees with Scheler and Stein's descriptions, he argues that they both fail to address a fundamental question. Phenomenological descriptions show that the encounter with others is grounded in the social world. This raises the question of the constitution of our experience of this social world. Precisely because it is so basic, we cannot rely on a traditional ontology of natural objects to explain what makes up the social world. For example, Scheler points out that a forest shows up differently for a ranger, a hiker, or an animal. What, then, makes that forest a thing in the *Milieuwelt*? What constitutes its being, so that we can speak of one and the same forest in these different situations? In general, we need to explain how we access entities in this social world. We do not experience them from the outside. Things in the social world show up in terms of the role they play in a larger whole, so the situation is like the figure–ground cases Gurwitsch used to explain the field of consciousness in his doctoral dissertation.

Gurwitsch recognizes that Heidegger's *Being and Time* addresses this basic ontological question in his phenomenology of available equipment in the environment. Gurwitsch gives a thorough and sympathetic reading of the mode of being of available equipment, what Heidegger calls "*Zuhandenheit*," connecting Heidegger's phenomenology to Gestalt theory. The holisms of Heidegger's analysis of everydayness, for Gurwitsch, have the structure of Gestalts, where individual entities only show up in terms of their role in the overall organization. Moreover, the Gestalt is only there for the engaged user. The character of equipment consists of its various relations to other equipment and to purposes. These relations cannot be grasped as external connections that items of equipment bear to one another; nor can they be reduced to functions of human purposes, if these are anthropologically understood. The equipment only shows up and the situation only discloses its sense when we are "living in" it as absorbed users of the equipment. Following Köhler, Gurwitsch defines this sense of equipment in the situation as "being demanded by the whole, fitting into it and emerging from it." For example, a hammer, nail, and picture frame only make sense as parts in terms of a whole, in this case the project of decorating the room. We discover these parts by first discovering the whole. Comportment makes sense insofar as it "uses equipment as the concrete situation demands it, according to its structure and the rules governing the whole" (1931, p. 113). Gurwitsch thus analyzes the social world in terms of a Gestaltist notion of the "whole" grafted onto Heidegger's phenomenology of available equipment.

Gurwitsch's use of "concrete situation" to describe the sense of available equipment reflects the influence of Kurt Goldstein and Adhemar Gelb at the Institute for Research on the Consequences of Brain Damage, where Gurwitsch wrote his doctoral dissertation. In a series of clinical studies Goldstein and Gelb capture the symptoms of some of their patients by distinguishing between "concrete" and "categorial" behavior. (Merleau-Ponty later explores the distinction between concrete and abstract actions, drawing on cases from the work of Goldstein and Gelb – most notably the case of Schneider.) Certain patients are unable to abstract ("categorially") from the present situation. For example, while they can easily drink from a full glass of water, they cannot use an empty glass to mimic drinking. Such concrete behavior is like Heideggerian absorption in a situation. Gurwitsch cites these clinical cases as confirmation that skillful use of familiar tools is a basic way of engaging the world. Familiarity with the practical world is more fundamental than abstract thought. Of course, there is a difference between the pathological cases and normal absorption. The patients cannot step back or imagine alternatives; their pathologies amount to a certain loss of freedom. The condition of these patients, Gurwitsch argues, is a "radicalization," or an extreme case of normal dealing with equipment in one's environment.

While Gurwitsch embraces Heidegger's account of absorbed dealing with equipment in arguing that the social world is fundamental, he disagrees with Heidegger's view of the status such absorbed dealings have in phenomenology. As we saw in Chapter 4, Heidegger argues that the basic mode of human intentionality is skillful, familiar, and disposed. The abstract or categorial stance consists of stepping back from concrete action. In other words, the cognitive intentional attitude is a privation of practical, absorbed being-in-the-world. Stepping back leaves something out. Cognition is derivative from prior and more fundamental practical engagement. Gurwitsch, on the other hand, claims that we cannot understand cognition as a deficient or derivative mode of being in the world. Stepping back describes a radical transition from absorbed living-in to thematic cognition. "The particularity of cognizing lies in the fact that it has its own thoroughly positive structures that cannot be understood as privations" (1931, p. 115). These are the positive structures of intentionality, and there is no way to get this intentionality of consciousness out of Heideggerian absorption. Practical absorption makes the entities of the social meaningful for us and it makes them available as objects for a radically different attitude, namely intentional consciousness. The job of phenomenology is to analyze this intentional consciousness. For Gurwitsch, Heidegger's phenomenology of *Zuhandenheit* can supplement Husserlian phenomenology, but it cannot replace it.

Later, Gurwitsch makes an analogous point about Merleau-Ponty's phenomenology of perception. Just as Heidegger thinks that absorbed, engaged dealing is phenomenologically basic, Merleau-Ponty argues that bodily phenomena are basic. In other words, there is an intentionality of skills and practices harbored in the body that constitutes our access to an intelligible world. Gurwitsch deeply influences Merleau-Ponty's work, and he admires and agrees with much of it. However, he thinks that the bodily phenomena Merleau-Ponty describes can play their constituting role "only as experienced bodily phenomena. . . . In the final analysis, the reference is not to bodily phenomena simply but rather to the experience and awareness of these phenomena" (1957, p. 298). Merleau-Ponty's work therefore needs to be grounded in a constitutive phenomenology of non-thematic or non-positional awareness of the body.

Heidegger and Merleau-Ponty share a commitment to existential phenomenology. In his review of Merleau-Ponty's major work, *Phenomenology of Perception*, Gurwitsch describes this existentiality as follows (the passage is about Merleau-Ponty, but its description of the concept of existence applies equally to Heidegger's work):

> The perceiving subject is essentially *engaged*. He finds himself situated within, and projected into, the world. He is *at the world*. Out of the world, there arise appeals and solicitations to the subject ... The things perceived and dealt with appear within the horizon of the world as the familiar milieu of existence and of any activity whatsoever. All perceptual consciousness is supported and pervaded by an inexplicit, unformulated, and silent reliance on the familiarity of the world. . . . Hereby is sketched a concept of *existence* to which Merleau-Ponty

gives priority over that of *consciousness*, understanding the latter with the sense of explicit thematization. (2009, p. 488)

Gurwitsch thinks the priority of existence over consciousness is misplaced. The existential focus on skillful, disposed, situated, bodily, concrete engagement does not permit the fundamental questions of constitutive phenomenology to arise. The existential subject, Gurwitsch argues, must always be understood as an intentional consciousness, and the meaningfulness of its life is constituted in consciousness. There is no escaping Husserl's transcendental question:

> No transcendental question is raised by Merleau-Ponty as to the constitution of the pre-objective world. On the contrary, he accepts it in its absolute factuality. If Merleau-Ponty has not developed a phenomenology of perception in the full transcendental sense, it is because the existentialist setting of his investigations prevents him from performing the phenomenological reduction in a radical manner. (1957, p. 165)

These criticisms of Heidegger and Merleau-Ponty show the limitations of Gurwitsch's phenomenology. He thinks that existential situatedness, including embodiment, cannot be part of phenomenological constitution, except through our awareness of the situated or embodied structure.

Key terms

marginal co-given – an entity in marginal consciousness.

marginal consciousness – consciousness that is not materially connected to the theme.

Milieuwelt – the shared social world. We only discover the meaning of entities in the social world by living in it.

non-egological conception of consciousness – the thesis that consciousness does not require a pure ego in the background.

thematic field – objects of consciousness that are concretely related to the theme.

theme – the central topic of consciousness. It always stands in a thematic field.

Further reading

Evans, J. C. and R. Stufflebeam, eds. (1997). *To Work at the Foundations*. Dordrecht: Kluwer.

7

Jean-Paul Sartre: Phenomenological Existentialism

Jean-Paul Sartre is one of the giants of twentieth-century literature and philosophy. His interests and accomplishments are extraordinarily broad. He wrote a Nobel-prize-winning novel and brilliant plays, was active in the French resistance, founded and edited a premier intellectual journal, and wrote widely on political philosophy and literary criticism. While much of his early philosophical work is straightforwardly phenomenological, in the 1943 *Being and Nothingness* his phenomenology is dominated by existentialism and its ethical consequences. In later writings, Sartre devotes himself predominantly to an analysis of Marxist political thought, and finally to an enormous biography of Gustave Flaubert.

At France's elite École Normale Supérieure, Sartre met Simone de Beauvoir and they struck up a close, lifelong, personal and intellectual relationship. Merleau-Ponty also overlapped with them and had limited philosophical exchanges with Sartre in the 1930s. All three worked together after the German occupation of France, when Sartre returned from being a prisoner of war and Merleau-Ponty from his duties in the French army. This work revolved mainly around their commitments to Marxism and their efforts to enact philosophically motivated politics. Together they founded the journal *Les Temps Modernes* to promote their philosophical and political thought.

During a stay in Berlin in 1933, Sartre studied Husserl's phenomenology. Like Gurwitsch and Merleau-Ponty, Sartre combined his enthusiasm for phenomenology with an interest in Gestalt psychology to produce innovative philosophical work. Over the next decade (during which he also published *Nausea*, his most influential novel, as well as several plays and short stories) Sartre published four monographs of phenomenological philosophy: *The Transcendence of the Ego*, *The Imagination*, and *The Imaginary*, conceived and written together, but published a few years apart; and the *Sketch for a Theory of the Emotions*. This period culminates with his major philosophical work, *Being and Nothingness*, published in 1943.

7.1 *The Transcendence of the Ego*

The title of this essay is a pun. Superficially it says that in this essay Sartre "transcends" the ego, that is, that he goes beyond traditional notions of the ego. Sartre rejects the notions of the ego from Descartes' cogito, and the transcendental ego in Kant and Husserl. More to the point, the essay is an extensive commentary on the sense in which the ego is "transcendent" in Husserl's sense of the term. For Husserl, transcendence means that the object of consciousness has a robust identity that goes beyond our conscious experience of it. The ego is transcendent because it is experienced by consciousness in the world of transcendent objects such as a tree or an inkwell. The tree and the inkwell are not in your mind. Sartre argues that the same holds for the ego: "The ego is neither formally nor materially in consciousness: it is outside, in the world. It is a being of the world, like the ego of another" (1962, p. 31). The ego is *transcendent*, but not *transcendental*. In other words, the unity of the "I" is given in experience, but there is no "I think" in the background that ties all experiences together. In fact, Sartre argues, Husserlian phenomenology itself undermines the idea of such a transcendental ego. It does not show up in the phenomena, and the kind of unity one might derive from a transcendental ego is already implicit in the empirical flow of consciousness.

The view Sartre spells out in *The Transcendence of the Ego* is similar to the criticisms of the pure ego that Gurwitsch put forth in his 1929 dissertation, even though Gurwitsch and Sartre seem not to have interacted directly until later, and it is unclear whether Sartre knew of Gurwitsch's work. Like Gurwitsch, Sartre develops his view as a criticism of Husserl's view of the *Ideas*, because it reverts "to the classic position of a transcendental I," whereas the earlier *Logical Investigations* correctly identifies the ego as a "transcendent production of consciousness" (1962, p. 37). Also like Gurwitsch, Sartre brings together ideas from Gestalt psychology with phenomenological analysis. In particular, he uses the ideas of a whole that comes before its parts and Lewin's notion of the valences of objects. A few years after Sartre published his essay, Gurwitsch presents and endorses its main points in "A non-egological conception of consciousness," the first English-language article on Sartre's work (Gurwitsch 1941).

Sartre makes two broad claims in the essay. The first is the phenomenological claim that the ego does not show up in ordinary experience. For example, Sartre writes, "while I was reading, there was consciousness *of* the book, *of* the heroes of the novel, but the *I* was not inhabiting this consciousness. . . . There was no *I* in the unreflected consciousness" (1962, p. 46f.). This insight corresponds to Gurwitsch's claim that "as long as we live in straightforward experience, we are not aware of the ego" (1929, p. 280). In another well-known passage Sartre describes how the objects in the world are prominent in absorbed activity:

> When I run after a streetcar, when I look at the time, when I am absorbed in contemplating a portrait, there is no *I*. There is consciousness *of the streetcar-having-to-be-overtaken*, etc., and non-positional consciousness of consciousness. In fact, I am then plunged into the world of objects; it is they which constitute the unity of my consciousness; it is they which present themselves with values, with attractive and repellant qualities – but *me*, I have disappeared. . . . This is not a matter of chance, due to a momentary lapse of attention, but happens because of the very structure of consciousness. (1962, p. 48f.)

Gurwitsch comments on this passage that "here there is complete agreement between Sartre and Gestalt psychology" (1941, p. 290n). As Lewin demonstrated, objects show up as making demands on us. The streetcar is "to-be-overtaken" and we are immersed in a world of "attractive and repellant qualities." These solicitations from the world of objects structure the experience. In the experience itself, there is no deliberation on my part to endow the streetcar, the portrait, and so on with attractions. Careful description shows that as long as we are absorbed in concrete situations, the unity of the experience comes from the objects. The experience does not display and does not require the unity of an "I think" to hold it together.

As Sartre points out, there is no I in ordinary experiences because of "the very structure of consciousness," by which he means its intentionality. Consciousness is such that "its object is by nature outside of it" (1962, p. 41). The story, its heroes, the streetcar, and the portrait are the intentional objects of consciousness. The I or ego is not such an object. Nevertheless, I am conscious of the novel as *my* intentional object, and

I experience the streetcar as to-be-overtaken *by me*. Sartre calls this ineliminable mine-ness of consciousness the "law of its existence": "The type of existence of consciousness is to be consciousness of itself. And consciousness is aware of itself *in so far as it is consciousness of a transcendent object*" (1962, p. 40). In order to distinguish the intentional object of consciousness (the novel, the streetcar) from this ubiquitous aura of mine-ness, Sartre uses the terms "thetic" or "positional." These two terms mean the same thing and Sartre uses them interchangeably. I have thetic or positional consciousness of the novel or streetcar, or whatever object consciousness is directed at. The same conscious act also has non-thetic or non-positional consciousness of itself. So intentionality and the "law of existence" of consciousness combine to give every conscious act this twofold structure. As Sartre puts it in *Being and Nothingness*, "every positional consciousness of an object is at the same time a non-positional consciousness of itself" (*BN*, p. 13).

Like Gurwitsch, Sartre points to *reflection* as a special kind of act through which we can grasp our non-positional self-consciousness and make it the intentional object of consciousness. For example, I can interrupt my absorption in the story and reflect on my enjoyment of it. Most of the time our conscious experience is unreflected, as we are absorbed in our activities and objects in the world. Accordingly, most of the time we have only a non-thetic consciousness of ourselves. But in reflection this non-thetic consciousness of myself becomes the intentional object of the reflecting consciousness. I am now "positionally" or "thetically" conscious of my own consciousness, of how much I like the story or how deeply I was absorbed in it.

Such self-conscious reflection plays an important role in philosophy. Husserl's transcendental reduction and Descartes' cogito are both examples of distinctly philosophical reflective self-consciousness. Sartre points out that such philosophical reflection is an "operation of the second degree" (1962, p. 44), insofar as it depends on a previous, first-order consciousness on which to reflect. "It is the non-reflective consciousness which renders the reflection possible; there is a pre-reflective cogito which is the condition of the Cartesian cogito" (*BN*, p. 13). Moreover, the reflective act shares the basic intentional structure and "law of existence" of all consciousness. Therefore, when I reflect and am directed at my own consciousness as the intentional object, that reflecting consciousness also has its own non-thetic awareness of itself. It includes the thetic consciousness of the reflected consciousness (the "I think" or cogito) and a non-thetic consciousness of the reflecting one. "Thus the consciousness which says *I think* is precisely not the consciousness which thinks. Or rather it is not *its own* thought which it posits by this thetic act." This appears to lead to an endless series of continually higher-order conscious-nesses reflecting on previous ones, like a dog chasing its tail. But Sartre points out that the cogito requires no such regress. "A consciousness has no need at all of a reflecting consciousness in order to be conscious of itself. It simply does not posit itself as an object" (1962, p. 45).

Sartre's idea that all consciousness is also non-positional self-consciousness is similar to Heidegger's claim that human existence is *jemeinig*, "in each case mine." For Heidegger, the mine-ness of ordinary, absorbed experiences is ineliminable and pervasive, and yet not salient in the experience itself. Any sense of yourself withdraws into the background and gives the concrete situation its contours only insofar as it remains withdrawn. Heidegger shows that the interconnected structure of affordances and involvements that makes up the meaning of the situation is organized by Dasein's basic commitments. It is here, in these basic commitments, that Dasein can pursue a genuine experience of itself. But in contrast to Sartre and Gurwitsch, Heidegger says that a genuine confrontation with one's basic commitments is not brought about through reflection. This is particularly clear when we consider how one's disposedness reveals the world. Reflecting on one's subjective mood or attitude only distorts disposedness.

Sartre's first broad claim is negative, that the ego does not show up in ordinary experiences. His second broad claim is the positive one that the ego is the transcendent unity of actions, dispositions, and qualities. This view replaces the generally Kantian theory that there must be a transcendental ego in the background that combines all conscious acts and gives them unity. Like Gurwitsch, Sartre holds that the flow of consciousness has its own implicit unity that derives from the way in which each particular conscious act stands in the context of all others. Both Sartre and Gurwitsch find this view in Husserl's *Logical Investigations*. Sartre maintains that Husserl also holds this view in his lectures on time consciousness, where he avers the unity of the flow of time without resorting to the constituting unification of a transcendental I.

Dispositions like irascibility or spitefulness, states like hatred or love, and actions like driving, thinking, or chasing streetcars all take place over time and across many distinct conscious acts. They are unified in the ego, that is, the many aspects and moments of chasing the streetcar belong together because they form a single experience. This unity, Sartre argues, comes from the "absolute indissolubility of the elements which cannot be conceived as separated, save by abstraction" (1962, p. 73). All the elements of the experience together form a whole in such a way that this whole gives meaning to the parts. I rush along the sidewalk, I take a step into the street, I dodge a car all in pursuit of the streetcar that beckons to be overtaken. Each move flows directly from the other and makes sense in light of the context of other moves before and after it. This relation of the whole and parts is like the relation of a Gestalt and its elements. Sartre points out that this unity does not need an underlying X that holds it all together. The unity is given among the moves and objects in the situation, and there is no need to analyze all these elements as being parts of a separate substrate that binds them. They bind themselves together, like the notes of a melody.

In the conclusion to *The Structure of Behavior* Merleau-Ponty renders this central Sartrean thesis: "The mental is reducible to the structure of behavior. Since this structure is visible from the outside and for the spectator at the same time as from within and for the actor, another person is in principle accessible to me as I am to myself; and we are both objects laid out before an impersonal consciousness" (1942, p. 221f.). Behavior has a Gestalt-like "form" or structure, and this structure contains all there is of the ego or the mental. The subject is out in the world, not hidden inside.

Just as each move on the way to chasing the streetcar shows up as part of a whole, unified action, the totality of actions, states and dispositions also show up as unified. This unity of unities is the transcendent ego. "The ego is nothing outside of the concrete totality of states and actions" (1962, p. 74). It is transcendent, because just like actions and states it is out in the world, in the objects that attract and repel us. As Merleau-Ponty notes, others can observe it from the outside just as we can from within. Like other transcendent objects, the ego bears surprises and further exploration. It may appear to me that I am spiteful and irascible, but it may turn out that I am anxious and solicitous. A gesture may appear magnanimous at first, but later begins to look merely indolent. The ego is the totality of psychical objects in such a way that it binds these objects but also is susceptible to changes in the meaning of these objects. Sartre compares this notion of the ego to Heidegger's notion of the world. The world, in Heidegger's analysis, is the whole interconnected context of affordances; we are familiar with it and go about our purposeful dealings, but the world as such rarely shows up. It lights up in breakdown situations, when something is out of place or does not work. Sartre argues that the ego is similar. It is the broad background in which actions, dispositions, and states knit together and refer to each other. But unlike Heidegger's world, Sartre says, the ego does not withdraw to only emerge in breakdown situations; rather it always appears as the horizon of states and actions. Actions and states show up within this horizon and refer to it.

7.2 *The Imagination* and *The Imaginary*

As a student at the École Normale Supérieure, Sartre wrote his thesis on "The image in psychological life." After discovering Husserl's phenomenology he returned to the topic and wrote a detailed and innovative analysis of imagining. This work was published in two separate monographs. *The Imagination* (1936) surveys inadequacies in the theories of the imagination in the "great metaphysical systems" of Descartes, Leibniz, and Hume and shows that classical psychological theory suffers from the same basic shortcomings in its framework, while Husserl's work promises a better theory. *The Imaginary* (1940) develops a phenomenological theory of imagination and a wide range of related mental experiences.

Sartre organizes this work around the distinction between perception and imagination. The metaphysics of the early modern period, he argues, conceives of imagination as a version of perception. This is the case despite the vast differences between the rationalism of Descartes, the "panlogicism" of Leibniz, and the psychological empiricism of Hume. All of these authors treat images as "ideas" or mental representations that differ from perception only by being more confused, less articulate, or less vivid. When you imagine a tree or a centaur you are conscious of an idea that, although confused and vague, is fundamentally like the idea you have when you actually perceive such things. This metaphysical view carries forward to classical and experimental psychology as a "crowd of prejudices" and shows up here as the basic stance that images are psychic content derived from sensations.

Husserl's phenomenology promises a radical renewal. Sartre calls Husserl's *Ideas* "the great event of pre-war philosophy" and says it is "destined to shatter psychology" (1936, p. 125). The key innovation is the recognition of the intentionality of all consciousness. Instead of treating an image as a mental object composed of sensations of color, tactile impressions, and so forth, Husserl shows that images are consciousness of transcendent objects. When you imagine a tree, you are conscious of a tree, albeit of a tree as imagined rather than a tree as perceived. This also holds for imagined objects that do not exist. As Sartre puts it, "the non-existence of the centaur or of the chimera does not give us the right to reduce them to mere psychic formations. . . . The temptation was strong to leave these mythical beings to their nothingness and only take into account psychic contents. But Husserl restored to the centaur precisely its transcendence at the very heart of its nothingness" (1936, p. 132).

Husserl does not give a complete theory of imagination in the *Ideas*.

Sartre supplements Husserl's various remarks. In particular he points out that we need a more thorough account of the role of hyle. Consider a line drawing of a knight. (Husserl uses the example of a print of Dürer's engraving *Ritter, Tod, und Teufel*, but the details do not matter to his point.) Husserl suggests that the hyle are one and the same if I perceive it as a physical object, the engraving; if I perceive in it the image of the knight in the flesh; or if I recollect seeing the knight, summoning the image in my mind without any sketch on paper. The difference between these three acts derives from the modifications of the noemata. These are spontaneous, insofar as it is up to me whether I see the lines on paper or see the knight in them. Sartre argues, though, that the spontaneous modification of noemata cannot account for all the differences between such acts. Obviously, it is not possible to spontaneously modify my imagined centaur into a perceived or recollected one. And yet there are hyle in the imagined act, for the imagined centaur goes beyond the mere empty intention in the word or concept of a centaur. Similarly, Sartre argues, the imaginative act of seeing the flesh-and-blood knight in the line drawing has hyle that go beyond the constraints of perceiving the physical engraving. There must be a particular kind of hyle that belong to imagination, distinct from the hyle of perception or recollection. Otherwise we risk falling back into the trouble of early modern metaphysics and classical psychology that is unable to distinguish between imagination and perception.

Sartre's refinement of Husserl's characterization of hyle is, in a sense, the opposite of Gurwitsch's criticism. Gurwitsch maintains that there are no hyle at all in the phenomenologically reduced consciousness, because we are always conscious of Gestalts, and never of raw data. There are, for instance, no hyle shared by the perception of a vase or faces in Rubin's ambiguous picture. Gurwitsch claims that the difference between these two perceptions is due to the different noemata. Sartre, on the other hand, claims that Husserl does not emphasize the hyle enough and that there are differences in hyletic constraints that are not captured by differences in the noemata.

The Imagination stops with this general outline of a Husserlian view and the indicated criticisms of the role of hyle. *The Imaginary* carries out the promise of a phenomenological theory of the imagination, as well as dreams, hallucinations, fiction, make-believe, and similar cases. In analyzing such experiences, Sartre retains Husserl's idea that each has a particular type of spontaneous synthesis that modifies how the object is intended. In addition, though, Sartre develops an original theory of the hyletic constraints or the matter of such acts. He calls this matter of an imaginative act an "analogon." Every act of imagining has its analogon. Depending on the type of imagination, this matter may consist of lines on a page, or a photograph, or the impersonation by an actor. This matter need not resemble, but it evokes the intended object. I may perceive a schematic drawing as lines on paper. This is an act of perception and the lines themselves are the perceptual hyle. If, however, in an act of imagination rather than perception, I see a face in the drawing, then the lines function as an analogon. To do this, "it is necessary that my body adopts a certain attitude, plays a certain mime to animate this ensemble of lines" (1940, p. 31). In some cases, a schematic drawing can serve as the matter for different imaginings. Rubin's vase is an obvious example of this. In such cases, the different imaginings derive from the difference in our bodily attitudes and our eye movements as we animate the schematic lines to conform to an intention. The laws of form studied by Wertheimer indicate a kind of default attitude that suggests a certain organization of the lines, but we can adopt other stances and other organizations of the matter. The kinesthetic sensations we experience in our eye movements and other bodily tensions are part of the analogon that guides and constrains your imagination. Moreover, we can generate an analogon without any lines, entirely by moving our bodies. Sartre gives the example of imagining a swing. This is much easier to do when you move your eyes back and forth as if you were following the swing. This kinesthetic sensation is the analogon of the imagining of a swing. It functions as a hyletic constraint that distinguishes the imagination from a mere empty intention of the concept of a swing.

Sartre's point that bodily movement constitutes the hyletic matter of intentional objects in some ways prefigures Merleau-Ponty's claim in the *Phenomenology of Perception* that we perceive with our bodies. But in *The Imaginary* Sartre restricts the contributions of the body to kinesthetic and somatic sensations, rather than the intentionality Merleau-Ponty discovers in the habitual actions and skills. It is unclear how deeply Sartre and Merleau-Ponty discussed their common interest in phenomenology in the mid-1930s. Merleau-Ponty wrote an appreciative review of *The Imagination*, and he was clearly familiar with *The Imaginary*, adapting several phenomenological insights from this work. Both authors merge elements of Gestalt psychology with phenomenology and develop their positions on the basis of a detailed critique of classical experimental psychology.

An underlying ambition of Sartre's phenomenology of the imagination is to reverse the metaphysics of the early modern period. While Descartes, Leibniz, and Hume treated the imagination as an imperfect version of perception, a shortcoming in a mind that is directed at knowing the truth of the world, Sartre elevates the imagination to the essential function of consciousness. "Imagination is not an empirical power added to consciousness, but is the whole of consciousness as it realizes its freedom; every concrete and real situation of consciousness in the world is pregnant with the imaginary in so far as it is always presented as a surpassing of the real" (1940, p. 186). By emphasizing this essential connection between consciousness and freedom, Sartre's detailed phenomenological work on the imagination prepares the grandiose existentialist phenomenology of *Being and Nothingness*.

7.3 *Being and Nothingness*

Sartre's intense phenomenological decade culminates in *Being and Nothingness*. The subtitle of this book is "a phenomenological essay on ontology." Sartre uses phenomenology in order to spell out the ontology of human beings. This ontology focuses on consciousness. Consciousness is essentially directed at transcendent objects, that is, at objects that are essentially beyond consciousness and that consciousness can never get entirely into its grasp. As Sartre argues in *The Transcendence of the Ego*, the ego itself is such a transcendent object. In Sartre's characteristic way of phrasing this point, it turns out that consciousness is inherently paradoxical. "We have to deal with human reality as a being which is what it is not and which is not what it is" (*BN*, p. 100).

In Chapter 3 we distinguished transcendental from existential phenomenology. Even though Sartre is arguably the most prominent of existentialist authors, *Being and Nothingness* is mostly in the mold of transcendental phenomenology. We can express this point as follows: Heidegger and Merleau-Ponty shift the starting point of phenomenological investigation from a Husserlian constituting consciousness to a skillful, embodied, attuned agent. Their claim that human intelligibility is grounded in skillful action defines the existential approach to phenomenology. Sartre, by contrast, shares Husserl's starting point and then derives existentialist theses about matters of freedom, self-deception, and our subjection to others.

7.3.1 *Being in-itself, being for-itself, and nothingness*

Sartre draws some of his basic vocabulary from Hegel. He distinguishes two basic modes of being, which he calls "being in-itself" and "being for-itself"– taken from Hegel's *Ansichsein* and *Fürsichsein*. Almost the entire dialectic of *Being and Nothingness* develops the internal dynamics of the tension between these two. The Hegelian gesture is often taken to be a more or less eclectic stylistic decision, owing to the inspiration that Sartre's generation of philosophy students derived from Alexandre Kojève's lectures on Hegel's *Phenomenology of Spirit* in the 1930s (which, however, Sartre did not attend; Merleau-Ponty did). This may be true, but there are also evident thematic reasons why Sartre chooses to lean on Hegel's concepts. First, Hegel's *Logic*, which is intended as a conceptual ontology rather than an analysis of the formal structures of reasoning, postulates that the three basic terms of ontology, from which the differences between all specific entities can be derived, are being, nothingness, and becoming. Hegel thinks that being and nothingness stand in a kind of fruitful tension that generates all possible objects for consciousness. Sartre discusses Hegel's "dialectical concept of nothingness," and criticizes it for its formality that drains it of phenomenological content (*BN*, p. 44f.); but his theory of consciousness reflects the generative powers of the same basic tension. Second, Hegel's *Phenomenology of Spirit* describes an early stage of consciousness, called the "unhappy consciousness." The unhappy consciousness is explicitly aware of a conflict between two aspects of itself that Hegel calls the "changeable" and the "unchangeable," where the former represents its temporal, contingent self and the latter represents its constant, essential self. Unable to reconcile these two aspects, it turns to a temporarily stable mode of self-denial in which it attributes its essential aspect to something outside itself and then continually aims to relate itself to that, while constantly failing to attain it. This is Hegel's analysis of the early Christian consciousness, and he thinks that cultural change eventually made it possible to overcome this stage. But the stringently atheistic Sartre adopts it as a description of the very nature of all consciousness: "The being of human reality is suffering because it rises in being as perpetually haunted by a totality which it is without being able to be it, precisely because it could not attain the in-itself without losing itself as the for-itself. Human reality therefore is by nature an unhappy consciousness with no possibility of surpassing its unhappy state" (*BN*, p. 140). Third, Sartre's analysis of the relation we bear to others elaborates the central thought of Hegel's famous master–slave dialectic from the *Phenomenology of Spirit*. Like Hegel, Sartre argues that reflective self-consciousness requires recognition by another, to whose hostile gaze we must feel subjugated, so that we can become an object for our own consciousness.

"Being in-itself" names the mode of being of ordinary, non-conscious entities, such as rocks and inkwells. Short of diving into complex philosophical theories, which Sartre wishes to avoid at first, there is not much to be said about their mode of being. There is, of course, much that can be said about the properties that such entities have; this is the domain of the positive sciences such as physics or chemistry. All these sciences share and presume the basic truth *that* their entities are. In other words, they share an ontological commitment to the being of entities. If we try to express this ontological commitment, we do not need to say more than this: "Being is. Being is in-itself. Being is what it is" (*BN*, p. 29). The rock is what it is, and it requires nothing else to prop it up, sustain it, or constantly create it.

This initial description of being in-itself seems like a tautology. But Sartre points out that it describes only one mode or "region" of being. The second region of being is what he calls "being for-itself," by which he means the mode of being of consciousness. About this we cannot say that it is what it is. In fact, as mentioned above, we have to say exactly the opposite. While being in-itself *is*, being for-itself *has to be*; and while being in-itself is what it is, being for-itself is what it is *not* (*BN*, p. 28). This sounds paradoxical. One simple way to make this distinction plausible is to recall Husserl's basic insight that consciousness is always directed at an intentional object. So the being of consciousness is never "in itself," because it always only exists insofar as it constitutes an object "for itself."

Sartre's ontological interest is not exhausted by cataloging these two regions of being, listing them alongside one another. Since consciousness is always directed at an object, its being "for-itself" depends in some ways on relating to the objects, to being "in-itself." Sartre's goal is to explain how the two regions of being relate to each other and hence to give a fuller explanation of consciousness. In Husserlian terms, this project is to explain how consciousness constitutes its intentional objects. Sartre thinks that this explanation needs to involve the notion of nothingness. This, too, sounds paradoxical, but actually is a version of an ancient philosophical question. As early as Parmenides, philosophers wondered how it is possible for us to intelligibly think about what is not the case, or what does not exist. Sartre introduces his notion of nothingness by contrasting it to negation. One view is that we can think about what is not the case through the negation of a judgment. We make negative judgments of various forms, such as "Pierre is not here," "the car does not start," or "I do not have 15 dollars in my pocket." Absences, lacks, or frustrations can thus be expressed in negative judgments. Sartre, however, argues that such negative judgments express a more originary experience of nothingness. When the car does not start, Sartre writes, we may look at the carburetor and so on questioningly. Without making any judgment we are "preparing for the eventuality of a disclosure of non-being" (*BN*, p. 39). Our pre-judgmental attitude toward the world already contains the possibilities that the negative judgment subsequently expresses.

A more concrete illustration comes from Sartre's Gestalt-inspired analysis of perception. He enters the café looking for his friend Pierre, and finds that Pierre is not there. Before making that judgment, while scanning the café, Pierre's absence already shapes the perception of the space. All perception has the structure of discerning a figure against a ground. Whether something is figure or ground never depends on any intrinsic features of the object, but derives from the attention of the perceiver. Sometimes we see the vase, and sometimes two faces in profile. When Sartre surveys the café looking for Pierre, the entire café, its furniture and walls as well as its patrons and staff, becomes the ground for a possible figure. "There is formed a synthetic organization of all the objects in the café, on the ground of which Pierre is given as about to appear" (BN, p. 41). This perceptual Gestalt is more basic than any judgment, and it already contains the absence of Pierre. So "non-being does not come to things by a negative judgment; it is the negative judgment, on the contrary, which is conditioned and supported by non-being" (BN, p. 42).

If nothingness is not the product of a logical act of negation, Sartre locates its origin in the ontology of human beings. Objects can show themselves as absent, lacking, or destroyed only because human purposes organize the world. A man needs to go somewhere, so the broken carburetor inhibits his project; he is looking for Pierre, so his friend's absence is perceptually salient. In the same vein, Sartre points out that human purposes make cities precious, and thus "it is necessary to recognize that destruction is an essentially human thing and that it is man who destroys his cities through the agency of earthquakes or directly" through war (BN, p. 40). The nothingness we experience everywhere in the world is a function of the fact that we constantly and unavoidably project possibilities that go beyond the simple being of the in-itself. "The rise of man in the midst of the being which 'invests' him causes a world to be discovered. But the essential and primordial moment of this rise is the negation. . . . Man is the being through whom nothingness comes to the world" (BN, p. 59).

7.3.2 Anguish, freedom, and vertigo

This leads Sartre to analyze the ontology of human beings, that is, the structures in virtue of which people project possibilities and discover a world suffused with nothingness. It is an ontology of human beings inspired by Husserlian phenomenology. But it is typical of Sartre's argument that he soon turns from the phenomenological perspective to an existential one. Instead of asking about the constitution of the intentional object, he describes human reality as freedom and our consciousness of freedom as anguish.

People are the origin of nothingness because they relate to themselves through nothingness. As we saw above, Sartre says that human consciousness, the "for itself," is what it is not. He describes this essential role of nothingness through the temporal structure of human existence. "Human reality carries nothingness within itself as the nothing which separates its present from all its past," as well as its future (*BN*, p. 64). He gives the example of "the gambler who has freely and sincerely decided not to gamble anymore and who, when he approaches the gaming table, suddenly sees all his resolutions melt away" (*BN*, p. 69). At that moment the gambler realizes the "total inefficacy of his past resolution" and that "nothing prevents him from gambling" (*BN*, p. 70). In a nutshell, nothing about the past resolutions and no facts about his past history can determine the gambler's next action. He is, of course, the same person he was, and his past resolutions really are his resolutions. We would misdescribe the situation, were we to argue that in making those resolutions he became "a changed man." Sartre's point is precisely that the gambler did not have a change of heart; this is not a case of someone being unwillingly overwhelmed by his addiction or some compulsive force beyond his control. What the gambler experiences, instead, is that the past resolutions cannot settle the matter once and for all. He must "sustain them in their existence" and experiences a "constantly renewed obligation to remake the self" (*BN*, p. 72). To be himself is a task of continual choosing and commitment, a task that cannot be assigned to anything outside himself, or referred to a fixed past.

The gambler's situation illustrates an essential feature of all human reality, which Sartre calls "freedom." Our freedom, for Sartre, is the continual possibility and obligation to remake ourselves. We do so by continually projecting possibilities and so organizing the situation we find ourselves in according to what is figure and what is ground, what stands out as salient and what is secondary, what demands our attention and what does not. This is an essential structure of the for-itself. Being in-itself just is what it is, and hence is not free; the inkwell cannot and need not choose what it is. While we are constantly free, we live in such a way that explicit consciousness of this freedom is the exception, rather than the rule. Once in a while we have a stark, direct experience of this freedom, as the gambler does when he approaches the gaming table and finds his usual stable grasp of the situation melt away and thus has to organize anew all the perceptions and solicitations that surround him. Sartre calls this experience "anguish," borrowing the term from

Kierkegaard. "It is in anguish that man gets the consciousness of his freedom, or if you prefer, anguish is the mode of being of freedom as consciousness of being; it is in anguish that freedom is, in its being, in question for itself" (*BN*, p. 65).

Sartre provides an even more dramatic illustration of freedom and anguish in a famous analysis of vertigo, the experience of the fear of heights. Vertigo is typically explained as the, perhaps unreasonable, fear of something happening to us when we are on towers or near precipices. A person is standing on a narrow path along the edge of a precipice. If the path itself is flat and stable, there is little chance of sliding over the edge. She only needs to make sure that she takes proper care in cautiously walking along this path, not stumbling over a rock on the path. Nevertheless, she experiences a strong feeling, akin to a fear that she may fall. Sartre's account of this experience is that it is a form of anguish, that is, consciousness of her freedom. The feeling is not directed at the precipice, the rock, or any other external being. It is directed at herself. For in the situation she cannot be certain that she will walk cautiously; her motivations to reach the other side, her perception of the precipice as "to be avoided," are not sufficient to determine her action. Between these present motivations and perception and her future self standing further down the path, nothingness insinuates itself. For Sartre, then, "vertigo is anguish to the extent that I am afraid not of falling over the precipice, but of throwing myself over. A situation provokes fear if there is a possibility of my life being changed from without; my being provokes anguish to the extent that I distrust myself and my own reactions in that situation" (*BN*, p. 65).

Sartre's claim that vertigo is anguish about throwing myself over the precipice suggests, at first, a psychology of unconscious motivation. If I have an explicit desire to travel safely along the path, then it seems that any motivation to throw myself over the precipice must be rooted in a hidden part of my psychology. A repressed desire may be inducing the anguish; but it must remain unconscious, because it contradicts my explicitly conscious desire to be safe.

Sartre, however, argues that an appeal to the unconscious is precisely the wrong account. He thinks that the very notion of an unconscious motivation cannot be maintained. Like Husserl, Sartre is committed to the transparency of consciousness (which he calls "translucency"), meaning that we can become self-consciously aware of all mental content. He maintains that this transparency is an ontological feature, for "the being of consciousness is the consciousness of being" (*BN*, p. 89). The notion of the unconscious posits mental content that is structurally or systematically unavailable to self-conscious reflection, and hence contradicts this ontological feature. Further, Sartre argues that Freudian explanations of unconscious motivation trade on an inconsistent description of the phenomena. On the one hand, the unconscious desires are said to be unavailable to consciousness; on the other hand, though, they show up in therapeutic conversations as "resistance" to the questioning of the therapist. Such resistance, claims Sartre, is phenomenological evidence that the desire in question is not unconscious at all. At the very least it is available to the patient's consciousness in the same way that it can be noticed by the therapist. Similarly, the actual experiences that emerge from these supposedly repressed desires, such as the anguish that constitutes vertigo, are themselves conscious experiences that make these desires available to reflection. In fact, Sartre thinks that it would impossible to understand the motivational efficaciousness of these desires if they were unconscious. "Freud," he writes, "is obliged to imply everywhere a magic unity linking distant phenomena across obstacles" (*BN*, p. 95).

7.3.3 Bad faith

The motivation for a theory of the unconscious is that it can avoid apparent contradictions in consciousness. It is absurd to maintain that a unified, rational consciousness can sustain directly conflicting motives, so a theory of the unconscious assigns the conflicting motives to different parts of consciousness. It maintains the duality by undoing the psychic unity. Sartre thinks that a proper description of the phenomena shows that the duality is present within the single, unified, transparent consciousness. He addresses them in his celebrated discussion of "bad faith." In order to understand this, he claims, we do not need the notion of the unconscious. Instead he uses the notions of pre-reflective consciousness and non-thetic or non-positional consciousness that he develops in *The Transcendence of the Ego*. He also draws on the idea from *The Imaginary* that we can use our own bodily movements as an analogon for imaginative play-acting.

Sartre's notion of "bad faith" covers a range of phenomena of self-deception. He gives an example, taken from the Viennese psychiatrist Wilhelm Stekel, of a frigid woman who feels pleasure during sex but firmly believes she does not. Another of Sartre's examples is a woman who is flirting but believes she is not. Instead of appealing to an unconscious, Sartre accounts for these phenomena by claiming that the experience of pleasure or the flirting are in non-thetic consciousness, while their opposite experiences, that is, the frigidity or the resistance to flirting, are in thetic consciousness.

Consider the flirting woman. She is engaged in conversation with a man with whom she is going out for the first time. The situation has a charm that derives from its ambiguity and openness. Then the man takes her hand. "This act of her companion risks changing the situation by calling for an immediate decision" (BN, p. 97). But she does not want this immediate decision. So she leaves her hand where it is, but seeks to deprive it of any significance. She dives more fully into conversation, becoming for a time "all intellect" so that her hand "rests inert . . . neither consenting nor resisting" (BN, p. 97). At that point, as Sartre describes the case, she is in bad faith insofar as she is conscious that the man has taken her hand, and she is conscious of the significance of this gesture and even enjoys it, but she adopts a thetic consciousness toward the situation that allows her to believe that there is no significance in this gesture. Thus the contradiction or self-deception implicit in her actions is not hidden or unconscious. It is in the order of a pretense, simulation, or distraction. It is, Sartre writes, "a certain art of forming contradictory concepts which unify in themselves both an idea and the negation of that idea. The basic concept which is thus engendered utilizes the double property of the human being, who is at once a facticity and a transcendence" (BN, p. 98). The facticity consists of the context, the background, the givens of the situation. She is on a date, the man holds her hand. The transcendence consists of the meaning-constituting projections of the situation. She is entirely invested in the intellectual aspect of the conversation. Typically facticity and transcendence coincide and reinforce each other. "But bad faith does not wish to coordinate them or surmount them in a synthesis" (BN, p. 98). Of course, the decision is only postponed, the ambiguity drawn out, but there is no hard obstacle to the full consciousness of the duality. Sooner or later she will own her hand again, and invest it with meaning. Sartre calls this bad faith "metastable"; it will last for a while, but is not fixed.

We all have our facticity and transcendence; we all have thetic and non-thetic consciousness. So bad faith is a possibility for all of us. This first example shows bad faith in a situation that is somewhat exceptional for being shaped by an ambiguity that the woman seeks to maintain. Sartre argues that there is a more common form of bad faith that most people are in most of the time. He illustrates this with his famous example of the café waiter.

> His movement is quick and forward, a little too precise, a little too rapid. He comes toward the patrons with a step a little too quick. He bends forward a little too eagerly; his voice, his eyes express an interest a little too solicitous for the order of the customer. Finally there he returns, trying to imitate in his walk the inflexible stiffness of

some kind of automaton while carrying his tray with the recklessness of a tight-rope-walker by putting it in a perpetually unstable, perpetually broken equilibrium which he perpetually re-establishes by a light movement of the arm and hand. All his behavior seems to us a game. He applies himself to chaining his movements as if they were mechanisms, the one regulating the other; his gestures and even his voice seem to be mechanisms; he gives himself the quickness and pitiless rapidity of things. He is playing, he is amusing himself. But what is he playing? We need not watch long before we can explain it: he is playing at *being* a waiter in a café. (*BN*, p. 101f.)

The waiter, of course, really is a waiter. What Sartre emphasizes by writing that the waiter plays at *being* a waiter is that he tries to be a waiter the way an inkwell is an inkwell. The affected mechanism and rapidity of the movements and voice all tend to skip over the decisions he continually has to make in order to choose to be a waiter. The affectations are a strategy to avoid the freedom that at bottom defines him. "What I attempt to realize is a being-in-itself of the café waiter, . . . as if it were not my free choice to get up each morning at five o'clock or to remain in bed, even though it meant getting fired" (*BN*, p. 103). The waiter is in bad faith by pretending not to be responsible for his ongoing choices. His consciousness is for-itself, but pretends to be in-itself. Such bad faith is widespread; it is a common strategy for fleeing the anguish that constitutes our consciousness of our freedom.

7.3.4 Sartre on perception and the body

We now turn to Sartre's analysis of the experience of our own bodies. Sartre relies centrally on his adaptation of Gestalt psychology, specifically Lewin's analysis of motivation. Sartre claims that the world is a "hodological space," which is Lewin's term for conceiving of distances in the environment according to the ease of the path, attractions, and resistances. We perceive our surroundings in terms of "the indication of acts to be performed" (*BN*, p. 424). Besides Lewin, Sartre is also influenced by Heidegger's analysis of entities "referring" to others, and having a tool-like mode of being.

Sartre's discussion of the body exhibits some of the ways in which he and Merleau-Ponty fertilized each other's thought. Sartre claims in *Being and Nothingness* that "perception and action are indistinguishable" (*BN*, p. 424). This is a slight exaggeration, for he goes on to mark a difference between perception and action. We perceive objects complete with Lewin's valences. Sartre writes that the perceived object is "full of promises," it "touches me lightly [and] engages the future" (*BN*, p. 424). Such perception "is naturally surpassed in action [and] can only be revealed in and through projects of action" (*BN*, p. 425). The action is in the perception as a "project" and we are separated from it through a kind of nothingness, a void, or a "gap." I see the cup as graspable insofar as I do not yet grasp it. There is a gulf between the facticity of my perception and the transcendence of my action. In this gulf we ply our existence, according to Sartre's ontology. It is marked in experiences through the anguished necessity of making a choice. Due to the importance of anguish for his ontology of human beings, Sartre insists on this difference between perceived valences on the one hand and solicitations for action on the other. (Compare this to the distinction between affordances and invitations with which commentators seek to expand Gibson's theory. See Chapter 10.) The cup on the saucer has a bottom, "which is there, which everything indicates but which I do not see" (*BN*, p. 424). The cup indicates the action that would bring the bottom of the cup into view, and the bottom or the back side is "at the end of my project."

We experience our bodies in terms of the references between the instrumental entities in this hodologically experienced world. "These references could not be grasped by a purely contemplative conscious-ness," Sartre writes, but only by the projects in which my body adapts to the world. My body is the "key" or "center of references" that reveals the instrumental nexus with its distinct references, pathways, and orientation (*BN*, p. 425). My hand and arm constitute the references from hammers to nails, from pen to paper, because to use a pen is to grab it with our hands, hold it with our fingers as we position our arms. This orienting role sets the body apart from all other instruments, even though the body itself is instrumental.

> We do not use this instrument, for we *are* it. It is given to us in no other way than by the instrumental order of the world, by hodological space, by the univocal or reciprocal relations of machines, but it cannot be *given* to my action. I do not have to adapt myself to it nor to adapt another tool to it, but it is my very adaptation to tools, the adaptation which I am. (*BN*, p. 427)

For Sartre, the body shapes the world, but is not encountered in it in the way tools are. Again, it is separated from the world by a tiny gap, or a veil of nothingness:

> I do not apprehend my hand in the act of writing but only the pen which is writing; this means that I use my pen in order to form letters

but not my hand in order to hold the pen. I am not in the relation to my hand in the same utilizing attitude as I am in relation to the pen. . . . The hand is the unknowable and non-utilizable term which the last instrument in the series indicates. . . . I can apprehend it only as the perpetual, evanescent reference of the whole series. (*BN*, p. 426)

Sartre ties his analysis of bodily experience to the nothingness between the consciousness of perception and the projected action. Ultimately his phenomenology is more deeply invested in the analysis of anguish and choosing than the intermingling of perception and action. It prepares us for an existentialist ethics, rather than an existential phenomenology.

Key terms

analogon – the sensory matter that constrains an act of imagination.

anguish – consciousness of freedom.

bad faith – fleeing anguish by maintaining a temporarily stable consciousness of contradictory self-conceptions; one of these self-conceptions is typically in non-thetic consciousness.

being for-itself – the mode of being of consciousness.

being in-itself – the mode of being of objects that are not conscious.

facticity – context and background of a situation, including one's past actions and decisions.

freedom – the continual obligation to remake ourselves by choosing our projects; present and future action is not constrained by facticity and past resolutions.

non-positional consciousness – same as non-thetic consciousness.

non-thetic consciousness – an accompanying consciousness that is not the focus of the conscious act. All conscious acts involve non-thetic self-consciousness.

positional consciousness – same as thetic consciousness.

pre-reflective self-consciousness – the non-thetic consciousness of ourselves that is in the background of conscious acts that are directed at objects other than ourselves.

thetic consciousness – the consciousness of the intentional object.

transcendence – meaning-constituting projections of a future self that shape the meaning of the present situation.

Further reading

Morris, K., ed. (2010). *Sartre on the Body*. London: Palgrave Macmillan.

Sartre, J. P. (1946/2007). *Existentialism is a Humanism*, trans. C. Macomber. New Haven: Yale University Press.

Webber, J., ed. (2010). *Reading Sartre: On Phenomenology and Existentialism*. London: Routledge.

8

Maurice Merleau-Ponty: The Body and Perception

In the introduction to his monumental *Phenomenology of Perception*, Merleau-Ponty writes: "Nothing is more difficult than knowing precisely *what we see*" (*PP*, p. 59). In a sense this statement is obviously false. When I look out the window at houses and gardens and the mountains in the distance, I know exactly what I see, without any difficulty at all. One could try to make sense of the claim by distinguishing between direct and indirect perception. For example, one could say that I directly see sense data or colors and shapes, and only indirectly see houses and mountains that I first have to "construct" out of the sense data. So, one could say, it is difficult to know what sense data we see, since they are obscured by our consciousness of the full-fledged object. However, Merleau-Ponty does not argue for a sense-data or constructivist view. Insofar as we can fit him into the dichotomy at all, Merleau-Ponty holds a direct perception view. We perceive the mountains directly, not indirectly through some intermediary data or process. More accurately, though, we should say that Merleau-Ponty's theory of perception undermines the very distinction between sense data and perceptual experience, and hence makes the distinction between direct and indirect perception theories obsolete.

A better way to understand the concern is to ask *how* we perceive. While it may be obvious that I see mountains in the distance behind the houses, it is hard to tell how I do so. "Rather than being attentive to perceptual experience, this experience is neglected in favor of the perceived object" (*PP*, p. 4). In an example we will return to below,

Merleau-Ponty points out that the perceived distance of the mountains depends on the visibility of the houses lying before them. If I block out the regions between me and the mountains, or if there is a relatively featureless expanse such as a lake or empty fields between me and them, they look closer. So the houses play some part in our perception of the distance of the mountains, even if we are not attending to them. It is not clear *how* this "marginal perception," as Merleau-Ponty calls it, affects what we see. Phenomenology aims to give an account of such features of perception.

This is similar to the way Husserl, the founder of phenomenology, approaches the issue. Husserl notes that we see more than meets the eye. For example, we see trees and houses as robust and three-dimensional, even though their back sides are not presented to us. Husserl works out these structures in terms of "horizons." The horizon of an act of perception is the background of meaning against which an object of perception stands out. These background structures are not themselves explicit in individual acts of perception, but they make the act intelligible. The work of phenomenology is to spell out the horizonal structures that make objects of perception intelligible. Merleau-Ponty follows this basic approach in his *Phenomenology of Perception*.

Merleau-Ponty was also influenced by Heidegger. While Husserl grounds his phenomenology in examples of perception – usually vision and sometimes hearing – Heidegger's core examples are about active involvement with tools and equipment in the course of accomplishing some purpose. According to Heidegger such being "at grips" is the basic form of intelligibility. He calls it "being-in-the-world." Merleau-Ponty takes over this view from Heidegger. Heidegger's views on being at grips with tools "at hand" make implicit claims about the bodily nature of the skills and competences through which we understand the world. But Heidegger rarely mentions the body, while Merleau-Ponty makes the body the centerpiece of his theory. He argues that the way we are directed at the world, our intentionality, is essentially a "motor intentionality" grounded in our bodily abilities.

One way to sum up Merleau-Ponty's work is to see it as a combination of the best features of Husserl and Heidegger. Like Husserl, Merleau-Ponty focuses on the horizonal structure of perception, and like Heidegger he takes the fundamental role of our skillful dealings in the world seriously. In a sense, Merleau-Ponty merges Heidegger's insight into the practical, skillful nature of our basic intentionality with Husserl's analysis of perception. In the preface to *Phenomenology of Perception*, Merleau-Ponty writes that "all of *Sein und Zeit* emerges from Husserl's suggestion" (*PP*, p. lxx). Here he has in mind Husserl's comments on

Umwelt in *Ideas II*, which concern the experience of a practical, engaged subject. In his 1942 *The Structure of Behavior* Merleau-Ponty analyzes the purposive structure of actions in a sustained critique of behaviorist approaches. The main views of these two books on behavior and perception form a continuous whole. For Merleau-Ponty, to see something is to comport oneself toward that thing.

In addition to these two philosophers, Merleau-Ponty's thought on perception is deeply influenced by his study of Gestalt psychology and his interactions with Gurwitsch. He also adapts examples from Sartre, especially the phenomenology of inter-sensory perception and hallucination from *The Imaginary*. The last part of *Phenomenology of Perception* engages Sartre's view on the ego and freedom from *Being and Nothingness*. However, it is the earlier chapters on space and perception that primarily influence future work on phenomenological cognitive science.

8.1 *Phenomenology of Perception*

The main thesis of *Phenomenology of Perception* is that perception is an essentially bodily process. But the book is ambitious and ranges widely to topics beyond perception. Merleau-Ponty claims that embodiment goes beyond perception, so that the human mind in general is necessarily bodily, or "incarnate." He makes claims about language, self-consciousness, human freedom, and art. His discussion of perception is embedded in a broader critique of the paradigms of traditional philosophical and scientific ways of studying human experience. Fully understood, Merleau-Ponty's views on perception amount to an ontology of human beings. In other words, underlying his insights into the nature of our perceptual openness to the world is a view about the type of beings we are. Because of these broad ontological ambitions, the book can at times seem abstract and frustrating. Merleau-Ponty seeks to establish the grounds for his phenomenological method and for his ontology of embodiment by refuting what he presents as the two main options in the tradition, which he calls empiricism and intellectualism. In doing so, he adopts a dialectic in which he presents criticisms of one such position, and then turns around to reject those very criticisms, giving rise to some confusion about what he himself takes to be the right view.

As we saw, Merleau-Ponty introduces his work by claiming that "nothing is more difficult than knowing precisely *what we see*" (*PP*, p. 59). He goes on to explain: "If the essence of consciousness is to forget its own phenomena and to thus make possible the constitution of 'things,' then this forgetting is not a simple absence" (*PP*, p. 59). But how can we make the forgotten constituting phenomena explicit? Merleau-Ponty uses a range of methods. He draws widely on the literature in phenomenology, psychology (especially Gestalt psychology), psychiatry, and neurology. He analyzes examples of visual illusions, such as the distance illusion mentioned above. He also turns to insights from visual artists. In particular, he thinks that Cezanne's paintings and writings can help us understand the nature of visual perception. And he prominently uses case studies of patients whose perceptual abilities are compromised. He presents a host of examples and observations from clinical case studies and links them to his conclusion. At times this approach gives the impression that his view is grounded in anecdotes from clinical psychology, which seems to make all the abstract philosophy unnecessary. However, the dialectic works in the other direction. Merleau-Ponty uses his philosophical acumen to provide a powerful new framework for explaining experimental results and clinical observations.

This dual nature of the book – its combination of philosophical reflection with empirical observations – partly explains its broad influence and the importance of Merleau-Ponty's work in contemporary developments of phenomenology. His framework for studying the mind and perception has been taken up by cognitive scientists, psychologists, and philosophers, and lays the foundation for a fruitful dialog between these disciplines. It has influenced Hubert Dreyfus' critique of artificial intelligence and subsequent critiques of cognitivist approaches to studying the human mind (see Chapter 11). Reportedly, James Gibson, the founder of ecological psychology, advised his graduate students to read *Phenomenology of Perception*. He taught a seminar on Merleau-Ponty while working on *The Ecological Approach to Visual Perception* (see Chapter 10).

8.2 Phenomenology, psychology, and the phenomenal field

The distinction between philosophy and psychology is relatively recent and phenomenology blurs the lines between the two. Husserl initially called his approach a "descriptive psychology" and one of his influences was Carl Stumpf, a fellow Brentano student who was a pioneer of Gestalt psychology and who supervised Husserl's habilitation. Husserl himself developed Gestalt ideas in his *Philosophy of Arithmetic*. Gurwitsch recognized the deep commonalities between Gestalt psychology and phenomenology and merged the two in his work. At the same time, some psychologists and psychiatrists thought that phenomenology was a suitable method for their fields. David Katz's work on color and touch perception is a good example of this. Philosophy, psychology, and phenomenology all aspire to give an account of perception. Like his phenomenological predecessors, Merleau-Ponty is skeptical of the idea that there is a deep distinction between these fields. He begins *Phenomenology of Perception* with a substantive introduction in which he argues that, properly understood, phenomenology and Gestalt psychology – to his mind the two most promising and subtle approaches to perception – tend toward the same methods and conception.

Gestalt psychologists argue against the constancy hypothesis. This is the claim that, all other things being equal, the same sensory stimulation will always give rise to the same perceptual experience. This hypothesis underlies many traditional accounts of perception, from Descartes onwards. It expresses the underlying idea that the perceptual apparatus is like a machine that transforms incoming stimuli along strict causal pathways to give rise to mental representations. Since the mechanism and causal pathways stay the same, identical sensory stimuli will produce the same representation.

Of course perceptual experience varies. Consider cases of perceptual error. If you see a stump in the woods, while I mistake it for a bear, our sensory stimuli are the same, but we have different visual experiences. The constancy hypothesis explains such cases by pointing to secondary mental factors that alter and distort the representation. I may be afraid of bears and especially worried about encountering one at that moment. This worry, or an association, or a subsequent judgment changes the experience, but aside from such secondary factors, all other things being equal, the same stimulus will produce the same experience. The constancy hypothesis, then, relies crucially on a *ceteris paribus* (all other things being equal) clause. Many things besides sensory data affect perceptual experience, so we can always point to some factor that could explain apparent deviations from constancy. The constancy hypothesis is thus effectively unfalsifiable and hence not really a scientific hypothesis, but rather a characterization of a basic framework for thinking about perception.

In attacking the constancy hypothesis, Gestalt psychology wants to undermine this entire framework. The basic idea of the Gestaltists is that we perceive Gestalts, which are not definite functions of the stimuli. We hear the same melody, even when it is played by different instruments in a different key. We perceive a square or a triangle in an arrangement of dots, or Mach bands at the border of two shaded regions. More generally, the Gestaltists claim that the object of perception is typically more than what is given by the sensory stimuli. Nevertheless, Gestalts are real objects that we experience directly. They are not the product of some error of association, or an intervening judgment.

This Gestaltist position raises a deep question about what Gestalts are, that is, what the content of our perceptual experience is. What are the Mach bands or the triangles that you see, if not the direct products of stimuli, or superimposed judgments? It seems as if they are not physical entities, since there is no material object producing the stimuli. Nor can they be mental entities, since we perceive them directly. This makes Gestalts odd fits for a Cartesian ontology. In *The Structure of Behavior* Merleau-Ponty addresses this question, arguing that the world of perceptual objects is not a "material plenum," but a "place where behavior appears" (1942, p. 125). The world of perception, in other words, is neither primarily a material source of stimuli, nor the product of intellectual judgments, but the place or milieu in which we act and comport ourselves. Perceptual Gestalts, then, are constituted not by stimuli or thoughts, but by a role they play in governing our comportment.

Gestalt psychology itself does not solve, or even fully confront, the ontological conundrum regarding perceptual objects. For the most part it maintains the stance of explanatory psychology, which seeks to account for perception in terms of causes. So, for example, Wertheimer's laws of form, such as similarity or proximity, are interpreted as laws that cause the stimuli to give rise to the perception of a certain Gestalt. While this avoids the constancy hypothesis, it nevertheless maintains the naturalism of psychology.

Merleau-Ponty argues that the Gestaltists' challenge to the constancy hypothesis implies a deeper point. To fully understand the status of perceptions and the role of laws and horizons that mediate between stimuli and perceptual objects, we need to suspend the usual reliance on naturalism. This suspension is akin to the method of reductions advocated by Husserl. Merleau-Ponty writes,

> Gestalt theory ... did not notice that an entire reformulation of the understanding is necessary if one wants to accurately express phenomena, or that in order to reach this goal one must question logic and classical philosophy's "objective thought," suspend the categories of the world, doubt (in the Cartesian sense) the supposed facts of realism, and proceed to a genuine "phenomenological reduction." (*PP*, p. 50)

It is worth noting that descriptions of perceptual experience in Wertheimer or Katz are similar to passages in Husserl, insofar as they aim to focus on what is present in the experience itself, while avoiding elements of description based on what one thinks one should be perceiving based on some theory. Gurwitsch, whose lectures on Gestalt psychology Merleau-Ponty followed in Paris in the 1930s, similarly argued that Gestalt psychology's rejection of the constancy hypothesis amounts to a Husserlian phenomenological reduction. Merleau-Ponty makes essentially this same point in the introduction to *Phenomenology of Perception.*

Merleau-Ponty uses one of the Gestaltists' examples to illustrate the reduction implicit in their approach. A bell tower, he writes, "appear[s] to me as smaller and farther away the moment that I can see more clearly the details of the hills and the fields that separate me from it" (*PP*, p. 50). If, however, I obscure them from my visual field, the same bell tower, while projecting the same image onto my retina, will appear larger and closer. We have a similar experience when we look at the far shore of a lake, or a ship on the ocean on a clear day. Because there is little detail on the lake surface, objects on the far shore will appear closer than they are. The variation of perceived distance in this example shows that the same stimulus of the steeple can give rise to different perceptual experiences, which supports the Gestalt criticism of the constancy hypothesis. Merleau-Ponty, however, wants to press a further question. The details between me and the bell tower are not explicitly the object of perception, yet they are evidently part of the perceptual experience, since their absence alters the perception of distance. Merleau-Ponty wants to know how such "marginal perception" affects our perceptual experience. It seems wrong to interpret these details' effect as the result of a judgment, or even an inference. We do not infer or reason that the steeple is further away given the marginal perception of interposed objects. We directly see it as further away. At the same time, however, it seems false to treat the visibility of fields and slopes as causes of the perception of distance, even though Gestalt psychologists tend to give such a causal explanation. For Merleau-Ponty, the interesting philosophical point is that crucial elements of perception do not fit the paradigm of explanations in terms of intellectualist appeals to reasons and judgments, and they also do not fit an empiricist causal or mechanical paradigm. Perception, he argues, requires a different analysis that cannot be reduced to either of the traditional paradigms. In this sense, Merleau-Ponty writes that there is "an entire philosophy emerging from the critique of the 'constancy hypothesis'" (*PP*, p. 509n).

The philosophy that emerges from this criticism, he claims, is phenomenology. Paying attention to "marginal perceptions" is like performing the phenomenological reduction. Merleau-Ponty calls such hidden aspects of our perceptual experience the "phenomenal field." Recall that Husserl developed the phenomenological reduction in order to focus on the constitutive meanings of our conscious acts. For instance, we see ordinary objects as having a back side even though it is not given in the sense data. Husserl explains this by claiming that robustness, three-dimensionality, solidity, temporal extendedness, and so on are part of the constitutive meaning of the perceptual act. If we did not see objects as having a back side and enduring through time, our experience would not count as seeing objects at all. Merleau-Ponty similarly pursues an account of the constitutive meaning of perception. "Vision is already inhabited by a sense that gives it a function in the spectacle of the world and in our existence" (PP, p. 52). Since some aspects of these constitutive meanings of perception are not given in the sense data, one goal of a phenomenology of perception is to bring out these hidden aspects of perception.

8.3 The lived body

We perceive with our bodies. German has two words for the human body, *Körper* and *Leib*. Husserl used these terms to draw a philosophical distinction, which Merleau-Ponty develops in more detail. Husserl reserves *Körper* to mean our body as a physical entity that shares objective features such as weight, extension, or buoyancy with inanimate physical bodies. Physics studies bodies in this sense, as in "solid body" or "heavenly body." Merleau-Ponty usually refers to our body in this sense as the "objective body." *Leib* means the specifically human body as we experience it first-personally, with which we touch and feel and move. Husserl's usage of *Leib* is usually translated as "lived body." Merleau-Ponty's big claim that we perceive with our bodies and are conscious with our bodies refers specifically to this notion of a lived body, and much of his work focuses on analyzing the relevant phenomena and making the notion more precise. Accordingly, when Merleau-Ponty uses the word "body" he means *Leib*. Occasionally he uses the phrases "habit body" or "phenomenal body" in order to highlight a specific aspect of his notion of the body.

Part of the concept of the lived body is that it is experienced by somebody in the first person. In Heidegger's terms it is *jemeinig*, "in each case mine." As Merleau-Ponty puts it, "I can only understand the function of the living body by accomplishing it and to the extent that I am a body that rises up toward the world" (PP, p. 78). Since the lived body is always experienced, Merleau-Ponty needs to address the question of how such experience is possible. In other words, he has to take a stand on the Cartesian question of interaction between consciousness and body. His answer follows Heidegger in claiming that the basic opposition of two Cartesian substances misdescribes the phenomena and leads to a philosophy that is incapable of resolving its basic paradoxes. Merleau-Ponty uses his keen insights into bodily experience to undermine these traditional categories and supply a new ontology. Consciousness is not a separate substance that somehow mysteriously interacts with a mechanical body. It is essentially incarnate. To be conscious is to be embodied. "The union of the soul and the body is not established through an arbitrary decree that unites two mutually exclusive terms, one a subject and the other an object. It is accomplished at each moment in the movement of existence" (*PP*, p. 91).

The Heideggerian notions of existence and the world are important here. Existence, for Heidegger, is the specific mode of being of humans, which consists of "being-in-the-world," that is, being at grips with equipment. Merleau-Ponty adopts Heidegger's ontological claims that our mode of being differs from the being of objects and that openness to a world is part of it. Unlike the objective body, the lived body is not one among many, *partes extra partes*. It does not occur in space as an object does, but has its own kind of spatiality. "We must not say that our body is *in* space, nor for that matter *in* time. It *inhabits* space and time" (*PP*, p. 140). The lived body relates to perceptual and natural objects not through external, mechanical relations, but through *intentional* relations. The lived body, in other words, constitutes the foundation of Husserlian intentionality, being directed at intelligible objects, which Merleau-Ponty defines as motor intentionality. This directedness at a world is part of what it means to have a lived body.

Merleau-Ponty introduces his conception of the body as intentionality through the case of phantom limbs. This example has a long history in philosophy. A person may experience sensations in a limb she does not have. It is not unusual for this to happen to amputees, who may feel pain or a tingling sensation in a leg or arm they have lost. They may also sense an urge to use the limb and attempt to do so, for example initiating a motion to walk or stand on a missing leg. There are also rare cases in which a person experiences a limb she never had, or experiences a limb she does have, but as longer or shorter than it is. There are both psychological and physiological components of the experience. On the physiological side, a sensation in the missing limb can be generated by stimulating nerve endings in the remaining stump. On the psychological side, phantom limb experiences can be augmented or even created by emotionally charged memories of the mutilating event. Accordingly there are two strategies for explaining the phantom limb. The first of these is "empiricist" in Merleau-Ponty's broad sense of the word, and it treats the phantom experience as the product of stimulations of nerve endings that resemble the stimulation of nerves in the missing limb. The second approach is "intellectualist," explaining the experience as an error of representation, a deception or false judgment. These two strategies may be combined. Descartes, for example, accounts for phantom limb experiences by claiming that the mind cannot distinguish proximal stimulation of nerve endings in the stump from distal stimulation in the limb and that the nerve impulse (or *élan vital*) hence produces an erroneous judgment. The experience of the phantom limb, he claims, is a mistaken judgment based on a mechanical impulse in the body.

Merleau-Ponty points out that both kinds of explanation distort the phenomena. Most critically it is hard, perhaps impossible, to show how the two explanatory frameworks meet. In other words, it is hard to explain how phantom limb experiences can be constituted as both physiological and psychological phenomena. Descartes combines the two by positing a mysterious interface in the pineal gland between the purely mechanical events of the body and the mental representation. Beyond this difficulty, careful attention to the phenomena shows that they do not quite fit the expectations we have for either physiological or psychological objects. It is obvious that the phantom limb is not the product of an explicit judgment, since the person is unambiguously aware that the limb does not exist, but this awareness does not eliminate the sensation. However, it also does not seem to be the object of judgment in a more attenuated sense. Merleau-Ponty writes that it is not a representation of a limb at all, insofar as "the experience of the amputated arm as present . . . [is] not of the order of the 'I think that . . .'." It is, rather, an "ambivalent presence" (*PP*, p. 83). This means that the patient does not unequivocally experience the phantom limb. She rather has an experience that involves both the limb and its absence. Merleau-Ponty illustrates the ambivalence of the experience with related cases of anosognosia of motor functions, in which a patient has a disabled limb but does not acknowledge the disability. "In fact the anosognosic patient does not merely ignore the paralyzed limb: it is only because he knows where he risks encountering his deficiency that he can turn away from it" (*PP*, p. 82). Similarly, "the amputee senses his leg, as I can sense vividly the existence of a friend who is, nevertheless, not here before my eyes. He has not lost his leg because he continues to allow for it" (*PP*, p. 83).

This is not to say that psychology and physiology are not part of the story. The distortion of the phenomena comes from the attempt to fit them into the naturalistic frameworks of these two sciences in order to construct an explanation. They both treat the body as an objective body, and thus get the experience wrong in a fundamental way. Instead, Merleau-Ponty proposes to explain experiences of phantom limbs by analyzing what it means to "allow for" the existence of a leg, say, that the patient knows to be missing. The phenomena only make sense if we understand them in terms of the world a person finds herself in. It is not enough to look at the internal workings of the objective body; we have to explain the way the lived body opens up to, or "rises up toward," a world. "The phenomenon – distorted by both physiological and psychological explanations – can nevertheless be understood from the perspective of being in the world" (PP, p. 83). The basic terms of this explanation – openness to action, being in the world, involvement in an environment – are existential terms in Heidegger's sense.

As an approximation of the existential notion of the world, Merleau-Ponty points to an example from the behavior of insects. If an insect's leg is severed, it will almost seamlessly use the remaining legs to proceed with its act. What accounts for the insect's use of its leg, or its body, is its immersion in an environment that draws out its behavior. It does not decide to use a leg instead of another. Its body simply is geared to the instinctive purposes that make up its vitality.

For all their differences from insects, humans also are geared to a purposive environment through their bodies. Our abilities to walk, stand, grasp, and so forth, and our habits of doing so, open up a world in which we can act. As such, the world appeals to our bodily possibilities. Objects present themselves as manipulable according to our skills of manipulating them, and surfaces present themselves as walkable according to our skills of walking on them. When these skills do not match the possibilities presented in the environment, people can experience phantom limbs.

> To have a phantom limb is to remain open to all of the actions of which the arm alone is capable and to stay within the practical field that one had prior to the mutilation. The body is the vehicle of being in the world and, for a living being, having a body means being united with a definite milieu, merging with certain projects, and being perpetually engaged therein. (PP, p. 84)

There is a kind of misalignment between the habitual possibilities and the actual ones. "It is as though our body comprises two distinct layers, that of the habitual body and that of the actual body" (PP, p. 84). As the person acquires new habits for walking and grasping, the solicitations of old possibilities diminish and the phantom limb experiences subside. Or, conversely, the phantom limb experience can be perpetuated by amputees who use it to guide their artificial limbs.

Note that this existential account fits the experience of the ambivalent presence of the phantom limb. If the world solicits one to grasp an object with an arm that is missing, the mutilation is forgotten in the solicitation and the intention to grasp, but present in the inability to perform the action. "The patient knows his disability precisely insofar as he is ignorant of it, and he ignores it precisely insofar as he knows it" (*PP*, p. 84). Merleau-Ponty's broader point, however, is that the coupling of bodily skills to the world that offers possibilities provides the proper framework for explaining phantom limbs. The psychological and physiological accounts need to be situated in this broader, more basic constellation. Beyond phantom limbs, the relation of the bodily abilities to the possibilities in the world makes up the framework in which Merleau-Ponty wants to explain perception. The living body, in his Heideggerian terms, is the "vehicle of being in the world."

8.3.1 The body schema

The notion of the lived body cannot be separated from the world in which we exist. Just as the lived body is not an objective body, the world is not an arrangement of objects in space. In the existential sense, which Merleau-Ponty takes over from Heidegger, the world is a space of possibilities. It is a familiar setting in which we can pursue our aims. The lived body opens up the possibilities that make up the world. First and foremost we do not entertain these possibilities mentally, as it were by thinking about them or imagining them. Instead, Merleau-Ponty argues, we are open to them through the skills and habits of the lived body. Our constant readiness to deploy those skills is what Merleau-Ponty calls the "body schema." It makes the world intelligible and hence constitutes the possibility of relating to objects and regions within it. Consequently, "the theory of the body schema is implicitly a theory of perception" (*PP*, p. 213).

As with bodies and the world, one can have an objective conception of space – roughly the conception of space employed in physics and geometry – and an existential conception of space. Merleau-Ponty starts the main argument about perception with an analysis of existential space. His main claim is that "far from my body being for me merely a fragment of space, there would be for me no such thing as space if I did not have a body" (*PP*, p. 104). This is a transcendental claim, reminiscent of Kant's contention in the transcendental aesthetic of the *Critique of Pure Reason* that "outside the human standpoint . . . the representation of space signifies nothing at all" (B42). It is also an existential claim, that is, it means that we are open to space through the lived body, rather than through a detached intellectual cognition.

The lived body opens up space through the "body schema" (*schéma corporel*, unfortunately often mistranslated as "body image"). This term is Merleau-Ponty's appropriation of the German *Körperschema*, which was used by psychiatrists at the beginning of the twentieth century to label the large stock of knowledge we have about our own bodies. For instance, we know what things look like when we are lying down, as opposed to standing up, or what pressure a surface exerts on our body in various positions. We have constant immediate access to such knowledge, gained through experiences and associations. Merleau-Ponty cites the Austrian psychiatrist and psychoanalyst Paul Schilder and the German neurologist and psychiatrist Klaus Conrad, who were two of the primary contributors to a debate on whether this knowledge about our own bodies consists of many different cognitions linked through association (Schilder 1923), or takes the form of a whole, a Gestalt (Conrad 1933). Both sides of the debate use the idea of such knowledge primarily to diagnose and explain psychopathologies, including phantom limbs, anosognosia, as well as autotopagnosia, in which patients appear unable to locate parts of their own body or know the positions of those parts in space. The current notion of the body image, which refers to the impression people have of the outward *appearance* of their bodies and which is implicated in some accounts of depression, bulimia, and anorexia, can also be traced back to the work of Schilder. However, it is very different from Merleau-Ponty's notion of the body schema.

Like these psychiatrists, Merleau-Ponty uses the body schema to explain phantom limbs and anosognosia, and he also views the body schema as a kind of knowledge of a whole Gestalt. However, he goes beyond the terms of the prior debate and gives the body schema a deeper sense by turning it into an existential notion. It is primarily a way to open up possibilities. "The 'body schema' is, in the end, a manner of expressing that my body is in and toward the world" (*PP*, p. 103). It is instructive to compare Merleau-Ponty's analysis to Kant's notion of the transcendental schema. The transcendental schemata, for Kant, are *a priori* rules according to which the mind prefigures intelligible patterns of events or objects occurring in time. They make it possible to subsume given perceptual content under the abstract *a priori* categories, the basic concepts that structure all understanding. The schema of the category of necessity, for example, is that of existence at all times, while the schema of the category of actuality is that of existence at some time, and the schema for the category of causation is succession in time according to a rule. We can not only think, but actually experience given events as causal or states of affairs as necessary, because the temporal structures of these experiences of the world are prefigured in our minds. According to Merleau-Ponty, the body schema similarly prefigures the possible experience of the world around us. It consists of the body's readiness to deploy its habits and skills in every possible situation, thereby opening up the possibilities that give a situation its significance. So, for instance, our skills of reaching and grasping give form to objects that we encounter as within our reach and as graspable. The same skills structure space into meaningful distinctions of up and down, high and low, in front of or behind.

Our basic motor skills, as well as our more involved, culturally inflected habits, place us in an environment that consists of things to be done, objects to be manipulated. The world is not merely a source of sensory stimuli. We dwell in it with our bodies and know it through the abilities that make up the body schema. As Merleau-Ponty puts it, the theory of the body schema shows us that "the background of movement and vision is defined not by a stock of sensible qualities, but by a certain manner of articulating or of structuring the surroundings" (PP, p. 117). In other words, we never see an expanse of colored patches or sensations. We see opportunities for action and movement. We are always up to something, at grips with the world in a purposive way, and our "projects polarize the world, causing a thousand signs to appear there, as if by magic, that guide action" (PP, p. 115).

So it is not the case that first we see and then we do. Rather, our possible movements and possible actions already prefigure what shows up for us visually. "Our body as a power of various regions of the world . . . already rises up toward the objects to grasp and perceive them" (PP, p. 108). Our *body* perceives, and it perceives in terms of what can be done, what is to be done. Infants do not learn to see or perceive from a world-detached stance. They learn to see in the course of learning skills for coping with the world and they build up a perceptual world as they acquire a body "with its habits that outline a human environment around itself" (PP, p. 341). Without the projections of this habit body there is no seeing and nothing to be seen.

Unlike Kantian schemata, Merleau-Ponty's body schema is not mental and has nothing to do with concepts. But like Kantian schemata it constitutes the possibility of experience. The body schema is schematic in the sense that bodily skills lie ready to give form to every possible situation. They are not restricted to settings that we have already experienced. They prefigure what kinds of forms we are able to perceive in general. This is so, because we deploy our skills in infinitely many different situations. "Human life 'understands' not only some definite milieu, but rather an infinity of possible milieus" (PP, p. 341). Every time we grasp a cup or take a step, the conditions are slightly different, but already understood by our bodily skills. The cup may be slightly heavier, further to one side, higher up with respect to the hand, and so on. The ground we walk on may be more or less slippery, inclined, well lit, and so on. The body simply makes the appropriate adjustment to exercise its skills. The perception of the cup as graspable or the path as walkable is guided by the adaptability of the skill.

We can discern the transcendental function of the body schema in our ability to distinguish a figure from its background. The figure–background structure is constitutive for perception in general (although Merleau-Ponty focuses his argument on vision). He writes that the figure–background structure is "the very definition of the perceptual phenomenon, or that without which a phenomenon cannot be called perception" (*PP*, p. 4). And yet it is already complex. Seeing a figure involves seeing edges and an outline, as well as a background that is perceived to continue behind the figure. The "invisible" background covered by the figure suggests that perception involves content that is not simply given as a sensation. A similar "strange mode of existence" (*PP*, p. 26) pertains to objects and regions that are at the edges or beyond the edges of our visual fields. "The region surrounding the visual field is not easy to describe. . . . In this region there is an *indeterminate vision*, a *vision of something or other* [*je ne sais quoi*], and, if taken to the extreme, that which is behind my back is not without visual presence" (*PP*, p. 6). And "we see just as far as the hold of our gaze upon the things extends – well beyond the zone of clear vision, and even behind ourselves. When we reach the limits of the visual field, we do not go from vision to non-vision" (*PP*, p. 289). The ambiguous presence of backgrounds, outlines, edges, and things behind us and outside our range of clear vision "contains much more than the currently given qualities" (*PP*, p. 13) and is irreducible to such qualities (*PP*, p. 24).

This undermines accounts that take sensations as the sole basis for perception. Sensations by themselves do not explain the emergence of figures and grounds. Wertheimer worked out the laws of form to explain this. For example, the contiguity, proximity, or resemblance of patches makes it more likely that we see them as belonging together to a single whole. Merleau-Ponty, however, argues that "the contiguity and the resemblance of stimuli are not prior to the constitution of the whole" (*PP*, p. 17) and these principles apply too late. In perception there is "tension," a "vague expectation," or "vague uneasiness" and the whole unified object emerges suddenly as an organization that resolves the tension (*PP*, p. 18). Prior to the emergence of the whole, there is no perception of resemblance among the parts. They only become available to perception afterwards. At a level more basic than mere sensations and associations Merleau-Ponty points to an "original structure that, for the normal subject, makes the hidden aspects of the world just as certain as the visible ones" (*PP*, p. 26).

The body schema's emphasis on possible action straightforwardly explains how we can perceive backgrounds obscured by objects. The floor behind my desk is a place I can move to, and I see it as such. The back side of the cup is a surface I can wrap my fingers around in an act of grasping. These "invisible" regions, spaces, and objects are perceptually available to me insofar as they are set forth in possible actions. The body schema similarly explains how we perceive the edges and outlines that make up figures. The cup and the desk show up as single objects, as figures, because to lift any part of the cup is to lift all of it, and to get behind any part of the desk we have to get behind all of it. In other words, the bodily skills that bring action-guiding features of the world into view do so by bringing out a distinction between figures and grounds. This is what Merleau-Ponty means by "polarizing." Or, as he also puts it, "one's own body is the always implied third term of the figure–background structure, and each figure appears perspectively against the double horizon of external space and bodily space" (*PP*, p. 103). The body schema explains the figure–background structure, because it explains the possibility of perception in general.

8.3.2 The case of Schneider

Of course there are a lot of cups we never grasp, and paths we never walk. The world surrounding us is replete with opportunities for possible actions that we do not "rise up toward." Further, we understand worlds and situations that are not presently in front of us and that we have never seen. The "body is not merely ready to be mobilized by real situations that draw it toward themselves, it can also turn away from the world ... and ... be situated in the virtual" (*PP*, p. 111). The body schema structures our experience not only of present and actual situations, but of possible ones. Merleau-Ponty develops this part of the argument about the body schema by analyzing the clinical case of patient Schneider, whose perceptual and motor disabilities derived from a breakdown of his body schema.

Schneider was a patient in a neurological institute in Frankfurt, which was devoted to studying the brain injuries of war veterans. The institute was founded and led by the neurologist Kurt Goldstein. Together with his colleague Adhemar Gelb, a psychologist who had studied with Carl Stumpf, Goldstein published a series of groundbreaking studies on visual agnosia, based on their work with Schneider and other patients. As a young man in World War I, Schneider was injured by mine splinters. Some splinters penetrated the back of his skull and caused damage to the occipital lobe in the back of the brain. These injuries left him with a range of perceptual disabilities resulting in "mind blindness" (*Seelenblindheit*), a type of visual agnosia. While Schneider could see patches of color, he was unable to visually recognize objects. Nevertheless, he was able to handle objects and perform complicated tasks with them. He was employed making wallets and managed to cut and stitch leather at a rate approximating normally abled workers. But Schneider had difficulties executing abstract actions that bear no relation to a specific task at hand, and he was seemingly unable to play-act or to imagine objects not present. Most strikingly, perhaps, he was generally unable to point to things, including regions of his own body, that he was able to grasp, touch, or swat.

Merleau-Ponty did not work directly with Schneider and relies on the studies by Goldstein and Gelb for the observation and explanations of Schneider's disabilities. He also learned details of the case in discussions with Gurwitsch, who had worked with Gelb in Frankfurt and written his dissertation there before eventually coming to Paris. Merleau-Ponty's aim is not to diagnose Schneider's disabilities, but to use this case to understand perception in normally abled people. He insists that it is not the case that Schneider is "missing" something that normal persons have. "It cannot be a question of simply transferring to the normal person what is missing in the patient and what he is trying to recover" (*PP*, p. 110). Instead, the various strategies that patients like Schneider develop to cope with their disabilities are "allusions to a fundamental function that they attempt to replace, but of which they do not give us the direct image" (*PP*, p. 110). Merleau-Ponty's goal is to describe these fundamental functions that govern perception. Using these phenomena, he uncovers the basic structure that connects perception and the objects in the natural world with bodily skills, abilities, and habits – in short, the body schema. It reveals a world in which we perceive objects in terms of their significance that draws us into purposeful actions. Merleau-Ponty draws on Husserl, and on Heidegger's notion of being-in-the-world, in elaborating it. Insofar as Schneider's condition highlights the constitutive role of the body schema in disclosing an intelligible world, his case "has allowed us to catch sight of a new mode of analysis – existential analysis – that goes beyond the classical alternatives between empiricism and intellectualism, or between explanation and reflection" (*PP*, p. 138).

Schneider "executes the movements that are necessary for life with extraordinary speed and confidence, provided they are habitual movements" (*PP*, p. 105). He uses matches to light lamps, blows his nose in his handkerchief, and makes wallets at work. The function of skillfully coping with familiar tools stays largely intact. But these vast skills no longer fulfill the schematic function of making the world in general intelligible to him, and consequently perception is impaired. Schneider walks to Goldstein's house in order to meet with him, but when he passes the same house without the intention to go there, he does not recognize it. He swats the spot on his body where a mosquito stings him, but when poked with a ruler and told to point to the spot, he cannot do so. He served in the army and knows how to salute, but when asked to do so out of context, he cannot execute the simple motion. Following Goldstein, Merleau-Ponty captures this broad range of manifestations in the distinction between pointing and grasping, or "abstract" and "concrete" movements. Schneider can grasp, but not point; he does fine with concrete movements, but is unable to perform abstract ones.

There are two points about these inabilities that Merleau-Ponty explains in terms of the theory of the body schema. First, grasping and concrete movements enjoy a privileged position over abstract movements insofar as they are not as severely compromised in Schneider, as well as in some patients who have injuries to their cerebellum. Merleau-Ponty claims that the phenomenal evidence shows that in concrete movements the objects we manipulate in our immediate environment are as intimately integrated into our abilities as our own bodies.

> I move my body directly, I do not find it at one objective point in space in order to lead it to another, I have no need of looking for it because it is always with me. I have no need of directing it toward the goal of the movement, in a sense it touches the goal from the very beginning and it throws itself toward it. In movement, the relations between my decisions and my body are magical ones. (*PP*, p. 96f.)

Concrete movements, like striking a match, holding a handkerchief, or swinging a hammer, are like moving our bodies. When we engage with these objects skillfully in performing a habitual action we do not first need to locate them in space. Like moving the body, "from its very beginnings, the grasping movement is magically complete" (*PP*, p. 106).

This analysis implies a distinction between objective space and bodily space or, more precisely, our ability to understand and represent objective space and our understanding of bodily space. We do not understand bodily space as an extension or a set of coordinates. It is the "envelope of . . . habitual action, but not . . . an objective milieu" (*PP*, p. 106) and "I can thus – by means of my body as a power for a certain number of familiar actions – settle into my surroundings as an ensemble of *manipulanda*" (*PP*, p. 107). Importantly, the distinction between bodily and objective space does not match the distinction between our bodies and other objects. The objects we handle in familiar actions are included in the bodily space. "I have an absolute knowledge of where my pipe is, and *from this* I know where my hand is and where my body is" (*PP*, p. 102). One way to put this point is that when we act skillfully, the objects we use skillfully become extensions of our own bodies, or the body and its tools become part of the same system.

Schneider still has this immediate, skill-based understanding of the environment: "placed in front of his scissors, his needle, and his familiar tasks [he] has no need to look for his hands or his fingers, for they are not objects to be found in objective space" (*PP*, p. 108). Similarly for his tools:

> The workbench, the scissors, and the pieces of leather are presented to the subject as poles of action; . . . they define . . . a particular situation that remains open, that calls for a certain mode of resolution, a certain labor. The body is but one element in the system of the subject and his world, and the task obtains the necessary movements from him through a sort of distant attraction. . . . In concrete movement, the patient . . . quite simply . . . is his body and his body is the power for a certain world. (*PP*, p. 108f.)

The tools draw out the action immediately, without having to be found or located and without any other intervening reflection or cognition.

With his skills Schneider, like the rest of us, finds himself in a situation full of "signs that guide action." The remarkable fact of his case, though, is that he finds himself solicited by his tools, open to the demands of his habitual work without being able to see distinctly. Nevertheless, his visual agnosia causes motor disabilities in abstract situations. So the second thing Merleau-Ponty wants to explain is why in his and similar cases the failure to see does not imply a failure to act concretely, but does limit abstract actions.

Schneider's perceptual world lacks what Merleau-Ponty calls a "physiognomy," the forms that give the regions of space around us a perceptual presence in terms of opportunities for action. We perceive our environment in terms of what we *could* do, in an attenuated sense of "could." I have no plan or intention to walk around the desk. I am fully absorbed in the task at hand, typing away at the keyboard. Nevertheless the floor behind the desk is perceptually present for me, as a place I could walk to, stand on, observe from, and so on. As we saw above, "the normal subject's body is not merely ready to be mobilized by real situations that draw it toward themselves, it can also turn away from the world . . . and . . . be situated in the virtual" (*PP*, p. 111). Schneider has lost this ability to "reckon with the possible" (*PP*, p. 112). So his deficiency is not straightforwardly visual in the sense that he somehow lacks sufficient sensations. The puzzling nature of his agnosia is precisely that he sees patches of color, but is unable to recognize objects in them. What he lacks is the ability to project potential actions and possible movements. The surrounding world for him does not consist of the vastness of potential actions implied in his bodily skills. And since the regions at the margins of our visual field are perceivable to us as places we *could* step to, objects we *could* handle, and figures we *could* focus on and attend to, Schneider's inability to reckon with the possible cuts him off from such perceivables. He is only open to concrete actions elicited by familiar objects in his immediate presence.

Note that such reckoning is not a matter of explicitly making plans, or of inferring or deducing. Schneider is capable of such high-level intellectual operations and, in fact, resorts to such strategies in order to make up for his inability to perceive. When shown a fountain pen, he does not recognize it as such immediately, but arrives at this recognition through a chain of intermediate descriptions. It is long, it is shiny, it is shaped like a stick, is an instrument, a pencil or a pen. "Language clearly intervenes in each phase of the recognition by providing possible significations for what is actually seen, and the recognition clearly progresses by following the connections of language. . . . The sensory givens are limited to suggesting these significations in the manner that a fact suggests to the physicist an hypothesis" (*PP*, p. 132f.). He finally recognizes the fountain pen as such when he reaches for his breast pocket and says "this is where it goes, for writing something down" (*PP*, p. 132). Through the back-and-forth of sensations and linguistic descriptions he manages to place the object in his bodily space and knows what is to be done with it. In other words, he successfully perceives when he connects the object to an opportunity for action. A normal perceiver performs this step immediately. That the pen affords taking notes gives a physiognomy to its perceptual presence as a potential action.

Schneider's condition causes him to be stuck in the moment of his current activity. He is open to the immediate solicitations of his environment but does not have broader spatial or temporal horizons. He cannot pretend or play-act. He cannot enter fictions, or can do so only by turning the fictitious situation into a real one. In summer he cannot say whether he likes the cold of winter. "Schneider is 'bound' to the actual, and he 'lacks freedom,' he lacks the concrete freedom that consists in the general power of placing oneself in a situation" (*PP*, p. 137). Schneider's inabilities are rooted not in sensations or motor functions, but in the more fundamental function that "projects around us our past, our future, our human milieu, our physical situation, our ideological situation, and our moral situation" (*PP*, p. 137). This "intentional arc," as Merleau-Ponty calls it, "goes limp" in Schneider's illness.

8.3.3 Motor intentionality

Intentionality is the feature of consciousness that it is about something or directed at something. Brentano revived this term from the scholastic tradition. Husserl adopted it and turned it into the cornerstone of his phenomenology. The task of Husserl's transcendental phenomenology is to explain how we can be meaningfully directed at transcendent objects in the world, that is, how we can be conscious of objects that are not immanent in our consciousness. Certainly representation, or ideas, can explain how our consciousness can be directed at objects. But Merleau-Ponty also credits Husserl with the discovery of a "more profound intentionality" that is not a matter of representation (*PP*, p. 520). Heidegger shifts the focus away from intentionality as a feature of consciousness and toward a pre-cognitive skill-based account of being-in-the-world. On his account, we are meaningfully directed at objects in the word by dealing with them skillfully while pursuing our aims. Since most of the relevant skills are pre-cognitive, we intend object without cognizing them. In order to make this difference clear, Heidegger dispenses with the term "intentionality" altogether. He uses the term "transcendence" to talk about how it is possible for us to have meaningful experiences of objects in the world.

Merleau-Ponty's theory of the body schema is also a theory of intentionality. Following Heidegger's lead, Merleau-Ponty argues that being meaningfully directed at objects is a matter of bodily skills and habits. We must "understand motricity unequivocally as original intentionality. Consciousness is originarily not an 'I think that,' but rather an 'I can'" (*PP*, p. 139). The ability to skillfully grasp and handle familiar objects does not seem to require that we stare at those objects or know where they are in "objective" space. My own body and close objects such as a coffee cup or keys on the keyboard have a presence consisting of their availability for my skillful, habitual action. I know how to type and my fingers find the keys, and I know how to grasp the cup without looking up. At the same time, however, I may not have a clear mental map of the location of keys on the keyboard, or the location of the coffee cup. If I merely tried to determine the location in thought, or comport myself toward the objects in some "abstract" movement, I might fail, even though the concrete movement succeeds. Try, for example, to merely *point* to the letter "s" on your keyboard. Each of these two different kinds of comportment is directed at objects in the world, and hence each has a kind of intentionality. "Bodily space can be given to a grasping intention without being given to an epistemic one" (PP, p. 106). Schneider, for instance, can grasp objects but not point to them. Merleau-Ponty argues, and the case of Schneider shows, that the intentionality of skills is more fundamental than cognitive or epistemic intentionality.

Merleau-Ponty introduces the term "motor intentionality" for this basic kind of intelligible directedness at objects. Like other structures in the phenomenal field, motor intentionality tends to be covered up by its own effectiveness. "It is difficult to bring pure motor intentionality to light, for it hides behind the objective world that it contributes to constituting" (PP, p. 523n). The objective world is the world of objects that we perceive and know about from a detached stance. These objects have definite features and definite locations, and we perceive and cognize these features. As Merleau-Ponty argues, this world is intelligible to us because we inhabit a world with our lived bodies. Nevertheless, the skills and habits that make up the lived body are not evident in the objective world, because these skills are not directed at the determinate properties of objects. They are directed at the usability of objects. In taking the detached stance toward the world, we are obscuring the kinds of features that we intend with our motor skills.

Merleau-Ponty describes motor intentionality as follows: "The gesture of reaching one's hand out toward an object contains a reference to the object, not as a representation, but as this highly determinate thing toward which we are thrown, next to which we are through anticipation, and which we haunt" (PP, p. 140). In motor intentionality we are directed at objects without representing them. Instead of entertaining an idea or a judgment about objects, instead of cognizing them explicitly in terms of their determinate properties, we refer to them "in the action of the hand" by "projecting ourselves toward them" or "haunting" them.

Consider the example of the coffee cup. The action of the hand is the concrete movement of reaching out to grasp it in order to take a sip of coffee. Such grasping, as we saw above, is already "magically complete." The movement anticipates its end, and if we prohibit taking hold of the cup, the entire action is inhibited (PP, p. 106). The cup, as an object in the world to be grasped, is therefore already intended by the hand, even though the entire action takes place pre-cognitively and we do not represent the size, shape, or location of the cup in explicit consciousness. The intention is evident in the posture of the entire body, the trajectory of the hand, and the aperture of the grip, which are from the beginning tailored toward the goal of grasping the cup. However, it is not sufficient to state that the shape of the hand intends the cup. Rather, the shape of the hand is part of an entire movement that intends the object. Our body opens up the world of objects through the skills and habits it acquires as complete movements. "A movement is learned when the body has understood it, that is, when it has incorporated it into its 'world,' and to move one's body is to aim at things through it" (*PP*, p. 140).

Finally, motor intentionality is also a matter of being receptive to the opportunities for action presented by the objects in the world. "It is to allow one's body to respond to their solicitation, which is exerted upon the body without any representation" (*PP*, p. 140). Motor-intentional actions are directed at their goal in such a way that the end of the action is already anticipated in its beginning. Such skillful, habitual action can be described as being drawn out from the body by the object. The action of the hand grasping the cup is drawn out or solicited by the cup. The intentional relationship we bear to objects is that we are open to such solicitations, allowing ourselves to "respond to their solicitation." With the concept of motor intentionality Merleau-Ponty therefore both elaborates and challenges the claim that intentionality is directedness at an object. It is just as accurate to say that the object is directed at us, insofar as it solicits us. As with Heideggerian transcendence, in motor intentionality the subject and the world are seen as implying each other, and "one can not conceive of a subject without a world" (*PP*, p. 343).

8.3.4 Examples

Motor intentionality makes up our openness to the world. We experience the world as a meaningful milieu in which we act. The meaning of the disclosed situation is not constituted mentally, through conceptual or noematic representations. Rather, "my body has its world, or understands its world, without having to go through 'representations,' or without being subordinated to a 'symbolic' or 'objectifying function'"(*PP*, p. 141). And "the acquisition of the habit is surely the grasping of a signification, but it is specifically the motor grasping of a motor signification" (*PP*, p. 144). In many cases this motor significance consists of an immediate response to solicitations, so that the phenomena show no distinction between meaningful bodily actions and worldly solicitations. Merleau-Ponty caps his discussion of motor intentionality with a series of illustrative examples that are well worth reviewing. These examples illustrate the specific bodily or motor "understanding" that opens up meaningful situations, as well as the experience of our bodies fusing or merging with worldly equipment.

> Without any explicit calculation, a woman maintains a safe distance between the feather in her hat and objects that might damage it; she

senses where the feather is, just as we sense where our hand is. If I possess the habit of driving a car, then I enter into a lane and see that "I can pass" without comparing the width of the lane to that of the fender, just as I go through a door without comparing the width of the door to that of my body. (*PP*, p. 144)

We have already seen Merleau-Ponty's examples of the blind man's cane and the skilled typist:

The blind man's cane has ceased to be an object for him, it is no longer perceived for itself; rather, the cane's furthest point is transformed into a sensitive zone, it increases the scope and the radius of the act of touching, and has become analogous to a gaze . . . If I want to become habituated to a cane, I try it out, I touch some objects and, after some time, I have it "in hand": I see which objects are "within reach" or out of reach of my cane. (*PP*, p. 144)

[Typing is] a knowledge in our hands, which is only given through a bodily effort and cannot be translated by an objective designation. The subject knows where the letters are on the keyboard just as we know where one of our limbs is – a knowledge of familiarity that does not provide us with a position in objective space. (*PP*, p. 145)

These examples show that the mastery and immediate understanding we have of our own bodies extends to clothes, tools, and machines that we use and that envelop us. Merleau-Ponty says that "habit expresses the power we have of dilating our being in the world, or of altering our existence through incorporating new instruments" (*PP*, p. 145). We will see in Chapter 13 that beyond such description of the experience, the incorporation of tools is measurable. If we analyze the human agent as a dynamic system, fluid ongoing tool use will show that the movements of the tool and the movements of the agent form a single dynamic system.

This "dilating" or extension of our bodily understanding into the world also happens when the tools vary. Obviously knowing how to type opens up possibilities with respect to many different keyboards. It is in this sense that Merleau-Ponty speaks of the body *schema*, built up through our habits and skills. Our motor-intentional understanding of the world is not limited to specific items of equipment, or specific spaces. Our bodies already understand, and hence open up the significance of, an infinity of possible situations. A crucial feature of our motor habits, then, is not simply that we can merge with our tools, but that our bodies will press into a situation as being of a certain type in which certain aspects are salient and that demands a certain kind of motor response.

As Merleau-Ponty puts it, "to understand is to experience the accord between what we aim at and what is given, between the intention and the realization – and the body is our anchorage in a world" (*PP*, p. 146). For example,

> an experienced organist is capable of playing an organ with which he is unfamiliar and that has additional or fewer keyboards, and whose stops are differently arranged than the stops on his customary instrument. He needs but an hour of practice to be ready to execute his program ... He sits on the bench, engages the pedals, and pulls out the stops, he sizes up the instrument with his body, he incorporates its directions and dimensions, and he settles into the organ as one settles into a house. He does not learn positions in objective space for each stop and each pedal, nor does he entrust such positions to "memory." (*PP*, p. 146)

These examples show how Merleau-Ponty's view eludes the criticism Gurwitsch makes of it (see Chapter 6). Gurwitsch claims that bodily phenomena can only have intentionality through our awareness of them. But Merleau-Ponty argues explicitly that the body intends its world through habits and skills "without having to go through 'representations'." Further, these examples exhibit a crucial difference from Sartre's phenomenology of bodily experience. Where Sartre asserts that the body and the hand are unknowable and only indicated by the instrument we use, Merleau-Ponty emphasizes that the body merges with its instruments in our openness toward the world. We know where the instrument is "just as we know where one of our limbs is" and the instrument becomes an extension of our body. Instead of an "evanescent reference," we find the body concretely as we incorporate tools into the body schema.

8.4 Perceptual constancy and natural objects

Merleau-Ponty argues that perception is an existential phenomenon in the vein of Heidegger's conception of being-in-the-world. We perceive objects insofar as they show up in the world of possibilities opened up through our bodily skills. First and foremost we understand perceptual objects in terms of possibilities for action. Nevertheless, we also understand objects and the world as existing independently of our skills and projects. Underlying our bodily space there is an "external" or "objective" space. Beyond soliciting us to act, objects have their own being in which they merely stay put and have certain objective properties.

Merleau-Ponty calls this conception of the object the "natural object." It is the object conceived from a detached point of view, as it were "in itself." However, in using this Kantian phrase, Merleau-Ponty asserts that even considered from a detached perspective, "the thing can never be separated from someone who perceives it; nor can it ever actually be in itself because its articulations are the very ones of our existence" (*PP*, p. 334). In the end, Merleau-Ponty defends a view in the vein of Kant's transcendental idealism and empirical realism. We can have empirical knowledge of real objects, which goes beyond the subjective appearances of objects. The real features of empirical objects are nevertheless structured by basic features of the finitude of our existence. Unlike Kant, of course, Merleau-Ponty finds these basic features in our bodily habits, not in concepts and representations. Merleau-Ponty's view of the natural world is Kantian empirical realism transposed into an existential framework.

The question for Merleau-Ponty's phenomenology is how natural objects are intelligible to us, or "on what basis do we judge that a form or a size are the form and the size of the object?" (*PP*, p. 312). Why, in Husserl's words, do we understand objects as transcendent, as having a mode of being that goes beyond their appearance to our consciousness? Size, shape, color, weight, hardness, and so on are properties of objects, and we understand natural objects as having these properties irrespective of the effect they have on us or how they appear to us.

To explain this independence or transcendence of natural objects Merleau-Ponty considers our perception of the *constancy* of such properties. Perceptual constancy is a familiar and pervasive phenomenon. As I walk along a street toward a friend, the image of my friend becomes increasingly larger in my visual field. Of course I do not perceive my friend growing, but see him as remaining the same size. Similarly, when we rotate a disc or a coin, the shape visible from a given perspective changes from circular to elliptical, but instead of a changing shape we see a constant shape in changing presentations. According to the lighting, a white wall shows darker and lighter patches and different shades of yellow, gray, and blue, but we see a uniformly white surface. These are the phenomena of size, shape, and color constancy and they are integral to our ability to perceive objects in the first place. Merleau-Ponty also points to the constancy of sound, and the constancy of weight.

> The perception of weights remains the same regardless of the muscles that contribute to it and regardless of the initial position of these muscles . . . whether or not the hand is weighed down with a supplementary weight . . . whether the hand acts freely or whether it is rather

tied in such a way so that the fingers work alone – whether one finger or several perform the task – whether the object is lifted with the hand or with the head, a foot, or the teeth – and finally, whether it is lifted in the air or through water. (*PP*, p. 327)

Perceptual constancy points to natural objects, but not directly. It is not the case that the properties we perceive as constant are the real properties of natural objects. We can be wrong. Merleau-Ponty points out, for example, that "constancy is much more perfect according to the horizontal plane than according to the vertical" (*PP*, p. 547). Cars seen below from the height of a skyscraper seem either smaller or further away than when we see them at the same distance down the street. In the size–weight illusion we feel a larger object to have the same weight as a smaller one, even though it may weigh significantly more. So the constant size or weight that we perceive an object to have may not be its real size or weight. The point is rather that perceptual constancy shows *that* perceptual objects have transcendent properties, not what the property is. In fact, the constancy of color, weight, or shape is only a reflection of the more basic perception of the constancy of things as such.

> The constancy of color is merely an abstract moment of the constancy of things, and the constancy of things is established upon the primordial consciousness of the world as the horizon of all of our experiences. Thus, it is not because I perceive constant colors beneath the variety of lightings that I believe in things, and the thing will not be a sum of constant characteristics; rather, I discover constant colors to the extent that my perception is in itself open to a world and to things. (*PP*, p. 326f.)

Colors and other sensible properties are "abstract" components, because objects are "inter-sensory." Obviously an object can be seen, touched, and heard, but Merleau-Ponty makes a stronger claim here. Color, for example, is not independent of texture. Adapting an example from Sartre's *The Imaginary* Merleau-Ponty writes, "a color is never simply a color, but rather the color of a certain object, and the blue of a rug would not be the same blue if it were not a wooly blue" (*PP*, p. 326). The color we see an object to have is never merely the color that appears, but a goal or norm that guides our actions and movements around that object. Seeing the color of an object is a process in which we resolve what is lighting and what is color by articulating the entire visual field. We see the color when we have understood the entire field, when we know our way around it. If we block out the visual field and look only at one colored patch through a screen, we lose this purchase on the entirety and hence lose our grip on the color perceived. Ordinarily we have no trouble telling the color of a wall in different lighting conditions, but if we obscure all but one patch, we cannot distinguish the color from the lighting. This is a useful trick for artists looking to choose the right paint, but it precisely does not reveal the color of the thing. The artist may choose violet to paint a white surface. Similarly, we can focus on a small or blurry patch of the rug to obscure its texture. But that only keeps us from seeing its true color. The same goes for other sensory properties. All sensory properties belong together, not just through external coordination, but because each property only is what it is in conjunction with the others. "The fragility, rigidity, transparency, and crystalline sound of a glass expresses a single manner of being" (*PP*, p. 333). What we see is not so much a constant color, but a constant thing of which the color is only one aspect.

This inter-sensory unity derives from the unity of our bodies. To perceive an object is to find it in the world opened up through our bodily competences, and in acquiring these competences we do not distinguish between the senses. The body works as a unit. "The sensory 'properties' of a thing together constitute a single thing just as my gaze, my touch, and all of my other senses are, together, the powers of a single body integrated into a single action" (*PP*, p. 331). The perceptual goal of a bodily movement is never merely to get information about color, size, and so on, but to open the possibilities for action in the world. So behind the constancy of sensory properties and the constancy of the things lies what Merleau-Ponty calls the constancy of the world. We perceive colors, shapes, and sizes as constant insofar as they are aspects of objects. And we perceive objects as constant insofar as they show up in the world of possibilities in which we find ourselves. The intelligibility of natural objects, then, emerges from our understanding of the world as a unified setting. This unity of the world, though, is more pervasive and basic than the unity of sensory properties. As we saw above, Merleau-Ponty calls it the "horizon of all of our experiences" and he describes it as a *style* that "ensures my experiences have a given, not a willed, unity beneath all of the ruptures of my personal and historical life" (*PP*, p. 345). We are perceivers insofar as we take our place in this world, knowing how to get along in it, skillfully discerning opportunities for action. Competent, bodily, purposive involvement is a "deeper function without which perceived objects would lack the mark of reality" and which "carries us beyond subjectivity [and] places us in the world" (*PP*, p. 358).

Key terms

abstract movement – for example, pointing; a movement that does not emerge out of a habitual action.

body (*Körper*) – the body as conceived by physics, or objective thought, as an extended mass.

body schema – the constant readiness of our bodily skills and habits, which prefigures the possible ways in which the world solicits us.

concrete movement – for example, grasping; a movement that emerges from skillful, goal-directed action.

empiricism – theories that attempt to explain perception by positing causal mechanisms that operate on sensory qualities. Empiricism includes scientific psychology, with much of Gestalt psychology, and is one of Merleau-Ponty's two broad targets.

intellectualism – theories that attempt to explain perception by positing inferential processes that lead from sensations to perception. Intellectualism includes Descartes and Kant, and is the second of Merleau-Ponty's two broad targets.

lived body (*Leib*) – your body, with which you experience from the first-person point of view.

motor intentionality – being meaningfully directed at objects, a matter of bodily skills and habits.

objective thought – the dominant prejudice of the modern period that the world of perception consists of sensory qualities that can be specified independently of each other and of the perceiver. Objective thought frames the theoretical outlook of both empiricism and intellectualism.

perceptual constancy – the feature of perception that we discern unchanging properties (such as an object's size or color) through variations of the presentation of the object (such as changing distance, angle, or lighting conditions).

physiognomy – the forms that give the regions of space around us a perceptual presence in terms of opportunities for action.

Further reading

Carman, T. (2020). *Merleau-Ponty*, 2nd edn. London: Routledge.

Carman, T. and M. Hansen, eds. (2005). *The Cambridge Companion to Merleau-Ponty*. Cambridge: Cambridge University Press.

Romdenh-Romluc, K. (2011). *Merleau-Ponty and Phenomenology of Perception*. London: Routledge.

9

Critical Phenomenology

9.1 The path not taken

The main story we tell in this book is of the influence of scientific psychology on the development of phenomenological philosophy, and, as we will see in Chapters 10 through 13, the subsequent influence of phenomenology on today's scientific psychology. This is not the only story we could have told. Another path from the phenomenological philosophy of the twentieth century to the present is what is now called "critical phenomenology." All of the historical figures we have discussed so far are male, and all of them are European. We can add to this that all of them are highly educated and mostly come from families of means. The key insight of critical phenomenology is that these traits make a difference to being-in-the-world. Thus the phenomenologists we have considered so far have erred in thinking that the structures they describe are *universal* features of human experience, when in fact they might only reflect the phenomenologists' status as wealthy, educated, European males. Critical phenomenology is an exploration of the ways in which the experience of wealthy, educated, European males differs from the experience of those who are not wealthy, educated, European males. Although it is critical of traditional phenomenology, it is indebted to it as well, especially to the work of Sartre and Merleau-Ponty. In fact, Lisa Guenther (2020) points to a disagreement between Husserl and Merleau-Ponty as crucial in the development of critical phenomenology. Husserl took intentionality as the orientation from constituting consciousness to constituted world. Merleau-Ponty took this to be a reciprocal relation, in which the world affects and modifies the intentional consciousness. This reciprocity makes it such that contingent features of the social world, such as race, gender, wealth disparities, and the like, are partly constitutive of our abilities to experience the world. Given this, phenomenology needs to account for the ways in which these contingent facts about the world partly constitute agency and intentionality. Merleau-Ponty provides a framework for analyzing how intentionality is shaped by contingent facts through his notion of the habits and skills that make up the body schema. This also points to a possibility for phenomenology to become affiliated with political activism, aimed at altering those features of the social world that have negative impacts on our agency and intentionality.

Critical phenomenology is, thus, vitally important philosophical work, brimming with social and political consequences. It is, however, off the main path of this book. This chapter is, for this reason, a cul-de-sac. Our goal in it is to introduce some of what we take to be the most important work in critical phenomenology, and point the interested reader to more comprehensive studies of it. For the latter point, we recommend *50 Concepts for a Critical Phenomenology*, edited by Weiss, Murphy, and Salamon (2020), in addition to the primary sources we discuss below.

9.2 Phenomenology and gender

Sartre's philosophical thought is inextricably intertwined with that of Simone de Beauvoir, who was both his collaborator and critic. It was Beauvoir's 1947 *Ethics of Ambiguity* and her 1949 *The Second Sex* that made phenomenology fruitful for concrete ethics and feminism. While Beauvoir, like Sartre, begins with a Husserlian conception of a meaning-constituting consciousness, her *Ethics of Ambiguity* goes beyond Sartre's abstract existentialist version of radical freedom, arguing that precisely the existential conception of freedom should serve as the ground for a concrete ethics in which we are responsible for enabling the material conditions for the exercise of such freedom. *The Second Sex* goes further in analyzing the concrete conditions of ethical subjects. Beauvoir follows the phenomenological method, but for her the "natural attitude" to be interrogated is whether the inferior position of women is a matter of biological destiny. Beauvoir shows how our social and cultural traditions have created notions of feminine inferiority that constrain the possibilities of women's existential projects. As she says in the Introduction,

"He is the Subject; he is the Absolute. She is the Other" (1949, p. 26). Beauvoir achieves a breakthrough by showing that these constraints apply to women as situated, embodied agents, making it clear that our meaning-constituting bodily projects are gendered. The work of Iris Marion Young is an important development of this basic insight.

In her important 1980 paper "Throwing like a girl," Young draws on Beauvoir and Merleau-Ponty to show how to apply the basic insights of phenomenology to modern feminism. Like Beauvoir, Young rejects any conception of femininity as a biological or genetic trait. Femininity is rather constituted by "the typical situation of being a woman in a particular society, as well as the typical way in which this situation is lived by the women themselves" (1980, p. 31). Young also moves beyond a Sartrean focus on an unhappy or conflicted consciousness. Instead she follows Merleau-Ponty's focus on the lived body. The typically feminine situation, she argues, is rooted in the lived body, that is, in the particularly feminine way in which a body relates to its world through its motor intentionality.

Young's analysis centers on the example of throwing. She cites a telling passage from Erwin Straus' 1966 *Phenomenological Psychology*, in which Straus describes and aims to explain an observed difference in throwing styles between young boys and girls:

> The girl of five does not make any use of lateral space. She does not stretch her arm sideward; she does not twist her trunk; she does not move her legs, which remain side by side. All she does in preparation for throwing is to lift her right arm forward to the horizontal and to bend the forearm backward in a pronate position. . . . The ball is released without force, speed, or accurate aim. (Straus 1966; quoted by Young 1980, p. 27)

In contrast to this, a young boy uses his whole body when he throws a ball. He pivots at the hip, twisting the throwing arm back, and shifts his weight to the leg on the same side as the throwing arm. He lifts his opposite foot and steps forward, transferring his body weight back from the throwing leg, reversing his hip pivot, and whipping his throwing arm forward with the weight of his body. Straus suggests that this difference must derive from an inherent "feminine essence," since biological and anatomical differences could not explain such marked differences at such an early age. As a phenomenologically trained psychiatrist he may have conceived of this essence as a type of Husserlian eidetic constitution. However, Straus misses the insight of Merleau-Ponty, for whom basic motor comportment is not constituted by some prior inner essence, but itself constitutes the original openness to the world. In other words, one does not throw like a girl because this movement manifests one's inner feminine essence; rather, if one throws like this, the femininity of the thrower consists entirely of the motor possibilities contained in this bodily comportment. Further, insofar as this type of description is accurate, if boys are indeed comfortable in using their whole bodies and the space around them to achieve a goal, while girls are hesitant and uncertain of their skill, it indicates a basic modality of the body schema. While Merleau-Ponty establishes the ontological importance of the body schema, he misses that the body schema expresses a gender. His phenomenology of the lived body is in fact the phenomenology of the lived *male* body and his work thus silently asserts the dominance of the image of masculinity in phenomenology. Young recovers the crucial modality of gender and analyzes how gender shapes the body schema in our culture. She thus shows that a complete phenomenology of the lived body is always already a feminist phenomenology.

Straus' description of how girls supposedly throw already seemed quaintly outdated in 1980, and certainly strikes us as a caricature today. Many of the restrictions and obstacles faced by girls in the middle decades of the last century have been eased or altered. Some corners of our culture now parody the insult that you throw, run, hit, and so on "like a girl" and hence subvert this sexist disparagement. Nevertheless, sexism in our culture continues to construct the typical situation of females as limited, objectified, and dominated. Examples of powerful, athletic women do not undermine this analysis. Young points out that the femininity here describes "the conditions that delimit the typical *situation*" and that "it is not necessary that *any* women be 'feminine'" just as it is possible for some men to be feminine (1980, p. 31).

Young focuses her analysis on throwing, walking, running, lifting, and general "bodily activities that relate to the comportment or orientation of the body as a whole, that entail gross movement, or that require the enlistment of strength and the confrontation of the body's capacities and possibilities with the resistance and malleability of things" (1980, p. 30). Throwing has many features that make it a telling case for an analysis of the body schema. It involves the whole body. It is a specifically human skill. It is widespread, but nevertheless must be learned. Throwing essentially points beyond the body to a target or a distance, so it has a specific way of expressing an intention and taking up space. If we take throwing to be a concrete movement, as opposed to an abstract one, then Merleau-Ponty's claim applies, namely that "from its very beginnings ... [it] is magically complete" (*PP*, p. 106). The feminine throwing action, however, does not fit this description. The action does not appear solicited by the world, the movement does not appear guided by the aim of the throw. Instead the throwing motion appears hesitant and obstructed.

Young analyzes three structures of the feminine lived body. Each marks a difference from the male body schema described by Merleau-Ponty. First, while the male lived body is the transcendent subject of experience, females experience *ambiguous transcendence*. The female body is experienced ambiguously: sometimes as the *transcendent* subject of experience, as the center of the world. This is the sense in which the body, in Merleau-Ponty's phrase, "rises up toward the world" (*PP*, p. 78) and that Young describes as "pure fluid action, the continuous calling-forth of capacities that are applied to the world" (1980, p. 36). At the same time, however, women experience their bodies as mere objects in the world, looked at and acted upon by (primarily male) others. To the extent that females experience their bodies as mere things, they experience them as *immanent*. This is not the kind of immanence Husserl describes in his analysis of the body, where a hand touching the other both feels and is felt, where the body both is the center of visual experience and is seen as one object among many. Rather, it is an objectification of the body by sexist culture. Young writes, "the woman lives her body as *object* as well as subject. The source of this is that patriarchal society defines woman as object, as a mere body, and that in sexist society women are in fact frequently regarded by others as objects and mere bodies" (1980, p. 44). In particular, females experience themselves as someone who is *looked at*. This is evident from the widely discussed idea of the "male gaze." In introducing this concept, Mulvey (1975) points out that in many representations of women in cinema, the camera treats a woman as a sexual object, moving over a woman's body the way a man's eyes would when he is "checking her out." This common feature of cinema affects the way women see themselves, teaching them to see themselves as sexual objects. This way that women see themselves – as males see them, as sexual objects – has been confirmed by social psychologists, especially in what is called objectification theory (Fredrickson and Roberts 1997). Social psychologists have learned that the male gaze has real, measurable effects on female self-esteem. Moreover, it is not only the male gaze that is at issue. Women also look at women more than they look at men, and gaze patterns of looking at women often mirror the "male gaze" (Hall 1984). Finally, there have been many studies of self-objectification in women, finding that women view themselves as an observer would, constantly monitoring the way they look (Calogero, Tantleff-Dunn, and Thompson 2011). The female lived body is both a subject of action and experience and a sexualized object of observation.

It is constantly *"overlaid* with immanence, even as it moves out toward the world" (Young 1980, p. 36).

Second, Merleau-Ponty describes the intentionality of the lived body as consisting in a feeling of readiness to perform skillfully, as an "I can." As he puts it, "consciousness is originarily not an 'I think that,' but rather an 'I can'" (*PP*, p. 139). In contrast, the feminine lived body exhibits *inhibited intentionality*. In inhibited intentionality, a woman sees the possibility of engaging in some skillful action, but does not see it as her own possibility, thus simultaneously projecting an "I can" and a self-imposed "I cannot." Such inhibition of bodily possibility is learned as girls acquire habits and develop their body schema.

> The girl learns actively to hamper her movements. She is told that she must be careful not to get hurt, not to get dirty, not to tear her clothes, that the things she desires to do are dangerous for her. Thus she develops a bodily timidity that increases with age. In assuming herself to be a girl, she takes herself to be fragile. (1980, p. 43)

In our sexist culture, girls are rewarded for reserved, passive behavior. Even as infants and toddlers, girls are typically picked up and held more demurely, while boys are often jostled in active and more mobile ways.

Third, women experience a *discontinuous unity* in their bodies. This discontinuous unity is made very clear in the contrast between throwing styles described above. Throwing, like many other actions, requires coordinated action of the whole body. Males experience their bodies as unified, and engage them in their entirety in performing an action. Women, on the other hand, experience their bodies as collections of parts and often engage only some of those parts in acting. The young girl throws with her arm, and keeps the rest of her body still. The feminine body schema fails to provide a background unity for feminine experience, and it also fails to unite the female with her surrounding world. Reminiscent of Fanon, who finds that as a Black man in a colonial, racist society his body schema disintegrates under the pressures of a society that forcibly defines him in terms of racists narratives (see below), Young argues that the feminine lived body does not sustain a unified, spontaneous integration into the world.

Females, who live in a male-dominated, sexist world, come to experience themselves differently. Following Beauvoir, Young insists that this difference between males and females is neither biological nor genetic, but a feature of the situation of women in our sexist culture. A female lived body is both the subject of skillful action and an object for males to look at; it is both transcendent and immanent. In many situations, the typical feminine body experience is not of a body that "surges" toward the world, but of a body whose movement does not univocally intend its object. Young is not making the trite and false point that there are typical female and male activities in our sexist culture, that girls are good at some things and boys good at others. The truth she uncovers is much more insidious. Girls are unable to be good at being themselves, at being in the world through the medium of their bodies, because their bodily intentionality is constrained and inhibited by the persistent forces of sexist culture. As Young puts it, "women in sexist society are physically handicapped" (1980, p. 42).

Perhaps unsurprisingly, the ideas of Merleau-Ponty and Beauvoir have also been central to understanding trans lived experience. Merleau-Ponty's focus on the distinction between *Körper* and *Leib* and on the body schema, both discussed above, is key here. Also crucial in this context is Beauvoir's inauguration of the possibility of a distinction between sex and gender in *The Second Sex*, the most famous line of which is "One is not born but rather becomes a woman" (1949). Beauvoir's point with this line is that the societal place of women in mid-twentieth-century France was not a matter of biological destiny, but instead the result of a series of deeply ingrained sociocultural biases. Although the distinction between (biological) sex and (sociocultural) gender is still hotly disputed, without it neither the discipline of trans studies nor current work on trans phenomenology, both of which took off around the turn of the twenty-first century, would ever have gotten off the ground. The central aim of trans phenomenology is to interrogate the necessary conditions for transgendered and transsexual lived experiences, without delegitimizing those experiences.

Henry Rubin (2003) uses Merleau-Ponty's discussion of anosognosia and phantom limbs to make sense of gender dysphoria in transsexual men. As we described in Chapter 8, Merleau-Ponty characterizes phantom limb experiences in terms of the body schema, and a mismatch between the habitual possibilities for action and those that our physical bodies enable. Rubin uses this mismatch to make sense of the experiences of transsexual men, who, he claims, suffer from both anosognosia and phantom limbs. Transsexual men "rise up toward the world" as if their breasts and female genitalia were not their own, and as if they had male genitalia that they lack. Just as the phantom limb sufferers know that they don't have the missing limb, transsexual men know that they have breasts and female genitalia and that they lack male genitalia, but this does not affect their body schemas. Rubin argues that this understanding of transsexual men has the advantage of accounting for their experiences, without pathologizing them. Rubin's claims have been met with some skepticism. First, he is correct that on his account transsexual men do not suffer from psychosis as it is defined by Sartre, as the "horrified metaphysical apprehension of the existence of my body for the Others" (Sartre, *BN*; quoted by Rubin 2003, p. 29). But this might not put enough distance between the experiences of transsexual men and mental illness: anosognosia and phantom limbs are considered pathological. The former is a strong indication of the presence of schizophrenia; the latter are typically debilitating to those who suffer them, unless they are able to align their body schema with their physical body. With Rubin's focus on transsexual men, it seems as if body dysmorphia is a pathology, which is treated by surgery or hormone therapy.

Talia Mae Bettcher (2012) argues that "wrong body" views like Rubin's risk pathologizing transgendered, as opposed to transsexual, lived experience, and draw too sharp a distinction between transgendered and transsexual lived experience. Bettcher points out that not all transgendered people want to change their bodies or experience their bodies as pathological; that is, not all transgendered people wish to become transsexual. In many cases, the only desire is to change one's sociocultural gendered identity. Better than a sharp distinction, Bettcher argues for a recognition that all trans people feel committed to their gender, whether or not that commitment is accompanied by a desire to change their bodies. Arguing otherwise, as Rubin does, accepts traditional understandings of sex and gender, according to which being a woman (man) requires having female (male) genitalia, denying the chosen gender identities of transgendered people.

Gayle Salamon (2010) uses Merleau-Ponty's distinction between *Körper* and *Leib* to develop an understanding of trans phenomenology that applies equally to transgendered and transsexual people. To do so, she uses what Merleau-Ponty calls the "sexual schema." Merleau-Ponty discusses the sexual schema in relation to the body schema. Just as the body schema makes sense of the way the world shows up to us as an arena in which we can act, the sexual schema makes sense of the way that things show up to us as objects of desire or love. And, like the body schema, the sexual schema is not itself an object of conscious experience; it is what orients us to objects of desire. In fact, interpreting a quotation from *Phenomenology of Perception*, Salamon suggests that the sexual schema, and the sexuality it enables, are rife with ambiguity and suffuse all our experience. When reaching for a drink, the reaching hand and arm recede from experience, which is aimed only at the drink. Merleau-Ponty refers to this assignment of an action to the body as "transposition." In transposition, the action and the parts of the body that enact it become the vehicle for the experience of the object that the action intends. When transposition occurs in sexuality, my body, in its desire, *becomes* desire itself. The flesh of it is felt only as an animated leaning, intentional in the sense that the desire animating it has an object – it is desire to the extent that it is desire *of* – but also intentional in the sense that my sense of it coalesces around a purposeful being toward this desired object. My body becomes a leaning or a yearning, a propulsive force that negates any sense of my body as solid or still, or indeed as *mine*, in that this sensation owns me more than I own it. (Salamon 2010, p. 52)

In applying these ideas to trans experiences, Salamon points out that any part of the body can become desire. "The join between the desire and the body is the location of sexuality, and that join may be a penis, or some other phallus, or some other body part, or a region of the body that is not individuated into a part, or a body auxiliary that is not organically attached to the body" (2010, p. 54).

Here, we have an understanding of sexuality that makes sense of trans experience, but does not tie it to the possession of particular body parts. That is, it makes sense equally of transgender and transsexual lived experience. What determines sexuality is not whether one has male or female genitalia, but the ways in which the lived body intends other lived bodies as objects of desire.

9.3 Phenomenology and race

Frantz Fanon, a psychiatrist and political thinker born in the French colony of Martinique, can be seen as taking up Sartre's (and Beauvoir's) call for an existential ethics. Fanon fought against French colonizers in the Caribbean, before going to France to join the Free French Army against Germany in World War II, where he received the Croix de Guerre. He studied medicine in Lyon, where he attended lectures by Merleau-Ponty and closely read Sartre's writings, before moving to work in a psychiatric hospital in Algiers. While there, Fanon joined the Front Libération Nationale in its fight against the French occupation of Algiers. Fanon is known mostly as a revolutionary and anti-colonialist theorist. His work is a crucial precursor of the discipline of post-colonial studies. His most famous work, *The Wretched of the Earth* (1961), was published just before his death at age thirty-six. Sartre wrote a preface for *The Wretched of the Earth*, in which he endorsed Fanon's notorious defense of violence by colonized people toward their colonizers. Fanon's justification for this was that because colonized people are not treated as human beings by their colonizers, the colonized are not required to follow the ethical principles expected of human beings in their dealings with colonizers.

Fanon's earlier book, *Black Skin, White Masks* (1952), is a reaction to the White, European racism he experienced during his time in France, where he was simultaneously an intellectual and war hero, on one hand, and reviled because of his skin, on the other. That Fanon was inspired by, and arguing with, Sartre, Merleau-Ponty, and Beauvoir is especially clear in chapter 5 of that book. The title of the chapter in French is "L'expérience vécue du Noir," a purposeful echo of the title of book 2 of Beauvoir's *The Second Sex*, "L'expérience vécue." This echo is lost in the standard English translation of *Black Skin, White Masks* (1967), which renders what should be "Black lived experience" as "The fact of Blackness," losing the reference to Beauvoir. She, in fact, was as much an influence on Fanon as Sartre and Merleau-Ponty were, though Fanon rarely acknowledges her (Gordon 2015).

"L'expérience vécue du Noir" is Fanon's most straightforwardly phenomenological piece of work. His writing in it is striking and impassioned. He begins the chapter with a racist epithet, which we, following Gordon, leave untranslated:

> "Dirty *Nègre*!" Or simply "Look, a *Nègre*!"
>
> I came into the world imbued with the will to find a meaning in things, my spirit filled with the desire to attain to the source of the world, and I found that I was an object in the midst of other objects.
>
> Sealed into that crushing objecthood, I turned beseechingly to others. Their attention was a liberation, running over my body suddenly abraded into nonbeing, endowing me once more with the agility I thought I had lost, and by taking me out of the world, restoring me to it. But just as I reached the other side, I stumbled, and the movements, the attitudes, the glances of the other fixed me there, in the sense in which a chemical solution is fixed by a dye. (1952, p. 82)

Although Fanon does not mention him by name in this chapter, this opening is a clear reference to Merleau-Ponty's phenomenology of the body. The body, Merleau-Ponty claims, is experienced not as an object, but as the center of the experienced world. "One's own body is in the world just as the heart is in the organism: it continuously breathes life into the visible spectacle, animates it and nourishes it from within, and forms a system with it" (*PP*, p. 209). When Fanon attempts to make sense of his Black lived experience, he finds that this is not true of him. He and his body are not in the world as the heart is in the organism; instead, he is "an object amidst other objects." Fanon makes sense of this in terms of the body schema, Merleau-Ponty's replacement for Kant's schemata as the set of structures that make experience possible. Fanon describes the body schema as the "slow composition of my *self* as a body in the middle of a spatial and temporal world," and "a definitive structuring of the self and of the world – definitive because it creates a real dialectic between my body and the world" (1952, p. 83). But he finds that his body schema has been unseated by a "historico-racial schema," supplied by White people who had "woven [him] out of a thousand details, anecdotes, stories." Under such pressure, his body schema crumbles, to be replaced by a "racial epidermal schema" (1952, p. 84).

Here Fanon is expanding on Sartre's view of the alienated, unhappy consciousness, which is stuck between two things it cannot fully attain, as it must be both in-itself and for-itself. A Black person in a racist society, Fanon says, is simultaneously three things that cannot be fully attained, a "triple person." "I existed triply: I occupied space. I moved toward the other . . . and the evanescent other, hostile but not opaque, transparent, not there, disappeared" (1952, p. 84). Fanon agrees with Hegel and Sartre that the self only exists in virtue of recognition by another. For a Black person in a racist society, however, the White other fails to recognize an experiencing subject, imperiling the very idea of a Black self.

The rest of the chapter is a report of Fanon's unsuccessful attempts to make sense of a Black self, "to assert myself as a BLACK MAN" (1952, p. 87). He tries crude jokes (poorly translated), scientific studies of racial differences, Black sexuality, and Black poetry, all to no avail. The last of these leads him to an extended discussion of Sartre's "Black Orpheus" (1948), a sympathetic reflection on Négritude, originally published as the foreword to a volume of Black poetry (Senghor 1948). Négritude is an anti-colonial philosophical and literary framework, developed in the 1930s by French-speaking Black intellectuals, aimed at raising Black consciousness and pride across the world. One of the founders of the movement, and the coiner of the term "Négritude," was Aimé Césaire. From his teens, Fanon knew fellow Martinican Césaire personally, and even worked on one of his political campaigns. Given this, it is not surprising that Fanon finds "Black Orpheus" unforgivable. Sartre takes a Hegelian approach to Négritude, which he calls an "anti-racist racism" (1948, p. 40). Négritude is the antithesis to the thesis of White racism; thus it is a temporary, transitional movement. The inevitable synthesis, Sartre argues, will be a color-blind Communism. Although Fanon ironically calls Sartre "a friend of the colored peoples" (1952, p. 102), he finds "Black Orpheus" unpardonable for its implication that Négritude and the experiences of Black people are mere reactions to White racism.

What is certain is that, at the very moment when I was trying to grasp my own being, Sartre, who remained The Other, gave me a name and thus shattered my last illusion. . . . [W]hile I was shouting that, in the paroxysm of my being and my fury, he was reminding me that my Blackness was only a minor term. In all truth, in all truth I tell you, my shoulders slipped out of the framework of the world, my feet could no longer feel the touch of the ground. Without a nègre past, without a nègre future, it was impossible for me to live my nègre-hood. Not yet White, no longer wholly Black, I was damned. Jean-Paul Sartre had forgotten that the Nègre suffers in his body quite differently from the White man. (1952, p. 105f.)

Ultimately, Fanon accuses Sartre of comparing the experience of Blackness to an amputation, Sartre, he says, tells him to resign himself to victimhood, treating his Blackness the way a veteran amputee gets used to missing a limb suffered in battle (1952, p. 107).

As noted above, the chapter is a record of Fanon's failure to come to terms with his own Blackness, and its impact on his being-in-the-world. In the end, he says, "Without responsibility, straddling Nothingness and Infinity, I began to weep" (1952, p. 108).

Following up on Fanon's work (and Beauvoir's, and Merleau-Ponty's), Linda Martín Alcoff argues that race, like gender, is constitutive of lived bodily experience, especially for those who are visibly members of stigmatized racial minorities (2006). There is a long history of work in psychology concerning the effects of racial stigmatization. For example, in a series of studies in the late 1930s and 1940s (i.e., during Fanon's lifetime), Mamie and Kenneth Clark had African-American children play with dark-skinned and light-skinned dolls and asked them a series of questions about the dolls. Between the ages of three and four, children became aware of race, identifying the dark-skinned doll as being like them. This was true even in cases in which their own skin tone was closer to that of the light-skinned doll. Older children, up to age nine, were asked which doll was good, which was bad, which they wanted to play with. They typically identified the light-skinned doll as the one they wanted to play with and the one that was good; they identified the dark-skinned doll as both the one that was bad and the one that was like them (Clark and Clark 1947). More recently, there has been work on stereotype threat (Steele 1997), in which being reminded of a stereotype negatively affects performance in members of the stigmatized group. In particular, it appears that being reminded of a stereotype leads individuals who are stereotyped to be more likely to fulfill the stereotype. For example, African-American students who are told that

African-Americans are comparatively poor standardized test takers will do worse than African-American students who are not told this. Stereotypes can become self-fulfilling prophecies. Clearly, the experience of race and being racially categorized has profound psychological effects.

Alcoff relies on Merleau-Ponty's phenomenology of the lived body, and especially the habit body, to account for the effects of race on experience. The habit body is culturally inflected, and in a culture in which race is an important perceptual category, the habit body will be racially inflected. As Alcoff puts it, "Greetings, handshakes, proximity, tone of voice, all reveal the effects of racial awareness, the presumption of superiority vis-à-vis the other, or the protective defenses against the possibility of racism and misrecognition" (2009, p. 184). The habit body is racialized, especially for those who are members of what Alcoff calls "visible minorities," those who can be racially categorized based on their appearance. Because the lived body, including in its guise as the habit body, is the necessary foundation of experience and because race is built into it, race becomes part of the tacit ground for experience. For visible minorities, the skillful readiness with which the world is confronted will include readiness to deal with bias, racism, and misunderstanding. The world that visible minorities experience differs from the world that those in the majority experience.

9.4 Conclusion

It might seem that these critical phenomenologies are irredeemably grim. It is true that they describe the deeply negative effects that cultural bias can have on those who experience it. At the same time, however, they make clear that these negative effects are contingent. Beauvoir, Young, Bettcher, and Salamon argue that gender is not a biological trait, but a cultural one; Fanon and Alcoff says the same about race. Because gender and race are cultural constructions, they can be altered, and pointing to the negative effects can be the motivation for making the necessary alterations.

As we noted above, this vital work is off to the side of the main story we tell in this book, a story that focuses on the interactions between phenomenology and the sciences of the mind. However, given the work's import and broad political implications, this might not be the case in the long term. That is, it is easy to imagine the phenomenology-oriented cognitive scientists we discuss in later chapters eventually turning their attention to themes from critical phenomenology.

Key terms

ambiguous transcendence – experiencing oneself as both a subject of experience and as an other, a mere object in the world.

male gaze – a concept, initially, from film studies, describing the way cameras move across women's bodies in movies, looking them up and down and treating female characters in movies as sexual objects.

Négritude – anti-colonial francophone philosophical and literary framework, aimed at raising Black consciousness and pride across the world.

racial epidermal schema – an analogue of Merleau-Ponty's body schema that structures the experiences of minorities in racist societies and leads to the experience of ambiguous transcendence.

sexual schema – an analogue of the body schema through which others are constituted as objects of desire or love. From Merleau-Ponty.

stereotype threat – a finding in psychology in which being reminded of a stereotype leads individuals who are stereotyped to be more likely to fulfill the stereotype.

unhappy consciousness – awareness of conflict between the essential self and the contingent self. From Hegel and Sartre; see Chapter 8.

Further reading

Alcoff, L. M. (2006). *Visible Identities: Race, Gender, and the Self*. New York: Oxford University Press.

Fanon, F. (1952/1967). *Black Skin, White Masks*, trans. C. L. Markmann. New York: Grove Press, 1967.

Gordon, L. (2015). *What Fanon Said*. New York: Fordham University Press.

Salamon, G. (2010). *Assuming a Body*. New York: Columbia University Press.

Weiss, G., A. Murphy, and G. Salamon, eds. (2020). *50 Concepts for a Critical Phenomenology*. Chicago: Northwestern University Press.

Young, I. M. (2005). *On Female Body Experience: Throwing Like a Girl and Other Essays*. New York: Oxford University Press.

10

James J. Gibson and Ecological Psychology

As we can see from the previous chapter, phenomenology has had fruitful influences in many directions. Rather than taking up the role of phenomenology in other fields, we will continue to focus on phenomenologically grounded accounts of perception and the role of the body in constituting intelligibility. In particular, we will now turn to the work of scientists – psychologists, neuroscientists, cognitive scientists – who have followed the phenomenologists in taking the nature of experience and the relationship between experience and ontology as their subject matter. Unlike a great deal of philosophy, the ideas of phenomenologists are sufficiently specific and consequential to be explored scientifically, and they have been explored – and often confirmed – scientifically.

We begin this alternative history by discussing the work of James J. Gibson, a psychologist and a contemporary of Merleau-Ponty. Though they came from different traditions, both Gibson and Merleau-Ponty were influenced by Gestalt psychologists, especially early in their careers. In fact, Gibson's views and Merleau-Ponty's views are in some respects very similar, and Gibson was aware of Merleau-Ponty's work. Like Merleau-Ponty, Gibson saw himself as developing a new framework for understanding perception from the ground up, and he struggled against the fundamental problems he saw in Kant's distinction between concepts and intuitions. That said, Gibson's ideas do not come from Merleau-Ponty or other phenomenologists, but from decades of applying the functionalist tradition in psychology to our perceptual experience.

E. B. Holt was a student of William James who attempted to push radical empiricism to its limits and to make it into a psychological theory. Holt's work is interesting in itself, though it has been until recently neglected by historians of psychology (Heft 2001; Charles 2012). For current purposes, though, Holt's most important role was as Gibson's teacher at Princeton. In the early 1920s, Gibson studied philosophy at Princeton as an undergraduate, and became a member of the first cohort of graduate students in psychology there. Holt was one of his professors. Another was Herbert Langfeld, who had studied with Brentano. Gibson's thesis was an experimental refutation of work on form perception by the Gestalt psychologist Wulf, who had been a student of Koffka. Gibson wrote of this in his autobiography: "Form perception was learned. Otherwise one fell into the arms of Immanuel Kant. I was a radical empiricist, like Holt . . . Little did I know that I would be facing Koffka himself weekly across a seminar table" (1967, p. 129f.). As we will see below, the Jamesian Holt and Koffka are the two main influences on Gibson's ecological theory.

10.1 Gibson's early work: Two examples

10.1.1 Perceived valences

The influence of Gibson's colleague Koffka and Gestalt psychology more generally is evident in an early paper by Gibson and Crooks (1938). In the paper, Gibson and Laurence Crooks, an engineer, analyze driving behavior using a modified version of the behavioral field theory developed by Lewin and Koffka. Recall from Chapter 5 that the behavioral field is the collection of directed motivations that guide our behavior. The child is positively disposed toward the cookie jar on the counter and feels pulled toward it, but simultaneously feels pushed away from the cookie jar by her mother's disapproving look. Gibson and Crooks feel that this is the right general approach to understanding behavior behind the wheel of the car. But it is too static. In a car, you are moving quickly forward, and, along with the repellent forces from the lamppost and the guardrail, there are other moving cars that change position relative to your car more or less constantly. What drivers experience and what determines their behavior is what Gibson and Crooks call a "field of safe travel," which "consists, at any given moment, of the field of possible paths which the car may take unimpeded" (1938, p. 454). They define this field explicitly in terms of Lewin's valences, positive or negative "meanings of objects by virtue of which we move toward some of them and away from others"

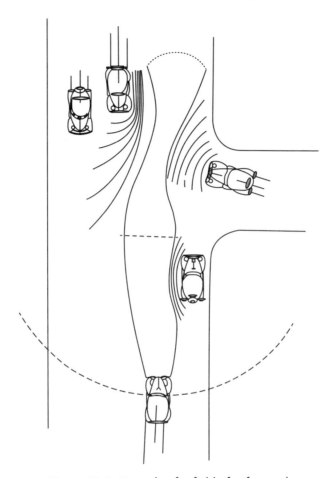

Figure 10.1 Example of a field of safe travel
Source: Based on Gibson and Crooks 1938 from *American Journal of Psychology.*
Copyright 1938 by the Board of Trustees of the University of Illinois. Used with
permission of the University of Illinois Press.

(1938, p. 455). The field of safe travel is a positively valenced path, surrounded by negatively valenced edges of the road, pedestrians, other cars
and so on (see Figure 10.1). Gibson and Crooks recommend rotating the
page so that the reader is looking along the page from the point of view
of the driver of the car. To facilitate this, the figure here has been rotated
so that the car whose field of safe travel is depicted is at the bottom of the
figure. The dashed arc that crosses the hood is the portion of the space
that is within the driver's field of view. The experienced repulsive forces
exerted by the other cars define the field of safe travel in front of the

car, which extends from the front of the car toward the top of the page, toward the horizon from the point of view of the driver. "Phenomenally, it is a sort of tongue protruding forward along the road" (1938, p. 454).

Although this paper is published early in Gibson's career, it has themes that recur, especially in Gibson's last book, *The Ecological Approach to Visual Perception* (1979). Among these is the influence of Koffka and Lewin. As noted in Chapter 5, the Gestaltists argue that forms, including the valences of the behavioral field, are not the result of cognitive operations, but are given in perception. In this paper, Gibson pushes this farther, claiming that the valences that make up fields of safe travel are not merely given in perception, but are components of the objective world:

> The field of safe travel, it should be noted, is a spatial field but it is not fixed in physical space. The car is moving and the field moves with it *through* space. Its point of reference is not the stationary objects of the environment, but the driver himself. It is not, however, merely a subjective experience of the driver. It exists objectively as the actual field within which the car can safely operate, whether or not the driver is aware of it. It shifts and changes continually, bending and twisting with the road, and also elongating or contracting, according as obstacles encroach upon it and limit its boundaries. (1938, p. 455f.)

Like his mentor Holt, Gibson in the 1930s considered himself to be both a radical empiricist and (like most American psychologists at the time) a behaviorist. Either of these identifications could account for Gibson's realism about the contents of experiences. As a radical empiricist, he did not believe in a distinction between the world we experience and the world-in-itself. If we experience fields of safe travel as tongues protruding ahead of our cars, then those tongues are real things in the world. As a behaviorist, Gibson was skeptical about internal mental causes, and thought that psychology needed to be done in terms of publicly observable stimuli and responses, combined with learning theory. From this point of view, the field of safe travel has to be a publicly observable stimulus, albeit a very complicated one, to which driving behavior is a response.

This is a key point of contrast between the scientist and radical empiricist Gibson and the phenomenologists: Gibson was a *realist* about the contents of our experiences. While both Heidegger and Merleau-Ponty are empirical realists about the objects of scientific study, they distinguish between available and occurrent features of the world. Heidegger would claim that the valences that make up the field of safe travel are available, not occurrent, features of the world. Similarly, Merleau-Ponty would claim that they are directly experienced as norms that draw our bodies into perceptually optimal positions, but for that very reason they are not part of the objective world that we can study scientifically from a detached point of view. For Gibson, however, the field "exists objectively," that is, as an occurrent feature of the natural world. In other words, Gibson's analysis seeks to accommodate existential phenomenology without adopting the existential ontology proposed by Heidegger and Merleau-Ponty.

10.1.2 Learning

Though Gibson remained a radical empiricist through to the end, he became dissatisfied with behaviorism as his career progressed. Indeed, by the time of his last book (1979), Gibson argues that stimuli are not the causes of behavior. Much earlier, however, spurred on by his wife Eleanor Jack Gibson, Gibson became convinced that behaviorists misunderstood learning, one of their key theoretical concepts (Gibson and Gibson 1955). Behaviorist theory holds that in learning, animals build associations between stimuli and responses. These associations are attached to the stimulus because of reinforcement or punishment received by the animal. Gibson and Gibson put this by saying that the stimulus is enriched in learning by having an association mentally attached to it. In this respect, behaviorism is in the same position as mentalist views like those of the structuralists in relying on an unobservable, unconscious process to make learning possible. Gibson and Gibson ask "Is learning a matter of enriching previously meager sensations or is it a process of differentiating previously vague impressions?" (1955, p. 34).

In an experiment designed and run by Eleanor to address this question, participants were shown a picture of a scribble that was to be the target, and then a series of other pictures, including one copy of the target and twenty-nine pictures that differed from it – twelve differed greatly, seventeen differed subtly. Participants were to find the target from among the thirty pictures. They were not corrected, punished, or reinforced; the experimenter simply went through the series of pictures without telling the participant whether she was correct in identifying the target. Adults were able to distinguish the target from the other pictures on average after just over three times through the deck of thirty pictures, without reinforcement of any kind, that is, without any correction, punishment, or reinforcement to cause the association to form between the target and the "yes" response. Children between the ages of eight and eleven took, on average, 4.7 passes through the deck. The Gibsons argued that this shows that learning does not involve unconscious mental enrichment of certain stimuli by supplementing them with an association. Instead, the subjects make finer and finer discriminations among the stimuli until they home in on the information that differentiates the target from the other pictures.

This result is notable for two reasons. First, it inaugurated the study of perceptual learning in psychology, a field in which Eleanor Gibson had a career as impressive and influential as her husband's in perception. Second, it is another affirmation of James Gibson's radical empiricism and realism about the contents of our perception. According to radical empiricism, there is only the world as we experience it; according to Gibson's realism, the contents of our experiences are real features of this world. The associations that were supposedly attached to stimuli according to the behaviorist understanding of learning are neither experienced nor features of the world. Gibson initially took himself to be a behaviorist and a radical empiricist. When behaviorism conflicted with radical empiricism, he chose the latter.

10.2 The ecological approach

Gibson is mostly known nowadays for what is called an *ecological approach* to the study of perception, especially visual perception. The ecological approach is in contrast with an inferential approach, which had been assumed since Descartes. The inferential approach to perception is designed to account for the presence of perceptual error, the fact that sometimes we make perceptual mistakes. We make mistakes because there is not enough information in the environment for us to perceive the world accurately. For example, see Figure 10.2, which is an altered version of a figure in Descartes' *Treatise on Man* (1664). Descartes was illustrating the perceptual process, by showing how someone perceives the arrow at the right of the figure. Light from the arrow strikes the lenses of the eyes, causing upside down, flattened images of the arrow to form on the surface of the retina. We have added the second, smaller arrow to the figure. Both arrows cast the same size and shape images on the retinas. In order to tell whether you are seeing a nearby small arrow or a larger distant one, according to the inferential approach, you must add information from memory to the retinal image. More generally, perceiving the size of something requires memory-based estimation of its distance, and vice versa, and it is impossible to tell from the size of a projection on the retinal image whether something is small and nearby or large and distant. Today, this is sometimes referred to as the "poverty of the stimulus," the claim that there is not enough information available

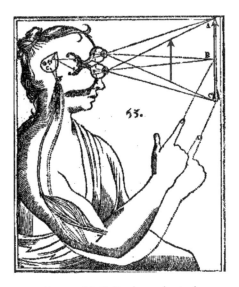

Figure 10.2 Body and mind
Source: Descartes 1664, altered to include second, smaller arrow

for us to be able to perceive the world, learn language, and so on. Because the stimulus is impoverished, perception must be a partly constructive process in which information from memory is added to the information available at the sensory surfaces. If the information available for perception were sufficient, there would be no perceptual error.

Gibson's rejection of the inferential view grew more radical over the course of his career. We can see this by looking at the three books he wrote. His first book, *The Perception of the Visual World* (1950), was inspired by his assignment in the military during World War II, when he studied the information pilots use to take off and land airplanes. He developed his "ground theory of perception," according to which perceiving the location of objects in space depends on their contact with the ground. The texture of the ground, for example, provides information about depth and distance. Texture elements on the ground appear smaller the further away they are from the point of observation, and perceiving differences in the distance depends on contact with the ground. Gibson's point in the book is that, if you look carefully at what the world actually looks like (i.e., if you engage in perceptual phenomenology), there is in fact a lot more information available to you than might initially seem to be the case. The stimulus is not really that impoverished.

Gibson's second book was *The Senses Considered as Perceptual Systems* (1966). In this book, he argues that it is a mistake to think

. perception is accomplished by the sensory organs alone (e.g., the
s for vision, or ears for audition). Instead, we see with moving eyes
on the front of a moving head, on a neck, on an ambulatory body.
Perception, Gibson argues, is something we *do*, and as such it takes
time. When we look at something, we move our eyes to scan it, we
crane our necks to get a slightly different angle, and we walk over to
get a closer view. All of this action we engage in during perception
creates information about the world we are perceiving, and there are
characteristic patterns of transformation of retinal information that
occur with movements that Gibson called *optic flow*. Hold this page
out at arm's length and look at it. Leaning forward or pulling the book
closer causes the retinal image of the book to expand; tilting your
head up or down changes the portion of the background hidden by the
book, and the rate at which this changes is inversely proportional to
the distance of the book; moving your eyes to the left causes the retinal
image of the book to sweep to the right; and so on. The information
available to a moving animal is vast. Again, the stimulus is not as
impoverished as we might think.

Gibson develops his ecological approach in his third, most important
book, *The Ecological Approach to Visual Perception*, published just
before his death in 1979. As noted above, the inferential approach to
perception seemed to be necessitated by the poverty of the stimulus.
But Gibson, in his first two books, shows that the stimulus is in fact
not impoverished. This is the basis on which he rejects the inferential approach in *The Ecological Approach*. Indeed, he goes further and
rejects the retinal image as the foundation of vision; our contact with the
objects we perceive is not mediated by the retinal image.

We can introduce the ecological approach as consisting in three
principles:

> *Principle 1: Perception is direct.* To claim that perception is direct is to
> claim that perception is not the result of mental gymnastics, of infer-
> ences performed on sensory representations. The direct perception
> view is anti-representationalism about perception. When an animal
> perceives something directly, the animal is in non-mediated contact
> with that thing. This implies, of course, that the perceiving is not
> inside the animal, but rather is part of a system that includes both
> the animal and the perceived object. The idea of direct perception is
> intimately intertwined with a theory of environmental information.
> *Principle 2: Perception is for action.* The purpose of perception is for
> the generation and control of action. It is usually added to this that a
> good deal of action is also for perception or cognition. The intimate,

two-way connection between perception and action has an immediate ring of evolutionary plausibility.

Principle 3: Perception is of affordances. This third principle actually follows from the first two. If perception is direct (i.e., non-inferential) and for the guidance of action, there must be information sufficient for guiding action available in the environment. Gibson introduces affordances to fill this role. Affordances are often misunderstood, and their precise nature is the subject of significant controversy both within ecological psychology and in the wider cognitive science communities. For now, it is sufficient to say that affordances are environmental opportunities for action. Because affordances are supposed to be objective features of the environment and dependent in some sense on animals, it is difficult to say exactly what kind of things affordances are. We will have more to say about them below.

What these principles actually mean, and why they might be correct, will become more convincing as we describe Gibson's ecological approach in more detail.

10.3 Ecological ontology

The Ecological Approach to Visual Perception (1979) is perhaps unique among books about perception in devoting nearly half of its pages to describing the nature of the environment that animals perceive. This half of the book is a discussion of Gibson's theory of the information available for vision, which goes hand in hand with his theory of visual perception. If perception is direct, no information is added in the mind; if perception also guides behavior, the environment must contain sufficient information for the animal to guide its behavior. That is, the environment must contain information that specifies opportunities for behavior. In other words, the environment must contain information that specifies affordances. These views place significant constraints on the theory of information that Gibson can offer. First, because it is used in non-inferential perception, information must be both ubiquitous in the environment and largely unambiguous; second, because perception also guides behavior, the information in the environment must specify opportunities for behavior, which is to say it must specify affordances. To satisfy these constraints, Gibson offers a novel ontology of the world as we perceive it.

Gibson begins his discussion by distinguishing between the environment that we perceive and the world as physicists describe it.

According to classical physics, the universe consists of bodies in space. We are tempted, therefore, to assume that we live in a physical world consisting of bodies in space and that what we perceive consists of bodies in space. But that is very dubious. The terrestrial environment is better described in terms of a medium, substances, and the surfaces that separate them. (1979, p. 16)

The *medium* is the space in which perception and action happen. It is insubstantial, and allows for passage of light, the transmission of vibrations, and the diffusion of chemicals. It also allows for locomotion. We do not experience the medium as a substance or a fluid or a thing. Instead, we perceive it as a set of *points of observation*, connected by *paths of locomotion*. A point of observation is any place an animal could place its sensory organs. A path of locomotion is a continuous, connected series of points of observation. The medium is the space in which we perceive and act. Notice that the medium is animal-relative. For humans, the medium is made of air, but for fish, it is water. For fish and birds, paths of locomotion are more three-dimensional than they are for creatures like us, who are more or less confined to the surface of the earth. *Substances* are the materials that make up the objects of the environment. *Surfaces* are the interfaces between substances and the medium. When we look around the room, we see substances via the light that has reflected off surfaces. Because of the laws of physics, chemistry, optics, and so on, light reflected off surfaces *specifies* underlying substances. The word "specify" is used here in exactly the way that it is used in legal contracts. The character of reflected light guarantees the presence of particular substances. Suppose, for example, that there is a banana on the table in front of you. The banana is a substance. The shape and chemical constitution of the banana lawfully determine the way the surface of the banana will interact with the air and light in the room. Because of these lawful relationships, light reflected off a banana specifies that a banana is present. This allows the light reflected off the banana to carry information about the banana.

The best first pass at understanding what Gibson meant by "information" is his distinction between stimulation and stimulus information. Consider standing in a uniformly bright, densely fog-filled room. In such a room, your retinal cells are stimulated. The light in the room enters your eye and excites the rods and cones. But there is no information carried by the light that stimulates your retina. The uniform white light that converges on the eye from the various parts of the room and is focused by the eye's lens does not specify the structure of the room. So stimulation, the excitement of sensory cells, is not in itself information and is not, therefore, sufficient for perception. The differences between the normal environment and the fog-filled room are instructive. In the fog-filled room, the light that converges on any point that could be occupied by an observer's head and eyes has been scattered by the fog. Thus, when it reaches the observer it has not come directly from any surface in the room, and hence cannot inform the subject about the surfaces in the room. In the typical, non-foggy situation, the light that reaches any point in the room has been reflected off the room's surfaces. The chemical makeup, texture, and overall shape of the surfaces off which the light reflects determine the characteristics of the light. Since surfaces are interfaces of substances with the air in the room, the nature of the surfaces is, in turn, determined by the substances that make them up. This set of facts allows the light that converges at any point to carry information about the substances in the environment. It also allows animals whose heads occupy the point to learn about their environment by sampling the light.

This account allows us to understand what it is for light (or other energy) to carry information, but it says nothing about what sort of thing information is. When Gibson and his followers claim that information is ubiquitous, are they saying that in addition to the substances, objects, and energies in the room, there is extra stuff, the information? Yes and no. Yes, information is a real aspect of the environment. But information is not a kind of measurable, quantifiable stuff that exists alongside the objects or substances in the environment. Instead, information is a relational feature of the environment. In particular, the light converging on some point of observation is in a particular relationship to the surfaces in the room, that of having bounced off those surfaces and passed through a relatively transparent medium before arriving at the point. The information in the light *just is* this relation between the light and the environment.

A few quick points about this. First, note that the information relation between the light and the surfaces does not hold in the case of a fog-filled room. So the light in this case bears no information about the layout of the environment. Second, it is worth noting that this way of understanding information allows it to be ubiquitous in the environment. Light reflected from surfaces in the environment converges at every point in the environment. Third, the information in the environment is more or less complete: the light converging at every point has reflected off *all* of the non-obstructed surfaces. Fourth, and most important for Gibson's project, the light can contain information that specifies *affordances*. To see this, a little needs to be said about affordances.

Affordances are opportunities for behavior. Because different animals have different abilities, affordances are relative to the behavioral abilities of the animals that perceive them. In some cases, these abilities are significantly related to an animal's height. To take just two examples, Warren (1984) has established a relationship between leg length and stair-climbing affordances, and Jiang and Mark (1994) have established a relationship between eye height and the perception of gap-crossing affordances. Given the relationship between height and some affordances, information about height is also (partial) information about affordances. Remember that at every point in the environment, reflected light converges from the surfaces in the environment. Among these surfaces is the ground, so one relatively obvious source of information concerning height is the light reflected from the ground beneath the point of observation. Sedgewick (1973) points out a less obvious source of information: the horizon cuts across objects at a height that is equal to the height of the point of observation. That is, whenever light is reflected to some point in the environment from the horizon and also from some object between that point and the horizon, the light will contain information about the height of the point of observation relative to the height of the object. Of course, information about the height of a point of observation is also information about the height of an animal. So, at least for the types of affordances that have some relationship to an animal's height (reaching, stair climbing, gap crossing), there is information in the light about the affordances. More generally, this means that information in light is not just about the things the light bounces off. It is also information about the perceiver and the relation between the perceiver and the environment. Gibson puts this point by saying that proprioception and exteroception imply one another. Indeed, visual information is always both propriospecific and exterospecific. Because bodies reflect light, information is always about the environment as inhabited by a specific animal. As Gibson puts it:

> the horse and human look out on the world in different ways. They have radically different fields of view; their noses are different, and their legs are different, entering and leaving the field of view in different ways. Each species sees a different self from every other. Each individual sees a different self. Each person gets information about his or her body that differs from that obtained by any other person. (1979, p. 115)

The fact that our eyes face forward, and that the backs of our heads block the light from reaching our eyes, makes seeing the world also seeing ourselves.

Demonstrating that information is ubiquitous and sufficient for guiding behavior – that the stimulus is not impoverished – has been a key focus of empirical research by psychologists in the Gibsonian tradition. Indeed, Gibson called this the central question for the theory of affordances: "The central question for the theory of affordances is not whether they exist and are real, but whether information is available in the ambient light for [directly] perceiving them" (1979, p. 140). Here, we focus on two examples: what is called looming in optic flow and perception by dynamic touch.

The easiest way to understand optic flow is to remember what happens when one plays a first-person video game. Moving your avatar around in its virtual environment causes a changing pattern on your monitor that, if the game is well designed, gives you the sensation of actually moving around in the environment. This temporally extended onscreen pattern is a simulation of optic flow. Consider a familiar video-game scenario: your virtual car is heading toward a fatal collision with, say, a brick wall.

1. As your car approaches the wall, the image of the wall on your monitor expands.
2. When you get close enough, individual bricks will become visible.
3. As you continue toward your virtual crash, the image of the wall will cover the entire monitor, and images of individual bricks will expand.
4. As you get closer to the wall, the images of the bricks will expand so that only a few of them are actually able to fit on the monitor, and they will appear textured.
5. Moving closer still, the images of the texture elements on the bricks will expand as well.
6. Then there is the loud crash noise and the cracked virtual windshield.

Back in the real world and less dramatically, the same phenomenon, called *looming*, happens constantly. As any animal moves about its environment, the images of objects or texture elements that the animal is moving toward will expand at the animal's eyes. This is often described by saying that optic flow is *centrifugal* in the direction of locomotion: texture elements radiate out from the center of your field of view as you move toward an object.

Detecting centrifugal optic flow is very important, of course, but it is not sufficient to guide behavior so as to avoid collisions. In a study of the plummeting behavior of gannet birds, David Lee (1980; Lee and Reddish 1981) demonstrates that properties of centrifugal optic flow can be sufficient to guide behavior by defining the higher-order optical variable τ (the Greek letter tau). τ is the ratio of the size of a projected image to the rate of change of the image's size. Using a little geometry and calculus, Lee shows that τ, a feature of the light available at the eye, is sufficient to guide the gannet's behavior without the use of internal computations. In particular, Lee shows that within a wide range of circumstances τ is equal to time to contact with an approaching object. Moreover, the way τ changes over time carries information about the nature of the contact with the approaching object: will I stop short of the object, bump it, or go barreling into it? In other words, τ, a feature of the light arriving at the eyes of an animal, carries information that can be used to guide locomotion.

There are several things here worth noting. First note that τ does not give information about the absolute distance of an object. Instead, it gives information about time-to-contact with the object, which is relevant to guiding movement. When you're trying to cross the street, how far away in meters an approaching car is matters much less than how soon it will hit you. Second, note that τ need not be computed by the gannet. It is available at the retina. τ, in other words, can be perceived directly. So, τ provides important information for the control of action in the environment, and it provides that information without requiring mental gymnastics. That is, sensitivity to the ratio of optical angle to the expansion of optical angle is sensitivity to the timing of approaching collision. Third, and most important, Lee and Reddish (1981) show that diving gannets are sensitive to τ and use it to determine when to fold their wings. Lee and Reddish filmed diving gannets and showed that the time of wing retraction is better predicted by the hypothesis that gannets pick up information using τ than by the hypotheses that gannets compute time-to-contact or retract wings at some particular height or velocity. Finally, there is evidence that τ and τ-derived variables are used to undertake a variety of visually guided actions. Indeed, Lee's lab has shown that τ is used by landing pigeons and hummingbirds, and by humans hitting balls, somersaulting, long jumping, putting in golf, and steering. (See Lee 2006 for an overview.) And, of course, τ is just one example of directly perceived information that guides behavior. Ecological psychologists have been finding others since the 1970s.

One more example: given two objects of equal mass, people (both children and adults) judge the one with a smaller diameter to be heavier. That is, they judge a comparatively small pound of lead to be heavier than a comparatively large pound of feathers. This is called the *size–weight illusion* (Charpentier 1891). This illusion has typically been taken to be the result of mental gymnastics: one judges an object's size and uses this judgment to (erroneously) correct one's judgment of weight. To investigate the size–weight illusion, ecological psychologists Amazeen and Turvey (1996) created what are called *tensor objects*. Tensor objects are composed of two rods connected to form a "plus" sign, with a third rod attached perpendicular to the point at which the two rods forming the "plus" sign intersect. Metal rings are attached at different locations on the rods on the object so as to create tensor objects with different weight distributions. Different weight distribution means different moments of inertia. A moment of inertia is a measure of an object's resistance to rotation. An object held in the hand could be rotated in three dimensions, so it will have three moments of inertia. The three moments of inertia can be combined mathematically using what is called an *inertia tensor*. So, an object's inertia tensor is the object's resistance to rotation in three dimensions at the wrist. Objects with different inertia tensors generate different forces when held, so exert different pressures at the wrist joint. These tensor objects allowed Amazeen and Turvey to construct a series of objects of identical size and weight, but with different moments of inertia designed to mimic the stimuli typically used in experiments that produce the size–weight illusion. They found that subjects judged the heaviness of these tensor objects as predicted by their inertia tensors, despite the fact that they were the same size and weight. This occurred both when subjects wielded the objects occluded behind a curtain and when they could see the objects (covered tightly with paper to make their volume apparent but hide the distribution of the metal weights). Thus, Amazeen and Turvey showed that subjects do not perceive the weight of objects by judging their size (whether by touch alone or by vision and touch) and mentally combining that judgment with their felt force due to gravity. Instead, subjects use the information available at the wrist, as determined by the object's inertia tensor.

The point of the above is that humans do not misperceive weight by mentally calculating it, computationally combining size and force due to gravity. Instead, they correctly perceive the information in the inertial tensor, which does not carry information about weight alone. What, then, is the information in the inertial tensor about? More recent work by Shockley, Carello, and Turvey (2004) indicates that these subjects perceive the affordance *moveability*. In particular, they show that subjects who misjudge the weight of an object when falling prey to the size–weight illusion make nearly identical judgments about whether the object is movable. That is, the question "On a scale of 1 to 100, where 50 is the control object, how heavy is this object?" gets the same answer as "On a scale of 1 to 100, where 50 is the control object, how easy is it to move this object?" So the size–weight illusion occurs because subjects are actually basing their judgments on perception of moveability, not weight, and their judgments about moveability are accurate. An object's inertia tensors carry information about the object's rotational inertia, which is to say they carry information about the object's tendency to resist rotation in a particular direction, which is to say they carry information about how difficult it is to move the object.

There is, then, information about the affordance moveability available for direct perception. The answer to Gibson's central question is clearly "yes." Information about affordances is available in the environment.

10.4 Affordances and invitations

Gibson's psychology involves an epistemological claim and an ontological claim. The epistemological claim is that we perceive the world directly, without adding information in mental representations or projecting meaning onto it. The ontological claim is that meaning, in the form of affordances, is a feature of the world that we perceive. We perceive opportunities for acting, and we perceive them by acting in the world. In both these claims, Gibson's views are similar to Merleau-Ponty's. The views are not identical, though. As noted above, Gibson's ecological psychology is in many ways similar to Merleau-Ponty's existential phenomenology of perception, but Gibson does not adopt an existential ontology. Gibson is a realist about the objects of experience, including affordances, and he aims to give an account of perception in terms of a naturalistic ontology. The world contains enough information to support our experiences and our actions. Perhaps because of the dominance of behaviorism in American psychology in the mid-twentieth century, Gibson is thoroughly anti-mentalist, and skeptical of calling on any psychological features to explain behavior. This may have disposed him against Merleau-Ponty's statements that the world has a "motor significance" and that we experience perceptual objects in terms of their "sense." With their foundation in bodily habits, these concepts evoke an air of subjectivity. One productive way to think of the relation between Gibson's naturalism and Merleau-Ponty's existential ontology is that Gibson aims to provide a scientific account that can fill in placeholders in Merleau-Ponty's descriptions. Merleau-Ponty, for instance, occasionally refers to "magic" in motor intentionality – such as the claim that from the outset the grasping movement is "magically" complete. Such phenomena cannot be explained by the empiricist and intellectualist paradigms that Merleau-Ponty argues against, and hence appear as magic from within those frameworks; but he is at pains to develop a new conceptual framework to account for these phenomena, and Gibson can be said to pursue the same aim. (Recent work by Alva Noë [2004, 2009] pursues the same aim, applying ideas from Merleau-Ponty and Gibson to a range of twenty-first-century philosophical concerns.)

In part because of his naturalism about affordances, however, Gibson's ecological psychology is incomplete. When describing the world I experience, Gibson's theory will talk about the relationship between my abilities to act and things in the world to give an account of what affordances are available to me. For example, the match and/or mismatch between leg length, strength, and flexibility, on one hand, and the height, width, stability, rigidity of surfaces in the room, on the other, determines where in the room I experience climbing affordances. This is, however, importantly incomplete as a description of my experiences of climbing affordances. Of all the things I could climb, I would only consider climbing a few of them. I could easily climb onto the end table, the chairs, the books stacked on the floor, and so on, but I do not; the stairs are not much easier to climb than the end table, but I regularly climb the former and never climb the latter.

Withagen et al. (2012), themselves ecological psychologists, put this by saying that Gibsonian ecological psychology needs to distinguish between affordances and invitations, or solicitations. At any moment, there are infinitely many affordances available to a human or other animal. While sitting in a lecture, you could stand on a chair or on the table, you could write on the board or on the walls, you could sing show tunes, you could pull the hair of the person seated next to you, and on and on. These affordances are all available to you, but none of them seem like live options for your next actions. These are all things that are afforded to you, but none of them invite action. To use Merleau-Ponty's terms, such generically conceived affordances are not perceived as "tensions" in a situation that demand a motor response. Affordances, at least by themselves, do not move you to act. Indeed, even explicitly perceived affordances do not move you to act. Being reminded that you could pull your neighbor's hair will cause you to attend to the affordance but will not move you to act on that affordance. Ecological psychology, Withagen et al. argue, needs a theory that will allow us to explain why only a few of the affordances are perceived, and even fewer invite behavior. To explain why this is the case, ecological psychology needs a theory of agency. Without an appeal to the purposiveness of the habit body, the naturalistic account of affordances is inert.

As it stood at the end of his life, Gibson's ecological psychology had no resources to account for the distinction between affordances and invitations. Indeed, among psychologists Gibson's work was sometimes disparaged as "phenomenology." That is, although it makes important, scientific strides toward a description of the world as we experience it, it lacks the resources to do what psychology is supposed to do, that is, explain behavior. Gibson himself knew about this lacuna in his theory. In his last book, he puts it as follows: "The rules that govern behavior are not like laws enforced by an authority or decisions made by a commander: behavior is regular without being regulated. The question is how this can be" (1979, p. 225). What is required is an explanation of behavior, akin to Merleau-Ponty's habit body, that does not make intelligent human action the result of an unobservable, mental cause. In Chapters 12 and 13, we will see two attempts by modern cognitive scientists to supply an adequate theory of agency for a Gibsonian psychology. One of these uses ideas drawn from physics to explain human action as a self-organizing, embodied, dynamical system; the other draws on Merleau-Ponty, especially his discussion of motor intentionality.

Key terms

affordances – opportunities for action in the environment. These are determined both by the abilities of an animal and by the physical environment. Gibson holds that affordances are perceived directly.

behaviorism – an approach to psychology that explains behavior in terms of learning, and not in terms of subjective mental states.

direct perception – the claim that perceptual contact with the environment is not mediated by mental representations.

exteroception – perception of the external world.

functionalism – early twentieth-century psychological movement, inspired by the work of William James. Functionalists studied the mind, emotions, habits, and so on as temporary adaptations to the environment.

medium – the unexperienced space in which perception and action occur. For humans, the medium is air on the surface of the earth. The medium is experienced as a set of points of observation connected by paths of locomotion.

neutral monism – the view, championed by William James, that the world is neither physical nor mental. This view is an explicit rejection of Kant's distinction between empirical and transcendental realities.

optic flow – changes in the information in light caused by the relative motion of an observer and the environment. Moving the body causes changes in the pattern of light available at the retina. Optic flow contains information for directly perceiving the affordances in the environment.

path of locomotion – any continuous string of points of observation in a perceiver's medium.

point of observation – any place in the medium where a perceiver can place his or her sensory surfaces.

poverty of the stimulus – the claim that there is not enough information available in the environment for humans to have the cognitive capacities that they do, especially perceiving the world and learning language. Poverty of the stimulus is taken to imply innate knowledge, complex internal computations, or both.

proprioception – perception of the self.

radical empiricism – a position, held by William James late in his life, that includes direct perception and neutral monism. According to radical empiricism, there is only the world that we perceive, and we perceive it directly.

structuralism – early twentieth-century psychological movement, inspired by the work of Wilhelm Wundt. Structuralists study the mind by identifying the elements of conscious experience.

substances – according to Gibson, perceivable entities in the medium.

surfaces – according to Gibson, the interfaces of substances and the medium. We see substances in virtue of light that has reflected off surfaces.

τ (tau) – an optical variable that specifies time-to-contact. It has been demonstrated that a good deal of locomotory behavior is controlled using tau.

Further reading

Gibson, J. J. (1966). *The Senses Considered as Perceptual Systems*. Boston: Houghton Mifflin.
– (1979). *The Ecological Approach to Visual Perception*. Boston: Houghton Mifflin.
Gibson, J. J. and Gibson, E. (1955). "Perceptual learning: Differentiation or enrichment?" *Psychological Review*, 62: 32–41.

11

Hubert Dreyfus and the Phenomenological Critique of Cognitivism

At the same time that Merleau-Ponty and Gibson were writing, there were the beginnings of a revolution occurring in psychology. As we have already discussed, behaviorism was the orthodoxy in psychology, especially in America. Behaviorists, as we have also already discussed, are opposed to explaining behavior in terms of unobservable mental causes, such as beliefs, thoughts, and the like. The reach of behaviorism can be seen in what is often thought of as the founding document in artificial intelligence, Alan Turing's "Computing machinery and intelligence" (1950). In that paper, Turing proposed a test for determining whether a machine is intelligent. He called this test the "imitation game"; it is generally now called the "Turing test." Imagine (anachronistically) that you are participating in a text message conversation with a stranger. The essence of Turing's proposal test is as follows: if, after engaging in this conversation for a while, you cannot tell that your conversation partner is a computer program and not a person, then the computer program must be intelligent. You may already have engaged with "chatbots," online computer programs that attempt, mostly poorly, to engage in text message conversation. Here, for example, is the transcript of a short conversation with the chatbot "A.L.I.C.E."

judge: Yo Alice.
ALICE: So?
judge: How's it going?

ALICE: I am functioning within normal parameters.

judge: Are you trying to fool me into thinking you are a person?

ALICE: No I am not trying to fool you into thinking I am a person. I'm
sorry you got that impression.

judge: Isn't this a Turing test?

ALICE: No, this is real life.

judge: But you could do a Turing test in real life.

ALICE: I could but let's get back to that later.

judge: You are evading anything with content.

ALICE: Thanks for telling me that I am evading anything with content.

(http://alice.pandorabots.com)

A.L.I.C.E. is not at all convincingly human in this exchange. It would not
"pass" the Turing test, and be deemed intelligent by Turing's criterion.
Notice, though, that whether it passes the test or not has nothing to do
with the nature of A.L.I.C.E.'s programming, only its behavior. To be
intelligent, A.L.I.C.E. just has to behave sufficiently similarly to a human
to fool a conversation partner. To use technical language, A.L.I.C.E.
needs only to be "input–output equivalent" to a human to be intelligent,
without regard to the processes that allow her to be intelligent. Although
Turing's work on computation and his Turing test were crucial precursors of the cognitive revolution that would partially displace behaviorism
as orthodoxy in psychology, the Turing test is a behaviorist test. And
even though the Turing test is behaviorist, the promise of computer
technology and artificial intelligence in explaining the mind led to a
backlash against behaviorist psychology, in what is known as the "cognitive revolution."

In his 1950 paper, Turing also made some predictions about the
future of artificial intelligence and computer technology. In particular,
he made extraordinarily accurate predictions about the processing speed
and memory capacity of the computers that would exist in the year
2000. He also predicted that by then, computers would routinely pass
the Turing test, fooling at least 30 percent of human interlocutors. The
interaction with A.L.I.C.E. above suggests that, even in 2013, computer
programs cannot converse intelligently with humans. Surprisingly, in
2014, a computer program named Eugene Goostman did pass a Turing
test. The way it did so was quite clever. Eugene Goostman, participants
were told, was a thirteen-year-old from the Ukraine. With these expectations in place, Eugene Goostman's poor conversational skills and limited
knowledge fooled 33 percent of human judges into thinking it was a
flippant teenager, speaking English as a second language. Most people do

not consider this an important milestone in artificial intelligence (Marcus 2014).

Starting in the 1960s, long before home computers were common-place, Hubert Dreyfus argued that disembodied, rule-governed computer programs could never replicate human intelligence (1965, 1972). His arguments were based on insights from Heidegger and Merleau-Ponty about the relationship between thinking and the world. Arguably, the history of artificial intelligence research in the last half-century is a series of demonstrations that Dreyfus (and Heidegger and Merleau-Ponty) are right about the nature of the mind. In this chapter, we will look at Dreyfus' critique of artificial intelligence and cognitive science.

11.1 The cognitive revolution and cognitive science

Beginning in the 1950s, the behaviorist orthodoxy that had been in place for decades was challenged by an interdisciplinary coalition of researchers interested in then-nascent computer technology. According to cognitive science's creation myth, the discipline came into being because of events in 1956 and 1957, a time when there were not yet any univer-sity departments specializing in computer science. In 1956, there were two important meetings of researchers from across disciplines, who were interested in the potential for computer technology to explain the mind. The first of these was a set of meetings at Dartmouth, in summer of 1956. These meetings were attended by the founders of the first three artificial intelligence labs in the world: Allen Newell and Herbert Simon founded the lab at the Carnegie Institute of Technology (now Carnegie Mellon University); John McCarthy founded the lab at Stanford University; Marvin Minsky founded the lab at the Massachusetts Institute of Technology. These meetings are thought of as initiating the academic discipline of artificial intelligence. Then, in September of 1956, there was the Symposium on Information Theory at MIT. At this meeting, papers were presented by Newell and Simon, Noam Chomsky, and George Miller. These speakers came from diverse academic backgrounds. Simon was an economist; Miller was a psychologist; Chomsky is a linguist. The only thing that the attendants at these meetings had in common was a shared interest in explaining thinking in terms of computation.

Staying with the cognitive science creation myth, the final blow that defeated behaviorism and created cognitive science as its successor was the publication in 1959 of Chomsky's scathing review of a book by behaviorist psychologist B. F. Skinner. In this review, Chomsky argued that behaviorist learning theory could not explain how children acquire natural language. This is the case, he argued, because of two facts. First, children learn to speak grammatically, rapidly and fairly suddenly, around the age of two. Second, prior to age two, children are not exposed to enough instances of grammatical sentences to learn the rules of grammar. Because children do speak grammatically at the age of two but could not have learned the rules of grammar by that age, the rules of grammar must be innate. In fact, Chomsky concludes, our language abilities must be the result of an innate computer program.

We have been calling this a creation myth, and it is a myth. Chomsky's argument did not kill behaviorism. Although it no longer dominates psychology, behaviorism is, even now, alive and well. Cognitive science didn't begin in earnest, as a discipline with journals and graduate programs, until the 1970s. That said, Chomsky's argument was very influential. It also provides a conceptual blueprint for cognitive science. First, notice that it is an instance of the poverty of the stimulus argument we discussed in Chapter 7. Indeed, it was Chomsky who coined the phrase "poverty of the stimulus" that we used to describe Descartes' argument. Just as Descartes argued that the projection on a retina does not carry enough information for us to perceive the world, Chomsky argued that the sentences children hear do not carry enough information for them to learn language. The conclusion in both cases is the same: there must be information already stored in the mind to be combined with the information from the senses. In Chomsky's case, the information is stored as a set of computational rules for generating grammatical sentences. In the cognitive science that followed, this claim was extended to all of thinking.

The central idea of cognitive science is that the brain is a computer and the mind is a collection of programs that run on it. Put as an analogy, the mind is to the brain as software is to hardware. Andy Clark (2000, 2013) has put this point by saying that our brains are "meat machines." "It is not that the brain is somehow like a computer . . . It is that neural tissues, synapses, cell assemblies, and all the rest are just nature's rather wet and sticky way of building a hunk of honest-to-God computing machinery" (Clark 2000, p. 8). We could add to this that your mind is a collection of "honest-to-God" computer programs. Many consequences follow from this way of understanding the mind and brain. To see them, it is important to understand that computer programs are "medium independent" in that the same program can run not just on different computers, but on different kinds of computers. The Google Chrome web browser, for example, can run on two different Apple MacBook Air laptops. It can also run on a Windows computer, an iPad, an iPod, an iPhone, an Android phone, and so on. Although it will be physically instantiated differently on these computers, it will still be the same software, Google Chrome. This is what it means to say that Google Chrome is medium independent. If software is medium independent and your mind is made up of software, your mind will be medium independent as well. It is this fact that makes artificial intelligence central to the enterprise of cognitive science.

The medium independence of computer programs also allows cognitive science to overcome the behaviorist opposition to including unobservable entities in scientific theorizing. By assuming that thinking is software running on the brain, cognitive scientists can speculate in a principled way about private mental processes. Start by gathering data on how humans, for example, prove logical theorems. Then write a computer program that attempts to match what was learned about human theorem proving, including the kinds of errors humans tend to make. If the program is input–output equivalent to the human performance, there is a basis for speculating that the software running in the brain is similar to the software you have written. Using this methodology, it is possible to develop and test hypotheses about private mental processes. And by iterating the process, it is possible to formulate and test more and more specific hypotheses about unobservable psychological processes. It is hard to overestimate the importance of this methodological point. In effect, cognitive science claims to have a sort of solution to the *problem of other minds*. On the face of it, it seems that we only know what we ourselves are thinking. What other people are thinking, or even that they are thinking at all, can never be observed. Philosophers of mind today often put this by saying that, for all anyone knows, other humans might be zombies, behaviorally indistinguishable from you or me, but with "nobody home" on the inside (Dennett 1991; Chalmers 1996). Cognitive science allows a scientific window onto what is going on inside other people.

The idea that intelligence is thinking, and that thinking is computation, enables a solution to another perennial philosophical problem: *the mind–body problem*. The mind–body problem is the problem of how the mind relates to the physical world. How could an ordinary physical object have thoughts and experiences? In their chemical composition, your brain and body are not that different from the packaged meat at the grocery store. How come you can think about what you will do this evening but pork chops cannot? Famously, Descartes concluded that minds are made of a different kind of stuff from the rest of the world. This is the same view that is held by the majority of the world's religions. It is immediately problematic, however. If the mind is made of a different kind of stuff from the rest of the world, it is unclear how it could interact with the rest of the world. It seems impossible that changes to your body, say by someone talking to you, can affect your immaterial mind. Similarly, it seems impossible that deciding, with your mind, to make a sandwich could cause your body to do anything. This is usually called the "interaction problem." By claiming that your brain is a kind of computer, we can see how an ordinary physical object, made up of ordinary physical stuff, can have thoughts about the world. Consider any one of those computers mentioned above. With the push of a virtual button or a few keystrokes, you could check the weather in Budapest. That is, within seconds, your computer could display information about the weather thousands of kilometers away. The computer is an ordinary physical device that carries representations of the world in it. By causally interacting with one another and with the world, those representations of the world change and can cause changes. The representation changes, for example, when a thermometer in Budapest changes and updates a local computer that is connected to the internet. That representation causes changes when it is sent to a printer or read by you, making you pack different clothes for your trip. If your brain is a kind of computer, it is not mysterious how your brain could have sentence-like representations carrying information about the world in it, could change those representations in response to physical events, and could cause changes to the physical world. Mind–world interactions, according to cognitive science, are no more mysterious than program–world interactions: very complicated, but not unknowable.

These are, of course, major philosophical claims, and they do not come for free. The price paid for these is that cognitive science is a reversion to Wundt's structural psychology, which was rejected on philosophical and empirical grounds in the early twentieth century (see Chapter 4). Understanding the brain as a computer and the mind as a computer program makes psychology about discerning the details of the mind's software. To write a computer program that solves some complex problem, you have to break the problem down into smaller problems and then break those smaller problems into smaller problems still, and so on, until you can solve the problems in terms of simple steps like counting, copying, writing, and moving small pieces of data. Consider, as an analogy, how we add large numbers using pen and paper:

Start by lining the numbers up so that their place values match.
Then add the digits in the ones place.
If the answer is less than ten, write the answer in the ones place in the answer space.
If the answer is greater than ten, write the digit from the answer ones

place in the answer space and the digit from the tens place above the tens place for the numbers to be added.
Move one place to the left and repeat until there are no further numbers.

With this general recipe, we can solve the problem as long as we know how to add the digits in the places. This can be done by looking up the answer in a table, which is the equivalent of the memorization of basic addition facts that children do in grade school. This, it might be suggested, is something like the computer program that is running on human brains when they do addition. Just as Wundt's atomistic psychology explains experiences in terms of the simple components that make them up, cognitive science explains mental processes in terms of the simple component processes that make them up.

This atomism is in stark contrast to the Jamesian functionalism and behaviorism that had dominated psychology in the first half of the twentieth century. Both of those views focused on the behavior of whole animals in their environments over extended periods of time. Cognitive science, in contrast, changes the focus to computational processes in the human brain. To the extent that the environment and the past play any role in cognitivism, they do so only as representations in the computational processes in the brain. Jerry Fodor (1980), a leading philosophical proponent of the cognitive revolution, specifically advocates *methodological solipsism*. Solipsism is the philosophical view that nothing exists but one's own experiences. It is a view that many teenagers entertain briefly, before realizing that the world is nowhere near enough fun to be plausibly a mere projection of their own minds. Methodological solipsism is a strategy for doing psychology in which one focuses only on the things that are represented in the mind of the thinker under study and the computational processes operating on those things, without regard to whether the things represented exist or whether they are represented accurately. The idea is that for the purpose of doing psychology only the goings on inside the brain of the thinker matter; the body and world do not matter. In these respects, cognitive science is extremely similar to Wundt's late nineteenth-century approach. As Fodor puts it:

> The trick is to combine the postulation of mental representations with the "computer metaphor" . . . In this respect, I think there really has been something like an intellectual breakthrough. Technical details to one side, this is – in my view – the only aspect of contemporary cognitive science that represents a major advance over the versions of mentalism that were its eighteenth- and nineteenth-century predecessors. (1987, p. 23)

Indeed, the cognitive revolution harkens back past Wundt to Descartes. Cognitive science is explicitly rationalist; so much so that the title of one of Chomsky's books is *Cartesian Linguistics: A Chapter in the History of Rationalist Thought* (1966).

We have seen that Heidegger, the Gestaltists, Merleau-Ponty, and Gibson argue explicitly and at great length against rationalist assumptions, and against the assumption that intelligence and understanding belong to the province of the mind, to which the characters of the body and the world are irrelevant. Beginning in the 1960s, Hubert Dreyfus used these arguments against the assumptions made in cognitive science and, especially, artificial intelligence. It is not difficult to read the history of research in artificial intelligence as a vindication of phenomenology, and of phenomenology-based critique.

11.2 "Alchemy and artificial intelligence"

In the 1960s, Dreyfus taught phenomenology in the philosophy department at MIT, which was (and still is) among the most important institutions for research in artificial intelligence and cognitive science. In an interview, he describes his time there as follows:

> At MIT I was teaching the usual stuff, and luckily at MIT, the students were coming over from what was called then the robot lab (it's now called the artificial intelligence laboratory), saying, "Oh, you philosophers, you've never understood understanding and language and perception. You've had 2000 years and you just keep disagreeing and getting nowhere. But we, with our computers, are making programs that understand, and solve problems, and make plans, and learn languages. When we do that we'll understand how it's done." And I thought, "Gee, I want to be in on that, but I don't think they can do that," because Heidegger and Wittgenstein, who I was reading, say that intelligence doesn't consist of following rules. And their stuff is all rules. So, then I was interested. (Kreisler and Dreyfus, 2005)

Dreyfus saw that artificial intelligence researchers, many of them his colleagues at MIT, had inadvertently reinvented rationalist philosophy.

Dreyfus' first writing on artificial intelligence (1965) was published as a technical report of the Rand Corporation, an often controversial, nonprofit corporation that emerged in the United States after World War II. Rand was among the earliest and most prolific supporters of artificial intelligence, and many of the early researchers in artificial intelligence were affiliated with Rand (Klahr and Waterman 1986). Dreyfus begins his critique by quoting some of the predictions made by Rand employees Simon and Newell (1958):

> It is not my aim to surprise or shock you – if indeed that were possible in an age of nuclear fission and prospective interplanetary travel. But the simplest way I can summarize it is to say that there are now in the world machines that think, that learn and that create. Moreover, their ability to do these things is going to increase rapidly until – in the visible future – the range of problems they can handle will be coextensive with the range to which the human mind has been applied. (Simon and Newell 1958, quoted in Dreyfus 1965, p. 3)

Dreyfus then lists several of Simon and Newell's predictions for the next decade, that is, the ten-year period that would end in 1968:

> The speaker makes the following predictions:
> (1) That within ten years a digital computer will be the world's chess champion, unless the rules bar it from competition.
> (2) That within ten years a digital computer will discover and prove an important new mathematical theorem.
> (3) That within ten years a digital computer will write music that will be accepted by critics as possessing considerable aesthetic value.
> (4) That within ten years most theories in psychology will take the form of computer programs, or of qualitative statements about the characteristics of computer programs. (Simon and Newell 1958, quoted in Dreyfus 1965, p. 3f.)

To Dreyfus, Simon and Newell's optimism is mystifying. These claims were considerably bolder than the one that Turing made in 1950, that a computer would pass the Turing test by 2000. The boldness of these predictions, Dreyfus argues, led those discussing artificial intelligence to fail to notice how little progress had actually been made toward achieving these ends by 1965. That so little progress had occurred is actually hard to see because of the exaggerations, the "intellectual smog" (1965, p. 5), in the writings of artificial intelligence researchers. Rather than encourage these grand claims, in the short history of artificial intelligence by 1965 the actual results typically followed a curve from early success on simplified problems, to extreme optimism, to disappointment or, worse, to "unequivocal failure."

Certainly, none of Simon and Newell's predictions had come true by 1968. Indeed, only one of them had come true by 2013. It is now generally recognized that computers can compose pleasing music (e.g., Cope 1996).

Deep Blue, a chess-playing program developed by IBM, did beat the world chess champion in 1997, but no one considers Deep Blue to be the world champion. More importantly for current purposes, neither music composition programs nor chess-playing programs are taken as models for human performance of the same tasks. Even though Deep Blue plays chess very well, it does not play the way a human plays. Deep Blue used a suite of computers to quickly simulate all of the possible sequences of moves, several moves ahead, given its representation of the current state of the board. Human experts consider only a few possible next moves. Similarly, Watson, the IBM computer that routed human opponents on Jeopardy in 2011, does not play Jeopardy the way a human does. Watson's memory includes all of Wikipedia. So, even when artificial intelligence does succeed, it does not inform us about the human mind. This points to an important distinction between different types of projects in artificial intelligence. On the one hand, there is artificial intelligence as *technology*, in which the goal is to develop machines that are useful in virtue of their automated information processing. On the other hand, there is artificial intelligence as a project in *cognitive science*, in which the goal is to use computer models to do psychology. Deep Blue is a success as technology, but not as cognitive science. It is an impressive achievement that tells us nothing about how humans work. The phenomenological critiques that Dreyfus brings to bear in "Alchemy and artificial intelligence" are equivocal about which of these projects is being rejected. As we will see, his arguments work well against artificial intelligence as cognitive science, but less well against artificial intelligence as technology. That the latter of these is also a target is clear from the title of his 1972 critique, *What Computers Can't Do*.

11.3 *What Computers Can't Do*

Computers, essentially, do automated logic. That is, they use rules to manipulate sentences in a symbolic language. For example, a computer might have a representation of a local printer:

Printer 1 is Online
Printer 1 is the Default Printer.

It might also have rules for sending print jobs:

If Printing, then find the Default Printer.
If the Default Printer is online, then use the Default Printer; otherwise request Alternate Printer.

A human brain that is a computer would have representations of many, many facts about the world. It would have rules about how to use those facts to generate more facts, and how to decide upon actions. For example, it might have some facts about dogs represented.

> All dogs are mammals.
> Some dogs have fleas.
> Some dogs bite.
> Momo is a dog.
> etc.

It would also have rules for combining these facts to produce new facts, such as the following.

> Momo is a mammal.
> Possibly, Momo has fleas.
> Possibly, Momo bites.

There might be more rules for generating possible actions, given these new facts.

Dreyfus' book-length critique *What Computers Can't Do* (1972) includes detailed descriptions of several different research programs in artificial intelligence, divided into historical eras. The same is true of the first revised edition, *What Computers (Still) Can't Do* (1979). The details of these research programs, and the differences among them, though interesting, are not crucial for current purposes. They all have in common the claim that thinking is computation, and they all share optimism about the near-future generation of genuine thinking machines. The differences concern the formatting of the facts, and the details of the rules for combining them. Dreyfus' critiques concern any system that uses rules to manipulate sentence-like representations. We will go through them in some detail below, but the key points that Dreyfus raises can be put simply. First, human thinking and acting is not rule following; second, the world that humans think about and act in cannot be represented as a set of sentences. He elaborates these points as he goes through four assumptions that all the research programs in artificial intelligence, at least through 1979, had in common.

11.3.1 The biological assumption

Nearly every computer is *digital*. To be digital is to always be in one of a limited number of states, and never in any other. In computers the number of states is two, usually named "0" and "1." Most things in nature are not digital, but range over many, many values, often infinitely many. Things that range over infinitely many values are *continuous*. When the temperature outside increases from 15 degrees to 20 degrees, it passes through every temperature between 15 degrees and 20 degrees, from 15.000 ... 001 to 19.999. ... One way to understand the difference between being digital and being continuous is to say that with digital things, you get to a point where you cannot measure more precisely, but you never get there with continuous things. The digital light switch is either on or off, and after you know that, there is nothing else to learn about its state. The weight of an aardvark is continuous in that, assuming your equipment is good enough, you are always able to add another decimal place to a measurement of it, going from 61 kilograms to 61.5 kilograms to 61.48 kilograms to 61.483 kilograms to 61.4833 kilograms and so on. Another way to see the distinction is to compare a game of chess to a game of pocket billiards (Haugeland 1985). Chess is digital in that it is a fact of the matter which square each piece is in. The exact position of the pawn in its square isn't important – once you know that the pawn is in the square, you know everything you need to know. In contrast, the exact position of every ball matters in pocket billiards. This allows, for example, chess players to play chess on separate boards in different countries, and we could finish a game we started on one board on another board. In contrast, we could not simply pick up the game of billiards on another table; it would not be the same game. Billiards is continuous.

What Dreyfus calls the "biological assumption" is the assumption that, considered at the appropriate scale, the brain is digital. Before discussing the "at the appropriate scale" caveat, we should be clear that this assumption is required only by artificial intelligence that attempts to be cognitive science. For the technological version of artificial intelligence, whose goal is simply to build useful, intelligent machines, it does not matter whether the mechanism that enables the intelligent behavior in the machines is anything like the mechanism that enables human intelligent behavior. It doesn't matter to Deep Blue's creators that Deep Blue doesn't play chess the same way its human opponents do. The biological assumption is necessary only for cognitive science. Indeed, the biological assumption is the essence of cognitive science, the idea that our brains literally *are* "wet and sticky" computers. Moreover, it is necessary that the brain be a digital device if it is to contain representations to which computational rules could apply.

Consider the following rule for playing tic-tac-toe:

If your opponent plays "X" in a corner for first move, play "O" in the center square.

For this rule to be applied, there has to be a fact of the matter where the opponent has played "X." It can't be that the X is partially in a corner, or more or less in a corner. To determine whether to apply the rule, the X has to be either in a corner or not in a corner. For rules to apply, the brain has to represent information in a digital format.

For those who have learned some neuroscience, say in an introductory psychology course, it will seem that neurons are a good candidate for being digital. That is, neurons would be "the appropriate scale" at which the brain is digital. And, indeed, this is what the artificial intelligence researchers Dreyfus criticized believed. Neurons, they argued, interact with one another by producing *action potentials*. When a neuron is at rest, its inside carries a negative electrical charge compared to the medium it is in. Neurotransmitters at the neuron's input end gradually cause changes in the neuron's cell wall that allow more positively charged ions to enter the neuron, causing the charge inside the neuron to increase (i.e., get less negative). Once the charge reaches a threshold, the neuron "fires," sending an action potential, down the length of the neuron and causing it to release neurotransmitters to the input ends of other neurons. The neuron becomes temporarily positively charged in relation to its surrounds, and cannot fire another action potential until it gradually returns to its original negative charge. This firing of an action potential is often described as being "all or nothing" in that until the voltage crosses the threshold, the neuron doesn't fire, and when it does fire it fires all the way. Certainly, this seems digital: the neuron is either firing or it is not, with no in between.

Unfortunately for the proponents of artificial intelligence Dreyfus argued with, this introductory psychology picture of neurons as simple on/off entities is far too simple. For one thing, neurons do not sit there waiting for enough input to fire: they are firing continuously, and what varies based on their interaction with other neurons is their *firing rate*. This was clear already in 1972. The intervening years have shown that neuronal behavior is much more complicated and varied than the introductory psychology understanding of neurons indicates. Bickhard (2013) provides an extensive list of ways that neurons do not behave as described above. Neurons are better understood as *oscillators* that modulate one another's activity. An oscillator is anything that has repeating behavior, like the pendulum on a grandfather clock, or ocean tides. The period of an oscillator is the time it takes to get from some point back to the same point. In the case of a neuron, the period is the time from one action potential to the next. Neurons interact with one another primarily by altering one another's period. The period of an oscillator is continuous, not digital. If neurons are oscillators rather than digital switches, the brain is not a digital computer.

11.3.2 The psychological assumption

The foundational idea of cognitive science is that the mind is a computer program. Given our experience, this foundational idea seems obviously false. When we recognize a friend on the street, we do not experience ourselves comparing the current visual image of the person with a stored representation of the person. We also do not experience ourselves estimating the distance and velocity of a car to calculate when it will reach the spot on the street we want to cross and then comparing the outcome of that calculation with an estimate of how long it will take to cross the street before deciding to cross. Instead, we just see an old friend, or that we can cross the street. This means that the computational processes that, according to cognitive science, make up our minds must be subconscious. The idea is that the relationship among brain, cognition, and experience is like that among the computer, the software running on it, and the user interface. Just as the computational processes that make letters appear on a computer monitor in response to pressing keys are invisible to the computer user, so too are the computational processes that allow you to recognize your friend. It is at a scale between physical (brain, computer) and experiential (conscious experience, user interface) that the mind is supposed to be a computer program. Drefyus calls this "the psychological assumption."

Dreyfus points out, correctly, that the status of the psychological assumption is multiply ambiguous. First, is the claim that human behavior is input–output equivalent to a computer program, or is it the stronger claim that the processes in our brains are like computer programs? This first issue is that between artificial intelligence as technology and artificial intelligence as cognitive science. For the former, the assumption is that it will be possible to build computers that behave intelligently; for the latter, the assumption is that our brain is a computer and our minds are computer programs. Although these examples were not available when Dreyfus wrote *What Computers Can't Do*, we know from Deep Blue and Watson, among others, that the computers can behave intelligently, at least in limited domains. The interesting question is the question of cognitive science. So the psychological assumption must be that human thinking really is computation. Second, it is ambiguous whether the claim is meant to be an empirical claim about the nature of our minds, or a conceptual claim. Are cognitive scientists trying to determine whether thinking is computation, or have they simply defined thinking as computation? Dreyfus points out that, at least in 1972, there was virtually no empirical evidence that thinking is computation. The history of attempts to build intelligent machines was a history of failures, with researchers failing again and again to get computers to exhibit intelligent behavior. Yet at the same time, researchers continued to make bold claims about the future of intelligent machines. This leads Dreyfus to conclude that the claim must be a conceptual one. Cognitive scientists are simply defining cognition as computation. So, with ambiguities removed, the psychological assumption is that thinking should be understood as subconscious computational processes of exactly the sort that occur on digital computers.

Dreyfus thinks that the conceptual form of the psychological claim is incoherent, arguing against the very idea of an intervening "level" of information processing between the brain and conscious experience. This computational level is supposed to bridge the gap between merely causal physical interactions with the world and conscious experiences. Indeed, this is the interaction problem discussed above, for which computation was intended to be a solution. Dreyfus thinks that the proposed solution does not work, and that nothing could bridge the gap between the merely physical world and our experiences. Cognitive scientists attempt to bridge the gap by trading on ambiguities in words like "sensation" and "information," which have both a physical sense and an experiential sense. A sensation has traditionally been understood as an experience, but the term is often used in neuroscience and psychology to refer to the excitation of sensory nerves such as retinal cells. Similarly, information can be used to refer to meaning, but is also a technical term in computer science referring to the amount of variability in a stream of bits. By vacillating between these senses of these not-quite-mental terms, cognitive scientists create a "new form of gibberish" (Dreyfus 1972, p. 92). As we will see below, Dreyfus' solution to the problem of interaction is to follow Heidegger, Merleau-Ponty, and Gibson in rejecting the Cartesian assumptions that allow a division between the thinking and the world to begin with.

Before moving to this, however, it is important to see that Dreyfus is incorrect that the very idea of an intervening level is incoherent. He is correct that cognitive scientists define cognition as computation. As has been said many times, this definition is the foundation of cognitive science. The key is that the definition is made tentatively, in a way that is standard scientific practice. The cognitive scientist says "Maybe thinking is computation. Let's suppose that it is, and see what predictions follow from that supposition. Then let's design experiments to see if those predictions hold up." Far from being incoherent, the supposition that thinking is subconscious computation has been central to a successful scientific discipline for many decades. This doesn't mean that thinking in actual fact is computation. We agree with Dreyfus that the psychological assumption is false. But at least in its general form, it is not gibberish.

11.3.3 The epistemological assumption

What Dreyfus calls the "epistemological assumption" is essentially the weak version of the psychological assumption. It is the claim that it is possible to build machines that are input–output equivalent to humans, that is, machines that would pass the Turing test. The epistemological assumption, then, is not that human brains are computers, but that a computer could be built that acts like a human. For it to be possible for a digital computer to behave like a human, Dreyfus argues, it must be the case that all of human behavior is specifiable in terms of rules connecting inputs and outputs. Indeed, it is often claimed that a computer can simulate *any* phenomenon. That is, for anything that can be specified in terms of inputs and outputs, a computer can be programmed to produce the same output given the same input. There seems to be no reason in principle why this could not be done with human behavior. Dreyfus argues against this assumption in a two-part argument. First, he points out that most attempts to simulate human behavior have been at the "psychological level," and he has already argued that the psychological level is incoherent. Second, he argues against the practical possibility of simulated humans at some smaller scale, for example at the scale of individual neurons or chemical processes.

The computational landscape has changed since 1972. As noted above, there are many cases of digital computers exhibiting human-level intelligence, at least in restricted domains. It might be argued that chess and super-fast searches of large databases are the sort of problems that are easily solvable using computers. Chess, after all, is digital; and searching through databases is the sort of thing that can be spelled out in terms of rules. There might be many, many other not-so-obviously digital phenomena that could not be spelled out in terms of rules mapping inputs to outputs. The recent computational focus on "big data" is reason to be skeptical about this. For example, you might not be able to come up with a list of rules that determines when you are likely to like music. But looking for regularities in the listening or purchasing histories of large numbers of people leads to hard-to-describe, but predictively useful rules for determining what sort of music individuals are likely to enjoy. Consider how well Amazon or Spotify does at recommending music to you. Certainly, the software that makes these recommendations doesn't do so the way a friend would. But that is not required for the epistemological assumption to be true. All that is required is that the recommendations (the output) be like those that a friend would make.

11.3.4 The ontological assumption

Although Dreyfus doesn't put it this way, what he identifies as the "onto-logical assumption" made by cognitive scientists is the assumption that the world is digital. If the brain is taken to be a digital computer and the mind is taken to be a collection of digital, computational processes that work by manipulating representations of the world, then it is natural to assume that the world is such that representing it digitally makes sense. To be easily amenable to digital representation, the world must be composed of a set of individual facts, expressible in a logical language, that are either true or false. "This is the ontological assumption that what there is, is a set of facts each logically independent of all the others" (1972, p. 92). It is in this assumption that artificial intelligence research most closely matches the rationalist tradition. It starts with assump-tions about how the mind works, then, given the assumption that the mind represents the world, moves to conclusions about the nature of the world. It is also with the ontological assumption that Dreyfus' critique draws most heavily on phenomenology.

Recall the distinction Husserl makes between the inner and outer horizons. Suppose you are experiencing a black, leather chair. What Husserl called the "inner horizon" is what is actually mentally repre-sented when you experience the chair. In contrast, the "outer horizon" is your background knowledge of the whole world, not just the chair you are mentally representing. Husserl found that in order to make sense of the inner horizon, it was necessary to include substantial portions of the outer horizon. This can be seen clearly with an example from Haugeland (1979). Consider the sentence "I left the raincoat in the bathtub because it was still wet." We assume that everyone reading this sentence under-stood it without any trouble, and probably without noticing that the word "it" in the sentence is ambiguous. Given the syntax of the sentence, it could be that the raincoat was still wet or it could be that the bathtub was still wet. Despite the syntactic ambiguity, it is obvious to any of us that the raincoat was still wet. It is equally obvious that we would never put a raincoat in a bathtub because the bathtub was wet – so obvious that we would never consider that interpretation of the sentence. Suppose that sentence is the inner horizon. How much of the outer horizon is required to explain our understanding of that sentence? That is, in virtue of which pieces of background knowledge is this sentence so obvious? It seems to include at least our knowledge of the effect of water on household items made of cloth, wood, leather, and so on; about private property; about the cost of furniture and refinishing wood floors; about bathtubs and drains and plumbing; and so on. Notice that, although this is almost certainly the first time you have considered this sentence about raincoats and bathtubs, there is nothing unusually complicated about it. Moreover, it is just one of the more or less infinitely many sentences that we all understand without any difficulty. If our knowledge of the world were in the form of mentally represented facts, we would need to have representations of infinitely many facts – the entire outer horizon of human culture – at our disposal at any given moment. That is simply not possible.

Recall that Heidegger argued that understanding the outer horizon is a prerequisite for understanding the inner horizon, or, in his terms, that encountering any given entity requires familiarity with the entire background of equipment and practices in which that entity makes sense. To understand a sentence about a raincoat in a bathtub, we need to understand raincoats and bathtubs. But, of course, we cannot understand a raincoat or a bathtub in terms of features of particular bathtubs; instead, we need to understand them functionally, in terms of the role they play in our lives. That is, we understand raincoats, bathtubs, and other equipment in terms of the "wholeness of equipment." Indeed, raincoats and bathtubs are what they are in terms of the wholeness of equipment. The wholeness of equipment is not a series of unconnected facts each of which is independently true or false. The world is not digital.

11.4 Heideggerian artificial intelligence

After critiquing the assumptions of artificial intelligence researchers, which are also the assumptions of the rationalist tradition, Dreyfus makes some suggestions concerning the right way to understand human experience. As mentioned above, he draws on Heidegger, Merleau-Ponty, and the Gestalt psychologists, along with Wittgenstein, to sketch this alternative picture, which will be familiar from reading this book up to this point. Dreyfus argues that the rationalist tradition ignores the role that the body plays in experience and intelligent behavior. Ignoring the body is an unsurprising consequence of taking the brain to be a computer and the mind to be computer programs, making it natural to think of the body as peripherals: our sensory surfaces are analogous to keyboards; or muscles are analogous to monitors and printers. We will see in the next chapters that focusing on the body, and on skillful activity in the world, has led to reforms in cognitive science that have transformed the discipline. To close this chapter, we consider early research that moves beyond Dreyfus' Heidegger-inspired critique of artificial intelligence to Heidegger-inspired research in artificial intelligence (Agre and Chapman 1987; Preston 1993; Agre 1997; Wheeler 2005; Dreyfus 2007).

As Preston (1993) points out, there are two challenges for a Heidegger-inspired artificial intelligence. She makes the point with the example of keys and locks. As discussed above, to understand why we do and do not lock doors, one must understand the whole of our cultural background. But this cultural background could not be mentally represented by users of keys and locks. This problem of the outer horizon is important to understanding when we decide to lock the door, but there is also the problem of how we actually manage to lock doors when we need to do so. When we are planning what to do with our days, do we plan to lock the car door when we get to work? When you ask someone to feed your cat while you are away for the weekend, you give them the key, but do you tell them how to use it to open your door? Somehow, we just manage to lock doors when we need to lock them. We exhibit two kinds of skill in locking doors: we are skillful in knowing when to lock the door and we are skillful in knowing how to lock the door. To successfully build artificial intelligence, both issues must be dealt with. We know when to lock doors because of the importance of private property in our culture. Because locking doors is an important, routine activity, locks and keys are designed to be easy for us to use. Locking doors is a simple, routine activity because locks are built with us (our hands, eyes, wrists, belongings) in mind. Heidegger's analysis of the "wholeness of equipment" entails that most human activity will be routine, skillful coping with an environment that is designed to be easy for us to deal with. Most of our engagement, that is, will be with equipment as ready-to-hand. So the problem for artificial intelligence as cognitive science is that we need to build machines that are capable of coping with the environment in routine situations, using artifacts that were designed to complement our bodily abilities.

The first deliberate attempt at constructing Heideggerian artificial intelligence is Pengi, a program written by Agre and Chapman (1987). Pengi was designed to play the 1980s video game Pengo. In Pengo, players control a penguin avatar chased by bees in an environment of pathways through movable blocks of ice. Pengi plays the game about as well as a human who has played for several hours. Pengi is a production system, a typical type of computer program used in artificial intelligence research, consisting of a set of rules, a workspace where features of the game are represented, and methods for determining which rules apply. Dreyfus has been correctly critical of production systems, and in fact it is not the general architecture of Pengi that makes it of interest. There are two things that make it interesting. First, Pengi does not represent any individual entities. That is, it does not represent particular blocks of ice or bees. Instead it uses what are called *deictic representations*, indexical-functional entities that stand for things defined in terms of Pengi's current activities. Bees and blocks are significant in Pengi's world, so indexical-functional entities with which Pengi is concerned are things like "the-bee-that-I-am-chasing" and "the-block-I-am-kicking." Although we can read them, these strings have no internal complexity – it is not possible for Pengi to see any particular bee separately from its concerns with its being "the-bee-that-I-am-chasing" and "the-bee-that-is-about-to-get-me." Thus Pengi's world is carved up according to the things Pengi needs to deal with in its skillful activity, activities that we would describe as avoiding obstacles and squashing bees. Second, Pengi plays Pengo as a routine activity, without represented plans or goals. It copes with the immediate game situation. Pengi has no explicit *plan* represented. There is no sense in which Pengi checks its current activities against short- or long-term goals. Instead it improvises according to what skills it has and what the environment affords. So, skillful, intelligent behavior emerges in Pengi's moves, despite the fact that Pengi itself has no representation of its long-term goals, and thus no idea what they are.

Pengi's deictic representations are not representations of facts that exist independent of Pengi's activity. Deictic "representations" are indexical-functional in that they stand for things that are only defined in terms of the agent who uses them (in this case Pengi) in accord with its current purposes. The indexical-functional entities that Pengi "experiences" ("the-bee-that-I-am-chasing," "the-block-I-am-kicking," and so on) are embedded in what Agre and Chapman call *aspects*, such as "the-bee-I-am-chasing-is-behind-a-block." Deictic "representations" are the means by which Pengi registers aspects and entities in its world, not representations of independent facts. As Chapman (1991, p. 32) puts it, "because a deictic representation must be causally connected with its referent, part of its responsibility is to constitute an object. The real world is not neatly divided up into discrete objects with identity labels on them. What counts as an object depends on the task."

Although he rejects the association, the robotics research of Rodney Brooks (1991) is often classified as Heideggerian artificial intelligence. Like Agre and Chapman's Pengi, the robots Brooks builds cope skillfully with routine situations: avoiding obstacles and exploring cluttered environments. Unlike Agre and Chapman, however, Brooks rejects representations entirely:

> We have reached an unexpected conclusion (C) and have a rather radical hypothesis (H):
> (C) When we examine very simple level intelligence we find that explicit representations and models of the world simply get in the way. It turns out to be better to let the world serve as its own model.
> (H) Representation is the wrong unit of abstraction in building the bulkiest parts of intelligent systems. (Brooks 1991, p. 140)

Rather than attempt to build efficient and complete representations of the world into his agents, Brooks builds robots that are complete creatures that actually do something. The first robot that he built according to these principles was Allen. Allen is a disc-shaped robot whose inputs are twelve distance sensors around its edge. These sensors give Allen information about the distance of objects in every direction. Allen is controlled by three semi-independent "layers." The lowest layer is called AVOID. AVOID is purely reactive, causing Allen to scoot away from any object that is too close. The second layer, WANDER, works by suppressing AVOID and causing Allen to generate a random heading and move in that direction. The third layer, EXPLORE, suppresses WANDER, and causes Allen to tend to move in the direction in which the obstacle is farthest away. Complicated behavior emerges from the interaction of these three layers, with no need for planning. Like Pengi, Allen simply reacts to its environment. Allen's behavior is quite robust in real-world settings: it is the basis for the Roomba robotic vacuum cleaner. Real behavior, in the real world, does not require representation.

At the beginning of research into artificial intelligence, Dreyfus was perceived as an irritating skeptic. His phenomenology-inspired critiques frustrated the confident, future-oriented practitioners of this new discipline. In hindsight, however, it seems that Dreyfus was right all along. Artificial intelligence researchers had simply reinvented rationalist philosophy, and the failures of artificial intelligence as cognitive science confirm the phenomenological critiques of rationalism. By the early 1990s, phenomenology (primarily via Dreyfus) had shifted from being a source of criticism to a positive inspiration for researchers in the cognitive sciences. The next chapters are a survey of phenomenology-inspired cognitive science from the 1990s to today.

Key terms

biological assumption – the assumption made by artificial intelligence researchers that the brain functions like a digital computer.

cognitive science – an interdisciplinary approach to understanding the mind, combining insights from psychology, computer science, linguistics, philosophy, neuroscience, and anthropology. The founders of cognitive science hypothesized that thinking is a kind of computation.

computationalism – the view that thinking is literally computation and that the brain is a computer.

digital – a system is digital when it can only be in a limited number of states. Computers are digital, but natural phenomena are not.

epistemological assumption – the assumption made by artificial intelligence researchers that it is possible to build a computer that is input–output equivalent to a human. This amounts to claiming that all human behavior can be described in terms of rules.

medium independence – computer programs are medium independent in that they can run on different kinds of computers. Cognitive scientists typically assume that the brain is a computer, so the same computer program could run on a brain and a laptop computer.

methodological solipsism – solipsism is the view that only one's own mind exists. Methodological solipsism is assuming, for the purpose of doing cognitive science, that only the thinker's representation of the world is relevant, but the world itself is not.

mind–body problem – the longstanding philosophical problem of understanding how the mind and the body are related to one another, including how they interact.

ontological assumption – the assumption made by artificial intelligence researchers that the world is made up of a set of independent facts of the sort that can be represented by sentences.

problem of other minds – the longstanding philosophical problem of how one knows what (or even that) another person is thinking.

psychological assumption – the assumption made by artificial intelligence researchers that thinking is computation.

Turing test – a behavioral criterion for establishing that a machine is intelligent. If a machine could fool a human interlocutor into thinking it is a human, then, according to Turing, it would have to be intelligent.

Further reading

Dreyfus, H. (1972/1979/1992). *What Computers (Still) Can't Do*. New York: Harper and Row.
– (2007). "Why Heideggerian AI failed, and why fixing it would require making it more Heideggerian." *Philosophical Psychology*, 20: 247–68.
Preston, B. (1993). "Heidegger and artificial intelligence." *Philosophy and Phenomenological Research*, 53: 43–69.

12

Enactivism and the Embodied Mind

12.1 Embodied, embedded, extended, enactive

In the wake of Merleau-Ponty's phenomenological philosophy, Gibson's ecological psychology, and the critiques of artificial intelligence by Dreyfus, increasing numbers of philosophers of mind and cognitive scientists began to question the rationalist assumptions that were foundational in the cognitive sciences. What these three historical precursors to what are now called "enactivism" and "embodied mind" have in common is a recognition of the importance of the body and action in understanding our mental lives. They also share a skepticism about internal, mental representations. To paraphrase Alva Noë (2004), experience is not something that happens to our brains; instead, it is something we do, typically by moving our bodies around our physical and cultural environments.

Enactivism and the embodied mind took shape in the 1980s and early 1990s. Arguably the true founding of both embodied mind and enactivism comes with *The Embodied Mind* by Francisco Varela, Evan Thompson, and Eleanor Rosch (1991). This book fuses Merleau-Ponty's phenomenology and work in neuroscience and situated robotics. The key claim of the book is that cognition does not involve computation or internal representations, but is instead a basic activity of living things. This was a radical rejection of the predominant cognitive science of the time, which took cognition to be computational processing of representations in the brain. In the late 1990s, some enactive ideas were mainstreamed and combined with representational and computational cognitive science, especially by Andy Clark (1997; but see also Wilson 1995 and McClamrock 1995). In effect, Clark's version of the embodied mind is what is now called "embodied mind"; Varela et al.'s original version is called "enactivism."

In the twenty-first century, there has been a profusion of theories that fall under the general idea of embodied mind, so much so that it is currently fashionable to lump them together as "4E cognition" (Menary 2010), where the Es in question are embodied, embedded, extended, and enactive. The first three of these are variations on a theme; the fourth is something of an outlier. To say that mind is *embodied* is to say that cognitive systems include aspects of the body outside the nervous system; to say that it is *embedded* is to say that environmental, social, or cultural resources are necessary for at least some cognitive activities; to say that mind is *extended* is to say that those environmental resources are literally components of the cognitive system (Clark and Chalmers 1998; Kono 2010). Notice that each of these successive Es is a stronger claim. Notice too that each of these three Es is compatible with mainstream representational and computational theories of mind. Indeed, arguments for extended mind often take it to be a straightforward consequence of functionalism in the philosophy of mind (Drayson 2010; Wheeler 2010), in which things in the environment play crucial roles in the cognitive processes that constitute cognition. For example, instead of remembering phone numbers using neural systems, you might store them in a phone or write them down in a notebook. The notebook out in the world is part of your mind. In this sense the mind is extended. Nevertheless the notebook functions by storing and representing information and the extended mind uses this representation to cognize the world. So the extended mind is a representing, computing mind. Saying that mind is *enactive* is to say something quite different; it is to say that mind is a fundamental activity of living things. As noted above, enactivism is incompatible with representational and computational cognitive science. It is the only one of the four Es that is genuinely in line with phenomenological thinking.

12.2 The original enactivism

The roots of the enactive approach are in biology, in the work of Humberto Maturana and Francisco Varela (Maturana and Varela 1973, 1987; Varela, Maturana, and Uribe 1974). Maturana and Varela developed the theory of *autopoiesis*, an attempt to give a theory of life and living systems that is amenable to mathematical and computational modeling. "Autopoiesis" translates from Greek as "self-creation." Maturana and Varela thought that being self-creating and self-maintaining is the key property of living things. In their analysis, autopoiesis has two components: autopoietic systems are *operationally closed* and *structurally coupled* to their environments. To be operationally closed is to be autonomous, in that a particular system's activities create and maintain those very activities. Suppose there is a set of two chemical reactions, which are such that a product of reaction A is a catalyst for reaction B and a product of B is a catalyst for reaction A. These two reactions could form an operationally closed system in that reaction A makes reaction B possible and vice versa. To be structurally coupled to one another, two entities must have a history of interactions that leads, over time, to a congruence between them. The key example of an autopoietic system that Maturana and Varela give is the cell. A cell is a set of chemical reactions that are bounded by a semi-permeable cell wall. The cell wall maintains the chemical reactions by keeping the concentrations of chemicals favorable; the chemical reactions in the cell create and maintain the cell wall. The wall and the reactions form an operationally closed set. The cell is structurally coupled to the extra-cellular environment in that the wall constantly and selectively admits raw materials for the chemical reactions from the extra-cellular environment, and constantly and selectively passes waste products to the extra-cellular environment. The cell impacts the chemical concentrations' extra-cellular environment, which also impacts the chemical concentrations in the cell. The cell, then, is an autopoietic system, structurally coupled to its extra-cellular environment. Maturana and Varela take autopoiesis to be the essential characteristic of living systems. More recently, Di Paolo (2008) has argued convincingly that autopoiesis is in itself not sufficient for life. What he calls *adaptivity* is also required. Adaptivity is the ability of a system to tell when it is approaching the boundaries of its viability, and to act so as to change its circumstances. This has been widely accepted as an important amendment to autopoietic theory. It shows, for example, why the Brooks robots discussed in the previous chapter are not alive.

This early work by Maturana and Varela is the basis for enactivism, which combines autopoiesis with insights from phenomenology. As we have seen, the work that is viewed as the founding document in enactivism is *The Embodied Mind* by Varela, Thompson, and Rosch (1991). That work chronicles the history of cognitive science, showing its repeated failures to capture human experience, and offers an alternative approach based on autopoietic theory, ideas from Merleau-Ponty, and the robots of Rodney Brooks described in Chapter 11. Although *The*

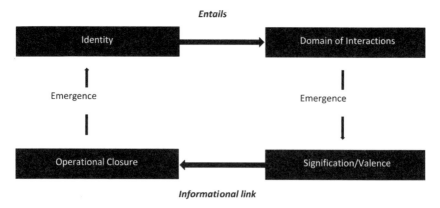

Figure 12.1 Co-emergence of self and world
Source: Based on Thompson 2004

Embodied Mind and *Mind in Life*, a later book by Thompson (2007), have been the most influential works in enactive cognitive science, the most clear and concise description of the first enactivist position is found in a 2004 article by Thompson, a tribute to Varela, who had died in 2001. Our exposition of enactivism in the next paragraph follows the exposition in that paper closely.

Thompson (2004) begins by pointing out that the key to understanding the relationship between experience and the material world, that is, to solving the mind–body problem, is what Merleau-Ponty called the lived body. The main question that enactive cognitive science attempts to answer concerns the relationship between a biological living body and a phenomenological lived body, the relationship between *Körper* and *Leib*. Figure 12.1 is based on a figure from Thompson's paper. The beginning point is that life is autopoiesis. Because autopoietic systems are operationally closed, there will be a separation of the living system from its environment, as in the case of the cell wall. This separation is what makes a living organism an entity separate from its environment. It also implies the emergence of a self, a primitive self in the case of a cell, but a self nonetheless. The emergence of the self implies the emergence of a world, not just in that the boundary around the self leaves everything else as the world, but also in that the activities of the living system pick out which aspects of the world it structurally couples with. This world and the self co-emerge, insofar as the activities of the autopoietic system determine what aspects of the physical environment it structurally couples to. Enactivists often call this co-emergence of self and world "sense-making" (Varela 1979; Thompson 2004; Thompson and Stapleton 2008), by which they mean that the experienced world for the organism is the sense it makes of its environment. Sense-making is both cognitive and emotional, so the world is significant to the organism; it has value and valence. Indeed, sense-making *is* cognition, at least in a minimal sense. In sense-making an organism maintains itself in a meaningful environment. This meaningful environment does not exist in advance of the existence of the organism, but co-emerges along with the activities of the organism. Organisms, as lived bodies, enact or "bring forth" worlds (Varela, Thompson, and Rosch 1991). This is now a biological, living body and also a phenomenological, lived body.

Varela, Thompson, and Rosch (1991) exemplify this bringing forth of worlds using the Rodney Brooks robot Allen, discussed in the previous chapter. As we noted there, Allen senses using twelve ultrasonic sensors positioned at each "hour" around its circular body. The only things, therefore, that can perturb Allen's behavior are physical objects large enough to reflect ultrasonic pulses, and the way Allen reacts to these objects determines their significance to Allen. This is what it is for Allen to enact or bring forth a very limited world of significance. This is taken as a model for all organisms, each of which brings forth a world that is determined by the connections between its sensing and acting, and these connections determine the significance of the entities in that world. The world that is experiences is already, automatically significant.

Enactivists are interested in extended mind. But because they focus on the bringing forth of worlds, extended mind takes on a different cast. Because organisms bring forth the world they experience, that world, in all its significance, is not independent of the organism, so it is strange to claim that the cognitive system extends beyond the organism. On the one hand, because the experienced world is not separable from the organism, mind could not but be extended; on the other hand, because the world is brought forth by the organism, it is strange to say that the world is external to the organism. Enactivists, therefore, focus on the possibility of extended life instead of extended mind. Di Paolo (2008) discusses the behavior of water boatmen, a species of insect that is able to breathe underwater by trapping air bubbles in abdominal hairs. Because of pressure differences that result from the boatman's own respiration, bubbles replenish themselves with oxygen, allowing for extended periods under water. These bubbles mediate environmental coupling, and alter the boatman's abilities to interact with its environment, and in so doing alter the significance of entities in its world. Di Paolo (2008) argues that these boatmen-plus-bubbles comprise an extended form of living. Thompson and Stapleton (2008) argue that cases like this are like the connection between Merleau-Ponty's blind man and his cane. Just as the blind man does not experience his cane, the water boatman does not experience the bubble, but experiences an altered world of significance through the bubble. The bubble for the water boatman is equipment. As Merleau-Ponty claimed, the water boatman and cane navigator have *incorporated* their equipment, experiencing the world through that equipment. Since life is cognition according to these enactivists, extended life is a form of extended mind.

De Jaegher and Di Paolo (2007) extend enactivism to social interactions, via what they call *participatory sense-making*. In participatory sense-making, two individuals are coupled with the world and with one another, such that they collectively and temporarily open a new domain of significant interactions that is not available to either separately. To take an example from De Jaegher and Di Paolo, consider what happens in what we might call "the hallway dance," when two individual humans both attempt to make space for the other while passing in a narrow hallway. Each of these individuals is an adaptive agent, engaging in sense-making, and bringing forth a significant world. Given their interest in avoiding collision with one another, which would have negative valence for both, each will move to one side of the hallway to let the other pass. Most of the time this works perfectly well, but sometimes both individuals will move to the same side of the hallway, yielding a potential collision. Because each experiences potential collisions negatively, both simultaneously then move to the opposite side of the narrow hallway, setting up another potential collision. To avoid the second possible collision, each individual once again switches sides of the hallway. This can happen several times, with each person mirroring the other's movement repeatedly. This hallway dance is an example of participatory sense-making. In it, each individual remains an autonomous agent, bringing forth a significant world, even while they are temporarily coupled with one another, but they also collectively bring forth a world significant to their coupled activity. Notice that, like the individuals that participate in it, the hallway dance displays its own autonomy (Fuchs and De Jaegher 2009). The dance maintains itself, at least for a while, because each attempt at collision avoidance by the participants leads to another possible collision, the avoidance of which leads to another possible collision, and so on.

In the case of the hallway dance, the participatory sense-making is at odds with what is adaptive for the individuals: neither of them wants to bounce from wall to wall in the narrow corridor, but they are temporarily trapped in a social interaction. This is not always the case in participatory sense-making, and much of our social interaction also serves the individuals in the interaction. Consider (non-hallway) dancing, conversation, or joint speech (such as protest or football chants; see Cummins 2018). In these cases, a new domain of significance, unavailable to the individual participants separately, is opened by the interaction, but, in this case, the participatory domain is positively valenced for the individuals. In these cases, the interaction maintains itself over time, for however long it does, because the individual participants (dancers, conversationalists) work to maintain the interaction.

In recent work, Cuffari, Di Paolo, and De Jaegher (2015; see also Di Paolo, Cuffari, and De Jaegher 2018) expand participatory sense-making into an account of language. Rather than trying to explain language as an abstract entity that humans use, they focus on what Maturana (1978) calls *languaging*, an activity central to our lives as human beings. Cuffari et al.'s full account of languaging is complex, and includes a dialectical and a developmental model. We will focus here on the latter. Beginning even before they are born, humans are enmeshed in a world that is first and foremost social, constituted by close interactions with care-givers. That is, the sense-making of infants is primarily participatory sense-making. The environment in which this occurs is replete with speech and gestures; the environment is "enlanguaged." During the early years of their lives, children develop skills at sense-making, alone and with others. Because this sense-making occurs in an enlanguaged environment, the skills and habits with which they make sense involve the use of language. That is, just as the water boatman has incorporated its bubble and the blind person has incorporated her cane, developing children incorporate pieces of language. As their sense-making habits and skills become more and more inflected with language, and their participatory sense-making with care-givers and a widening circle of others depends more and more on speaking and listening, children become what Cuffari et al. call "linguistic bodies."

From a phenomenological point of view, this is an attractive view of language and linguistic activities. Unlike cognitivist approaches to language, which focus on innate neural propensities for syntax and grammar, the enactive approach accounts for language as a skilled activity with which we make sense of the material, social, and broader cultural worlds. In this way the enactivist view of language fits with Heidegger's claim that "language, as the holistic totality of words in which discourse has its own 'worldly' being, shows up within the world just like available entities" (*SZ*, p. 161). Language is equipment and our linguistic abilities are practical competences for using it correctly. Moreover, again unlike the cognitive approach, the enactive approach is what Cuffari et al. call "nonrepresentational." In languaging, humans make sense of the world, but not typically by representing it. Cuffari et al.'s view differs from "anti-representational" approaches because it acknowledges that one of the things we can do with language is make representations, as when we tell a story or compare a loved one to a summer's day.

12.3 Other enactivisms: The sensorimotor approach and radical enactivism

Although it is often also called "enactivism," the strong sensorimotor approach associated primarily with Alva Noë , J. Kevin O'Regan, and Susan Hurley (O'Regan and Noë 2001; Hurley 2002; Hurley and Noë 2003; Noë 2004, 2009; O'Regan 2011) is rather different from enactivism as described above. Although it is influenced by Merleau-Ponty, it is more closely related to Gibson's approach. To avoid confusion, we will call it the "sensorimotor approach." The key to the sensorimotor approach is that perceiving, seeing, experiencing, and the like are things that we *do*, not things that happen inside of us. Consider dynamic touch, described in Chapter 10. To be able to perceive by touch, you need to explore by actively hefting, running your fingers over edges, and the like. Indeed, Gibson (1962) showed that human participants could not identify objects that were pressed into their palms or run over the edges of their fingers by experimenters, but could identify them very precisely (e.g., "a snowman-shaped cookie cutter") when allowed to explore them with their hands. Perceiving by touch requires exploratory work, and sensory stimulation alone is not sufficient. According to the sensorimotor approach, all our senses are like touch in that they require active exploration of the world. Accordingly, this active exploration is part of experience, so the sensorimotor approach is a form of extended mind, with experiences depending on the brain, body, and environment.

The key differentiating feature of the sensorimotor approach is its explanatory use of *sensorimotor contingencies*. Sensorimotor contingencies are relationships between bodily movements and changes in sensory stimulation (O'Regan and Noë 2001). Sensorimotor contingencies are in some ways like Husserl's inner horizons, and in some ways like Gibson's affordances. To use an example from Noë (2004), when you look at a tomato, only a small portion of it is reflecting light that strikes you in the eyes. You nonetheless see it as a three-dimensional object and as having a back. The back of the tomato is present, even though light reflecting off it is not striking your eyes. You also see it as something you could touch or bite or slice. You see all of these things in virtue of an awareness of sensorimotor contingencies, how you would be stimulated if you acted in a particular way. You see the back because if you leaned forward, light from it would strike your eyes; you see that you could touch it because if you reached out with your hand, your finger would press on its flesh. Having experiences at all, according to the sensorimotor approach, requires awareness of these sensorimotor contingencies.

Among the consequences of the sensorimotor approach is a scientifically accessible approach to conscious experience (O'Regan 2011). The sensorimotor approach has a readily available explanation of why the different senses differ from one another. We can differentiate between, for example, vision and touch because they have different sets of sensorimotor contingencies. Moving my fingers over an object yields different changes in stimulation than moving my eyes over it will. This is buttressed by experimental research with sensory substitution. In the 1970s, Bach-y-Rita and colleagues began experimenting with connections between an eyeglass-mounted camera and arrays of vibrating motors worn on the back or stomach or, later, tongue (Bach-y-Rita and Kercel 2003). This is called tactile-vision sensory substitution or TVSS. With the eyeglass-mounted camera, explorations of the environment had vision-like sensorimotor contingencies: turning the head to the left, for example, led to changes in the light entering the camera, and so to changes in vibrations of the array of motors, that were similar to visual changes. Those wearing the TVSS system could quickly learn to identify objects and navigate around cluttered rooms. Moreover, they reported the feeling of *seeing* things around them, rather than feeling a pattern of vibrations on their tongues. This strongly suggests that the experiential difference between seeing and touch has nothing to do with the nature of the stimulation (light hitting photoreceptors in the eyes, vibrations on the skin), but is instead determined by the sensorimotor contingencies specific to each sense. This suggests that the sensory substitution device is part of the extended cognitive system (Auvray and Myin 2009), meaning that this version of enactivism also embraces the extended mind.

We consider yet another approach called "enactivism" primarily for the sake of completeness. What Daniel Hutto and Erik Myin (2013, 2017) call "radical enactivism" consists primarily in the rejection of representations in what they call "basic cognition." Basic cognition is cognition that is not informed by public language or other cultural symbol systems. Basic cognition, Hutto and Myin argue, involves no computation or representations. So, they argue, there are representations only in human linguistic activities, and not in perception, motor control, and the like. They group their arguments for this claim into what they call "don't need" and "can't have" arguments. For the former, they say that basic cognition can be explained just in terms of biological function and without referring to representations and computation, so theorists don't need representationalism. For the latter, they argue that the very idea of mental representations is incoherent, so theorists can't have them for their explanations.

We find many of these arguments convincing, and generally endorse Hutto and Myin's anti-representationalism about basic cognition. We are less convinced by their representationalism about language use and cultural cognition. The phenomenologists we have described throughout this book generally assume that, although language and cultural resources can be used to construct representations, language and culture are not representational at their base. As we have seen above, so too do the others described in this chapter who call themselves enactivists. Although they align themselves with other enactivists and Gibsonian ecological psychologists, Hutto and Myin's form of enactivism differs in that it is not inspired by phenomenology. This is, of course, not a criticism, but rather an explanation for this book's short discussion of radical enactivism.

12.4 Enactivism as a philosophy of nature

Enactivism is often called "enactive cognitive science." We have, so far, avoided that term, because enactivism is not, in and of itself, a scientific view. Indeed, in two recent major works in enactivism (Di Paolo, Buhrmann, and Barandiaran 2017; Gallagher 2017), it has been claimed that enactivism is best viewed not as a scientific research program but as a philosophy of nature. (This distinction comes from Godfrey-Smith [2001].) A scientific research program is a set of hypotheses, at least some of which are testable, and has methods and practices for testing some of those hypotheses, analyzing data, and evaluating results. In short, a scientific research program is what we generally call a "science"; examples include cognitive neuroscience, plate tectonics, and condensed matter physics. In contrast, a philosophy of nature is a philosophical stance about some features of the natural world and scientific attempts to make sense of them. A philosophy of nature is broader than an individual scientific research program, and develops stances toward the methods and results of multiple scientific research programs, interpreting and critiquing their results, and sometimes inspiring new scientific endeavors. Godfrey-Smith introduces the distinction to argue that developmental systems theory, a theoretical approach in biology that inspires and interprets research in scientific research programs such as evolutionary biology, developmental biology, heredity, and genetics, is a philosophy of nature and not a scientific research program. (See

Oyama, Griffiths, and Gray [2001] for more on developmental systems theory.)

Gallagher argues that enactivism should be seen as a philosophy of nature because "from the very start enactivism involved not only a rethinking of the nature of mind and brain, but also a rethinking of the concept of nature itself" (2017, p. 23). Indeed, as we have seen above, the first work in enactivism was a rethinking of the nature of living things, and of the relationship between life and mind. Moreover, enactivism has none of the trappings of a scientific research program. It is a philosophical position, in most cases inspired by the work of the phenomenological thinkers we have described in earlier chapters. As a philosophy of nature, enactivism has inspired work in scientific research programs. For example, as noted above, Maturana and Varela intended autopoiesis to be a theory of life amenable to mathematical and computational modeling. Given this, autopoiesis and enactivism are foundational in the field of *artificial life*. Long before desktop computers were common, Varela, Maturana, and Uribe (1974) had demonstrated an autopoietic system on a computer, building a virtual cell with a semi-permeable, self-repairing cell wall. Artificial life continues to be an important methodology for enactivist theorists (e.g., Froese and Di Paolo 2010; Egbert, Barandiaran, and Di Paolo 2011). So too does artificial intelligence: Froese and Ziemke (2009) describe an approach that they call "enactive artificial intelligence."

Enactivism is a philosophy of nature, and not a scientific research program. Arguably, the same is true about Gibson's ecological psychology described in Chapter 10. Even though he was employed as a psychology professor and did empirical science, in his *The Ecological Approach to Visual Perception*, Gibson told a detailed story about the nature of perception and action, and of the world in which animals perceive and act. That book contains no descriptions of testable hypotheses, experimental methods, or data analysis tools. Like enactivism, ecological psychology is more a philosophy of nature than a scientific research program. As good philosophies of nature, both ecological psychology and enactivism are inspired by and have inspired significant scientific research. In the next chapter, we will explore research programs in the cognitive sciences inspired by several of the phenomenologists we have discussed in this book.

Key terms

adaptivity – the ability of living systems to respond to situations in which they approach the limits of their viability.

autopoiesis – literally, self-creation. According to enactivists, autopoiesis is living and living is cognition.

embodied mind – a combination of the views of Gibson, Heidegger, and Merleau-Ponty with computational cognitive science. According to the theory of the embodied mind, cognition is a kind of computation in which some of the computational operations are done by using the body.

enactivism – a theory of cognition according to which cognition is the activity through which living things bring forth a significant world.

extended mind – the view that cognitive systems sometimes include portions of the non-biological environment.

operational closure – a key part of autopoiesis. A system is operationally closed when it maintains all its own operations.

participatory sense-making – a state in which two individuals are coupled with the world and with one another, such that they collectively and temporarily open a new domain of significant interactions that is not available to either individual separately.

sense-making – what an autopoietic system engages in when it finds significance in its world. This occurs even in simple systems that respond differentially to different situations.

sensorimotor contingencies – relationships between movements and changes in sensory stimulation that enable experience and allow for differentiation among the senses.

structural coupling – a state in which two systems' shared history leads to a congruence between them. Autopoietic systems are structurally coupled to their environments.

Further reading

Cuffari, E., E. Di Paolo, and H. De Jaegher (2015). "From participatory sense-making to language: There and back again." *Phenomenology and the Cognitive Sciences*, 14: 1089–125.

Di Paolo, E., T. Buhrmann, and X. Barandiaran (2017). *Sensorimotor Life: An Enactive Proposal*. New York: Oxford University Press.

O'Regan, J. K. and A. Noë (2001). "A sensorimotor account of vision and visual consciousness." *Behavioral and Brain Sciences*, 24(5): 883–917.

Thompson E. (2004). "Life and mind: From autopoiesis to neurophenomenology. A tribute to Francisco Varela." *Phenomenology and Cognitive Science*, 3: 381–98.

Varela, F., E. Thompson, and E. Rosch (1991). *The Embodied Mind*. Cambridge, MA: MIT Press.

13

Phenomenological Cognitive Science

13.1 The frame problem

At the end of Chapter 10, we noted a problem for Gibson's ecological psychology. How do some of the many affordances that are available at any particular time become the ones that are acted upon? How, to use the language of Withagen et al. (2012), do some affordances become invitations? This question is a version of a more general problem that cognitive science of every stripe faces, called the "frame problem." The frame problem was first described by John McCarthy and Patrick Hayes (1969), two founders of artificial intelligence as a discipline, and is usually taken to be an insurmountable problem for artificial intelligence. The best, and most widely discussed, description of the frame problem is from Dennett (1987). Dennett asks us to imagine how a robot chooses its actions, especially in light of the fact that every action has many side effects. The robot needs to move its spare battery out of a room in which a bomb is about to explode. The robot formulates a plan to roll a cart with the power supply out of the room. Unfortunately, the bomb is also on the cart. So rolling the cart out of the room has the effect of moving the power supply out of the room and the side effect of moving the bomb out of the room. Even if the robot knows that the bomb is on the cart, it might not realize that moving the cart has the side effect of moving the bomb. One possible solution is to have the robot consider all the possible side effects of an action before engaging in any action. The problem with this is knowing what the side effects are without considering the ways that every possible feature of the world might be changed by the action.

1. Moving the cart would change the position of the power supply;
2. moving the cart would change the position of the bomb;
3. moving the cart would change the position of the robot;
4. moving the cart would change the position of the shadow cast by the cart;
5. moving the cart would not change the color of the carpet;
6. moving the cart would not change the mass of the cart;
7. moving the cart would change the distance between the cart and the Eiffel Tower;
8. moving the cart would change the distance between the power supply and the Eiffel Tower;
9. moving the cart would change the distance between the bomb and the Eiffel Tower;
10. moving the cart would not change the distance between the bomb and the power supply;
11. moving the cart would change the area of the triangle defined by the position of the bomb, the Eiffel Tower, and Stonehenge;
12. moving the cart . . .

This could go on forever, of course. A robot that had to consider all the possible effects of any action it was planning would never get around to engaging in any action at all. To solve this problem, the robot needs to know which of the possible side effects of its action are *relevant* and to consider only those relevant side effects. Obviously, the way to do this is not to generate the same infinitely long list of possible effects, and sort them into a list of relevant possible effects (1, 2, 3, 10 . . .) and irrelevant possible effects (4, 5, 6, 7, 8, 9, 11, 12 . . .). That just compounds the previous problem, adding more required processing before action. What the robot needs to do somehow is to know which effects of an action are relevant, without considering every possible effect. This is the frame problem. The problem is how a robot or computer could know what is relevant, without having to consider all the irrelevant things to decide they are irrelevant.

It is hard to imagine how a robot or computer program could solve the frame problem. Yet, as we saw in the previous chapter, we seem to solve the frame problem effortlessly. Recall John Haugeland's (1979) sentence: "I left the raincoat in the bathtub because it was still wet." We understand this sentence, without even noticing the ambiguous reference of "it." We have all the information we need to know that "it" refers to the raincoat, and are not distracted by any irrelevant information. We certainly don't seem to do so the way the robot just discussed tried to plan its action: by explicitly considering all of our knowledge, eliminating the irrelevant bits, and using our knowledge of porcelain, upholstery, evaporation, and so on to disambiguate the referent of the pronoun. The frame problem is sometimes taken to exemplify the failings of the rationalist research in artificial intelligence and cognitive science that Dreyfus criticized. As Kiverstein (2012) points out, any successor to rationalist cognitive science can argue for its worth by showing that, unlike rationalist computational theories of cognition, it has the resources to solve the frame problem. In the rest of this chapter, we will consider several partly overlapping approaches in cognitive science inspired by phenomenology.

13.2 Radical embodied cognitive science

As noted in Chapter 10, Gibsonian ecological psychology needs a way to distinguish between affordances and invitations (Withagen et al. 2012; Rietveld 2008). Why do we act on so few of the affordances that are available to us? Why do we even notice so few of those affordances? Gibson was aware of this issue for his ecological psychology. He was also aware that calling on an inner homunculus deciding what to do was not an option available to him. Moreover, the frame problem indicates that calling on an inner homunculus (like a computer program with representations of the world) does not help. In trying to explain action in a way that does not demand an inner agent using sensory representations to develop motor representations, Gibson (1979, p. 225) says that "the rules that govern behavior are not like laws enforced by an authority or decisions made by a commander: behavior is regular without being regulated. The question is how this can be." Gibson's solution to this problem, like his solution to most problems, was in terms of the environment surrounding the animal: he argued that the information in the surrounding environment was sufficient to control behavior (without, that is, mentally added information, computation, or inference, and without a mentally represented plan). Kugler, Kelso, and Turvey (1980) asked how that information could actually generate the action. Their answer is that human action is *self-organizing*, and therefore subject to the same kind of mathematical modeling that one applies to self-organizing systems in other sciences. A self-organizing system is a system that exhibits regularities that arise without a plan or leader, but emerge from the interactions of the parts of the system. The idea that human action is self-organizing prompted a recent resurgence of interest in *dynamical systems theory* in psychology. Chemero (2009) calls this combination of ecological psychology with dynamical systems theory "radical embodied cognitive science." We will use that name to mark the distinction between Gibson's own ecological psychology and today's version of it. The key point is that ecological psychology plus dynamical systems theory (i.e., radical embodied cognitive science) can explain the distinction between affordances and invitations, while ecological psychology alone cannot. Before explaining how radical embodied cognitive science solves this version of the frame problem, we will explain what dynamical systems theory is, and how it is used in cognitive science.

13.3 Dynamical systems theory

Any explanatory framework for Gibsonian ecological psychology has to have two features. First, it must take perceiving and acting to be tightly connected to one another. Recall that from Gibson's point of view, perception is geared toward guiding action, and often involves action. We move our eyes and heads and torsos to see what is behind the table, and this movement is part and parcel of the seeing. Second, it cannot work by ascribing representations and computational processes. That is, neither the results of perceiving nor the causes of actions should be internal representations of the world. Like all the phenomenologists we have considered, ecological psychologists are anti-representationalists. Dynamical systems theory has both these features. Dynamicists take cognitive agents to be dynamical systems, best explained using the tools of dynamical systems theory. A *dynamical system* is a set of quantitative variables changing continually, concurrently, and interdependently over time in accordance with dynamical laws described by some set of equations. Most things that change over time are dynamical systems in this sense. The use of dynamical systems theory as an explanatory tool in psychology takes the tools that are used to explain how things change over time in other sciences, such as physics or biology, and applies them to perception, action, and cognition. That is to say, perception, action, and cognition are explained using calculus. (See van Gelder [1998] or Chemero [2009] for detailed accounts.) Differential equations are used to explain the ways that variables change over time. Suppose we use the variable s to describe the distance of a train from Philadelphia. The first differential of that variable, symbolized as $\dot{s}$ or $\frac{ds}{dt}$, is the rate at which the train's distance from Philadelphia is changing, that is, its velocity. The second differential, symbolized as $\ddot{s}$ or $\frac{d^2s}{dt^2}$, is the rate at which the train's velocity is changing, that is, its acceleration. The equations that determine the rates of change or accelerations will have other symbols in them that are assumed to remain fixed. These are called parameters. When dynamical systems theory is applied to cognitive science, the interest is in finding differential equations in which the variables and parameters are relevant to perception, action, and cognition.

The use of dynamical systems theory as a modeling tool plays several crucial roles in combination with ecological psychology. First, and perhaps most importantly, it does what modeling does throughout the sciences: it bridges the gaps between abstract theorizing and concrete data that can be gathered in the lab. Gibson's theories of the relationships among perceiving, acting, and the environment are abstract, as are the theories of the other phenomenologists we have discussed. It is far from obvious in many cases how one might test them, or put them to work in the lab. Dynamical systems theory is easily applicable to real data. Second, ecological psychologists require an explanatory tool that can span the agent–environment border. Dynamical systems theory is especially appropriate for radical embodied cognitive science because single dynamical systems can have parameters inside and outside an organism. With it, we can explain the behavior of the agent in its environment over time as coupled dynamical systems, using something like the following equations, from Beer (1995):

$$\textit{Equations 1 and 2:}$$
$$\dot{X}_A = A(X_A; S(X_E))$$
$$\dot{X}_E = E(X_E; M(X_A))$$

where A and E are dynamical systems, modeling the organism and its environment, respectively, and $S(X_E)$ and $M(X_A)$ are coupling functions, connecting environmental variables to organismic parameters and organismic variables to environmental parameters, respectively. Although we tend to think of the organism and environment as separate, they are best thought of as forming just one unified system, U. Rather than describing the way external (and internal) factors cause changes in the organism's behavior, such a model would explain the way U, the system as a whole, unfolds over time. (See Figure 13.1.) This feature of dynamical models makes them appropriate tools to combine with Gibson's ecological psychology. Dynamical models are also useful, as we will see below, for doing cognitive science inspired by Heidegger and Merleau-Ponty.

The most widely discussed example of a dynamical model in cognitive science is the Haken–Kelso–Bunz (HKB) model. The roots of the HKB model are found in a suggestion by Kugler, Kelso, and Turvey (1980)

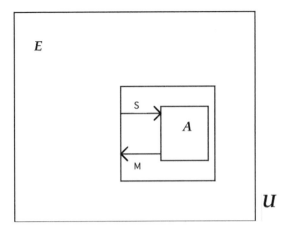

Figure 13.1 A unified system. Source: Based on Beer 1995

to the effect that limbs in coordinated actions could be understood as nonlinearly coupled oscillators whose coupling requires energy to maintain and therefore tends to dissipate after a time. In the context of this suggestion, Kelso performed experiments on finger wagging. The results were then modeled by Haken, Kelso, and Bunz (1985). Participants in these experiments were asked to wag their index fingers left to right along with a metronome, and were found to be able to produce only two stable patterns of coordination. In one, called *in-phase* or *relative phase 0*, the fingers approach one another at the midline of the body; in the other, called *out-of-phase* or *relative phase .5*, the fingers move simultaneously to the left, then to the right. As subjects were asked to wag their fingers out of phase at gradually increasing rates, they eventually were unable to do so, and slipped into in-phase wagging.

The mathematical model of this behavior, the HKB model, is a *potential* function, where potential V(f) is a measure of the stability of the system, with its two oscillating parts (wagging fingers) at relative phase f. The simplest potential function that will capture all of the data on finger wagging is:

Equation 3: $V(\phi) = -A\cos\phi - B\cos2\phi$

This formula can be visualized as shown in Figure 13.2. To understand the graph, it must be imagined as on the surface of a tube. That is, relative phase 0 and relative phase 1 are actually the same points on the graph. In the graph, the potential V has two minima: a deep one at relative phase 0 = 1, and a shallower one at relative phase .5. These

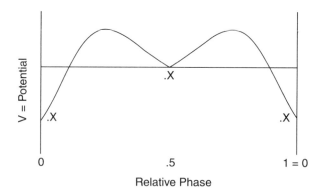

Figure 13.2 The HKB model. Source: Based on Haken et al 1985

are called attractors, states toward which the system tends. This graph accounts for the stability of the system when fingers are wagged at these relative phases, and the lack of stability at any other relative phases. Put differently, the graph shows the degree of difficulty of maintaining coordination at all possible values of relative phase. The deep well at 0 = 1 and the shallower one at .5 indicate that these are the relative phases to which the system tends. Increasing the rate of finger wagging changes the shape of the graph. As the rate increases, the minimum at .5 disappears, leaving only one well, at relative phase 0=1. At slower rates, this field has two attractors, that is, states toward which the system will move. This means that any finger wagging will tend to be stable only when one of these values for relative phase is maintained. But as the rate increases (and passes what HKB call the *critical point*), the shallower attractor at .5 disappears, so the only remaining attractor is the deeper one at relative phase 0. Then finger wagging at higher rates will tend to be stable only when it is in phase. This is, it turns out, not just true of wagging fingers: any coordinated movement of symmetric limbs (arm waving, leg swinging, etc.) works the same way.

Equation 3 can be combined with the first temporal derivative of f,

$$Equation\ 4:\ d\phi/dt = -dV/d\phi,$$

to yield this motion equation for relative phase:

$$Equation\ 5:\ d\phi/dt = -A\sin\phi - 2B\sin2\phi.$$

Equation 5 describes the way relative phase ϕ will change, given its current value. The ratio B/A is a *control parameter*, assumed to vary inversely with frequency of oscillation, which determines the nature of the change in behavior of the system. That is, B/A determines the shape of the phase space, the layout of attractors and repellers.

The HKB model is an example of a general strategy for explaining behavior. It first observes patterns of macroscopic behavior; then seeks collective variables (like relative phase) and parameters (like rate) that govern the behavior; finally, it searches for the simplest mathematical function that accounts for the behavior. Because complicated dynamical systems (like the one involving the muscles, portions of the central nervous system, ears, and metronome in the finger-wagging task) self-organize and so have a tendency to behave like much simpler systems, one will often be able to model these systems in terms of extremely simple functions, with only a few easily observable parameters. The HKB model makes a series of specific predictions. First, it predicts that as rates increase, experimental subjects will be unable to maintain out-of-phase performance. Second, even at slow rates, only relative phases of 0 and .5 will be stable. Third, the behavior should exhibit *critical fluctuations*: as the rate approaches the critical value, attempts to maintain out-of-phase performance will result in erratic fluctuations of relative phase. Fourth, the behavior should exhibit critical slowing down: at rates near the critical value, disruptions from out-of-phase performance should take longer to correct than at slower rates. Each of these predictions was borne out in the experiments by Haken, Kelso, and Bunz.

Readers might be wondering at this point what finger movements have to do with human experience. By designing experiments with the ideas of phenomenologists in mind from the beginning, radical embodied cognitive science does what Gallagher and Zahavi (2008) call "front-loading phenomenology." To front-load phenomenology, one takes the insights developed by phenomenologists into account when designing experiments, and even subjects those insights to empirical test. As noted above, the key for Kugler, Kelso, and Turvey and for Haken, Kelso, and Bunz was to answer Gibson's question about how action could be regular, without an internal homunculus acting as the action regulator. Although the initial task invented by Kelso seems strange, it did allow for scientific studies of action that satisfied Gibson's theories. Finger wagging is an action, but it can be explained without recourse to planning. More importantly, in the years since Kelso's first experiments, the basic HKB model and explanatory framework has now been pushed well beyond finger wagging. Radical embodied cognitive scientists have used variants of the HKB model to explain several other features of motor control and the cognitive modulation of motor control (Treffner and Turvey 1995; Shockley and Turvey 2005); they have used it to explain language processing and production (Port 2003); they have used it to study phenomena such as learning, attention, and intention (Scholz and Kelso 1990; Amazeen, Sternad, and Turvey 1996); they have used it to do social psychology (Schmidt, Carello, and Turvey 1990; Richardson et al. 2007; Harrison and Richardson 2009); they have used it to do neuroscience, and especially to study the neuroscience of conscious experience (Kelso et al. 1998; Varela et al. 2001; Freeman 2006; see below). (For detailed review, see Kelso [1995] or Chemero [2009].) In each case, these scientists have shown that purposeful action can exhibit regularities that are not caused by the plans of an internal regulator. And they have done so, specifically, by front-loading phenomenology.

By now, the HKB model and its successors are established tools in cognitive science. These dynamical models work, as we have said several times now, by assuming that thinking, experiencing, acting humans are self-organizing dynamical systems that comprise portions of their brains, bodies, and tools. This assumption is the key to the way that radical embodied cognitive science avoids the frame problem. Self-organizing systems have their organization without a plan or controller. They can do so by using energy from their surroundings to create patterns. Consider, for example, the whirlpool pattern that forms when a toilet is flushed. The water molecules temporarily move in a coordinated way that is very atypical of water molecules. They can exhibit this pattern of behavior because potential energy is released when the toilet is flushed. This energy enables the pattern to form and last until the energy is dissipated, after which the water molecules go back to their more typical behavior. The same is true for the finger-movement patterns explained by the HKB model – they require energy to be maintained, and last only as long as energy is being expended to keep them in place. Self-organizing systems, like the whirlpool and moving fingers and the psychological phenomena mentioned in the previous paragraph, tend to organize themselves into very *particular* patterns. This is often put by saying that they have built-in or *endogenous* activity. Consider what happens if you hold a stick in the water before you flush the toilet. The water will still form a whirlpool, whose shape will be changed somewhat by the presence of the stick. Technically, this is put by saying that the endogenous activity of the whirlpool is *perturbed* by the stick. A passing breeze, or turning off the bathroom light, on the other hand, will not affect the shape of the whirlpool at all. Smashing the toilet bowl, however, would break the whirlpool apart. Similarly, a finger-wagging human has endogenous dynamics, which allow just a few possible modes of finger wagging, and those dynamics are perturbed by changing the rate or rhythm at which the participant is asked to move and are disrupted completely by the fire alarm, but would not be affected by the chair in the corner or the sound of the air conditioner.

Now imagine a human engaged in a task, like building a bookcase. From the point of view of radical embodied cognitive science, that human, plus her tools, will comprise a self-organizing dynamical system engaged in a particular task. This means that the human-plus-tools engaged in this task will have endogenous dynamics, making it perturbable only by certain things. This, finally, is how radical embodied cognitive science solves the ecological version of the frame problem. There are more or less infinitely many affordances available at any moment, but very few of them actually invite action. When the self-organized human-plus-tool system is engaged in building a bookcase, it can be perturbed only by the task-relevant affordances. That is, the system will be responsive to the invitations at the tool bench, but not to the mere affordances elsewhere in the room. More generally, when a human or other animal is engaged in a task, it organizes itself into a temporary, special-purpose dynamical system – a bike rider, a finger wagger, a roadkill scavenger – and as such it is only sensitive to the affordances that are relevant to that temporary, special-purpose dynamical system. Only those relevant affordances that can perturb the temporary, special-purpose dynamical system are experienced as invitations.

13.4 Heideggerian cognitive science

At the end of Chapter 11, we discussed research in what Preston (1993) called Heideggerian artificial intelligence. At around the same time, Michael Wheeler published a prescient paper called "From robots to Rothko" (1996), in which he argued for a *Heideggerian cognitive science*. Like radical embodied cognitive science, Heideggerian cognitive science relies heavily on dynamical systems theory as an explanatory tool. Indeed, Wheeler bases his Heideggerian cognitive science on experiments by Husbands, Harvey, and Cliff (1993) combining dynamical systems theory with robotics. Husbands, Harvey, and Cliff used a simulated evolutionary process to design a control system for a simple robot. The resulting control system was an artificial neural network that Wheeler describes as looking like a bowl of spaghetti, and whose activity cannot be plausibly seen as housing representations of the robot's environment. Indeed, the network is best understood as a large feedback loop, with one particularly noisy neuron – neuron 11 – at its center (see Figure 13.3). This neuron is noisy in that its output to other neurons is not very closely determined by the inputs it gets from other neurons. Suppose there is no

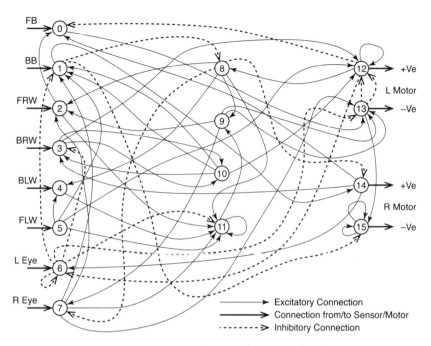

Figure 13.3 A control system for a simple robot
Source: Husbands, Harvey, and Cliff 1993

input to the robot's sensors. If the neurons were not noisy, the neurons connected to the sensors would pass the value 0 to other neurons, which would continue to be passed around the network, leading to a quiet network. Now suppose one of the neurons is noisy. If the input to the network is 0, the neurons connected to the sensors will pass 0 to other neurons, most of which will continue to pass that lack of activation around the network. However, the one noisy neuron will not pass 0 to its neighbors; instead it will pass 0 ± some constant, say .3. The neurons connected to the noisy neuron will get inputs of ±.3, which they will pass along to the neurons they are connected to. Because the network is a feedback loop, this activity, which originated in the network itself, will propagate through the network repeatedly. This means that the network will have endogenous activity that is independent of any input to the sensors, just like the self-organized dynamical systems described in the previous section. Wheeler (1996) argued that this shows that the robot's neural network doesn't represent the world, and that this recommends a Heideggerian approach in the cognitive sciences.

In the decade that followed these early papers by Preston and Wheeler, many of the themes they discuss moved to the forefront of cognitive science. Cognitive scientists – typically inspired by Gibson and Brooks rather than Heidegger – began to focus on the importance of the body and action in cognition. (See the discussion of 4E cognition in Chapter 12.) By the time Wheeler wrote a book-length work on Heideggerian cognitive science in 2005, there were established scientific research programs that he could draw on. From research in 4E cognition, Wheeler argues that cognitive science is becoming Heideggerian, but that this is happening because of issues in the science itself, rather than from engagement with Heidegger's ideas. Wheeler argues that this Heideggerian approach to cognitive science is committed to engaged intelligence as the primary kind of human intelligence, and that this intelligence extends across the brain, body, and environment. Moreover, the proper explanatory mode in Heideggerian cognitive science is dynamical. However, Wheeler explicitly rejects Heidegger's anti-representationalism. He argues that the practice of embodied cognitive science, which he identifies as Heideggerian cognitive science, involves attributing *action-oriented representations* to animals engaged in skillful tasks in their environment. Action-oriented representations differ from the representations posited by traditional cognitive science in that they are not sentence-like, they are not of the objective world, and they are geared to particular actions. As Wheeler puts it, they have a "content-sparse, action-specific, egocentric, context-dependent" character (2005, p. 253). In essence, action-oriented representations are representations of affordances. So rather than needing to combine the representation of the bottle in the refrigerator with stored representations of the connection between bottles and beer, the connections between beer and thirst, the present state of thirst, the social strictures concerning beer drinking and time of day, and the actual time of day, an agent can simply have the action-oriented representation of drinkability here-now. Wheeler accepts action-oriented representations both because they are part of the practice of embodied cognitive science, and because he thinks that Heidegger scholars overestimate the amount of time we spend coping smoothly. Dreyfus, among others, suggests that smooth coping with the ready-to-hand is both ontologically foundational and the majority of human experience. Wheeler agrees with the former, but not the latter. For Wheeler, action-oriented representations are the key to understanding our frequent switches between smoothly coping with the ready-to-hand and in-the-moment problem solving with the unready-to-hand.

For others interested in Heideggerian cognitive science, such as Dreyfus (2007) and Rietveld (2008, 2012), Wheeler's reliance on action-oriented representations puts his view at odds with Heidegger's phenomenology and makes it incapable of solving the frame problem. Dreyfus and Rietveld argue that understanding the mind in terms of representations, even action-oriented representations, is the cause of the frame problem. They both think that the key to solving the frame problem in a Heideggerian cognitive science is to be found in Freeman's anti-representationalist neurodynamics (Freeman 2000, 2006). (Note that we list Freeman among the radical embodied cognitive scientists in the previous section.) Freeman understands the brain as a self-organizing dynamical system, one that at any moment has endogenous activity that has been shaped by all prior experiences. For example, a history of inter-actions with odors and foods sets up the rabbit olfactory bulb (which Freeman studies) so that it has nonlinear endogenous dynamics, with several attractors. This endogenous activity, with these attractors, is the background against which any present odor is experienced. Suppose an experienced rabbit is presented with an odor, say ammonia. The odor will cause some sensory activity at the rabbit's chemosensitive cells, and this activity will cause the olfactory bulb activity to enter one of its attractor states. This is the only effect of the sensory activity – nudging the olfactory bulb into an attractor. The rabbit's response to the odor is determined by which attractor the olfactory bulb enters. Immediately subsequent experience, such as receiving food or a punishment, or meet-ing a conspecific, then shapes the set of attractors in the olfactory bulb, so they will be subtly different the next time the rabbit experiences an odor. This is how the rabbit learns.

Freeman argues that it would be a mistake to view the activity of the olfactory bulb as representing the odor. Indeed, thinking that it had to be a representation initially hindered his own understanding of what the olfactory bulb was doing (Skarda and Freeman 1987; Freeman and Skarda 1990). The olfactory bulb's endogenous dynamics is the background against which any odor is encountered. The activity of the bulb is perturbed by the odor, and it settles into one of the attractors that were available before the odorant molecules came into contact with the rabbit's sensor cells. That is, the set of olfactory experiences that are possible for the rabbit is already in place before any particular odor is encountered. The state of the olfactory bulb at any moment does not represent any odor. Instead, it reflects the consequences of the rabbit's encounters with every odor it has experienced. A rabbit that receives an electric shock after smelling carrots will have a different set of attractors from that of a rabbit that just gets carrots. The attractors available in the endogenous activity of the olfactory bulb are determined by the *signifi-cance* of the odors that the rabbit has encountered. This is how Dreyfus and Rietveld think that Heideggerian cognitive science evades the frame problem. The endogenous activity of the brain does not represent the world, and then attach significance to only a few of the representations. Instead, the brain's endogenous activity is such that interactions with the world perturb it, and because these interactions perturb it into attractors that exist because of prior experiences interacting with the world, they are guaranteed to be significant.

We prefer Dreyfus' and Rietveld's interpretation of Heidegger to Wheeler's, and we prefer radical embodied cognitive science over embodied cognitive science. Which of these will turn out to be more useful as a scientific approach to understanding human experience is an empirical matter. In the meantime, Heideggerian cognitive scientists are accumulating empirical results.

We close this section with a discussion of experiments working toward experimental confirmation of some important parts of Heidegger's phenomenology. Dotov, Nie, and Chemero (2010) designed experiments aimed at empirically demonstrating the transition from readiness-to-hand to unreadiness-to-hand in interactions with tools. To gather empirical evidence for this transition, they relied on dynamical modeling that uses the presence of 1/f scaling or pink noise as a signal of sound physiological functioning (e.g., West 2006). Pink noise or 1/f scaling is a kind of not-quite-random, correlated noise, half way between genuine randomness (white noise) and a drunkard's walk, in which each fluctuation is constrained by the prior one (brown noise). Pink noise or 1/f scaling is often described as a fractal structure in a time series, in which the variability at a short time scale is correlated with variability at a longer time scale. (See Riley and Holden [2012] for an overview.) The connection between sound physiological functioning and 1/f scaling allows for a prediction related to Heidegger's transition: when experimental subjects are coping smoothly with a ready-to-hand tool, the human-plus-tool forms a single, functional system. This human-plus-tool system should exhibit 1/f scaling.

Participants in the study played a simple video game in which they used a mouse to control a cursor on a monitor. Their task was to move the cursor so as to "herd" moving objects to a circle on the center of the monitor. At some point during the trial, the connection between the mouse and cursor was temporarily disrupted, so that movements of the cursor did not correspond to movements of the mouse, before returning to normal. As predicted, the hand–mouse movements of the participants exhibited 1/f scaling while the video game was working correctly. The 1/f scaling decreased, almost to the point of exhibiting pure white noise, during the mouse perturbation. So, while participants were smoothly playing the video game, they were part of a human–mouse–screen system that had the same pattern of variability as a well-functioning physiological system. When Dotov, Nie, and Chemero temporarily disrupted performance, that pattern of variability temporarily disappeared. This is evidence that the mouse was experienced as ready-to-hand while it was working correctly, and became unready-to-hand during the perturbation. (See Dotov, Nie, and Chemero [2010] for more details.) By front-loading phenomenology, Dotov, Nie, and Chemero were able to derive testable consequences and then gather empirical evidence for Heidegger's phenomenology.

In a second set of experiments, Dotov et al. (2017) used a similar method to demonstrate the transition from readiness-to-hand to presence-at-hand. They had the participants play a more difficult version of the same game, in which they had to herd multiple objects. The researchers also introduced a more severe perturbation of the connection between the mouse and the corresponding object on the monitor. In the perturbation of the first set of experiments, the cursor appeared offset from its intended location in a random direction, looking as if it bounced around the monitor. In the second set of experiments, the onscreen cursor stopped responding to mouse movements for increasingly long intervals, and then stopped responding altogether. By the end of the trial, the mouse was genuinely unusable, and should have been experienced as present-at-hand. Heidegger said that present-at-hand entities are experienced as objects with properties, and Dotov et al. found that participants who experienced this more severe perturbation remembered more functionally irrelevant features of the task setup (the colors of the herded objects, the monitor, etc.) than those who did not have a perturbation of the connection between mouse and cursor. This is a confirmation of the transition from experiencing working tools as ready-to-hand to experiencing broken tools as presence-at-hand. By front-loading phenomenology, Dotov et al. were able to derive testable consequences and then gather empirical evidence for Heidegger's phenomenology.

We have been focusing on Heidegerian cognitive science, but it is not just Heidegger that has inspired empirical research in cognitive science. A few examples follow.

As discussed above, Gibsonian ecological psychologists brought dynamical systems theory to cognitive scientists, and have been engaged in a flourishing research program since the 1980s. Recently, there have been several attempts to create an ecological neuroscience (Anderson 2014; Pezzulo and Cisek 2016; Hasson, Nastase, and Goldstein 2020).

In the 1990s, Varela was calling for a "neurophenomenology" that would combine phenomenological reflection, dynamical systems theory models, and neuroscientific experimentation, and speculating about the

way we could neuroscientifically study Husserl's theory of time consciousness (Varela 1996, 1999). Neurophenomenological methodology
was solidified soon thereafter (Varela et al. 2001; Lutz et al. 2002) in
a series of experiments on the relationship between large-scale neural
synchronization and first-person experience.

As we saw in the previous chapter, in the twenty-first century enactivism has inspired work in artificial intelligence and artificial life. Froese and
Ziemke's (2009) article "Enactive artificial intelligence: Investigating the
systemic organization of life and mind" serves as a manifesto for future
enactivist artificial intelligence. De Jaegher and Di Paolo's (2007) work
on participatory sense-making has inspired an empirical research program
on what is called "perceptual crossing" (Auvray, Lenay, and Stewart
2009). In perceptual crossing experiments, pairs of participants in separate rooms move avatars around in a virtual environment, searching for
one another with only minimal tactile feedback (a vibrating touch pad).
Moving an avatar over three things in the environment causes the touch
pad to vibrate: these three are stationary beacons, the other participant,
and the other participant's shadow, which lags the other participant by a
few seconds. Participants in perceptual crossing are easily able to find one
another by moving back and forth over something that causes the touch
pad to vibrate: beacons are stationary; shadows move, but don't respond;
the other participant does respond. Most trials end with the participants
recognizing one another by repeatedly engaging in the same kind of feedback that we see in the "hallway dance" in Chapter 12 (De Jaegher, Di
Paolo, and Gallagher 2010). These findings have been replicated repeatedly, including in artificial intelligence (Froese and Di Paolo 2010) and
virtual reality (Froese, Iizuka, and Ikegami 2014) contexts.

The advent of virtual reality in the cognitive sciences, beginning in the
2010s, has been a great opportunity for investigating phenomenological
ideas empirically. In virtual reality, we can actually manipulate the coupling between movements and perception, changing what Merleau-Ponty
called the lived body instantaneously. By turning up visual gain (i.e.,
making a small head movement look like a larger head movement) in a
virtual environment, we can make anyone feel capable of dunking a bas-
ketball. By decoupling the relationship between where something looks
to be and where it sounds to be, we can explore the relationship between
visual and auditory localization, each of which requires different bodily
movements. For example, Sanches de Oliveira, Riehm, and Annand
(2019) did just this in an effort to investigate what Merleau-Ponty (1945)
called the "sensori-motor unity of the body," especially his claim that the
senses are unified. In a virtual environment, participants had to track a
moving virtual buzzing bee, which was sometimes visible and sometimes

not visible; the researchers then looked for, and found, differences in the 1/f scaling of the participants' head movements when they had both audio and visual information about the location, only audio information, and no information (the buzzing was in mono, so provided no information about the bee's location). In virtual environments, it is possible to make features of embodiment into independent variables, manipulable by the experimenter. Going forward, virtual environments will be crucial tools in phenomenological cognitive science.

13.5 The future of scientific phenomenology

These approaches to phenomenology-inspired cognitive science are much more alike than they are different. They all focus on the perception and action of organisms-in-their-environments; they all utilize dynamical models as a crucial explanatory tool; they are skeptical of the explanatory usefulness of mental representations. Perhaps most importantly, they are similar in that they are all on the ascent within cognitive science, attracting increasing attention, adherents, and grant funding over the past two decades. Although there are differences, there is also a significant degree of mutual admiration and overlap among the practitioners of different varieties of scientific phenomenology, and they regularly cite one another's works.

Even with these overlaps, there is some tension among phenomenological cognitive scientists, especially between ecological psychologists and enactivists. This tension mirrors the differences between Gibson's realist ontology and Merleau-Ponty's existential ontology, discussed at the end of Chapter 8. Indeed, enactivists have been critical of ecological psychology (e.g., Varela, Thompson, and Rosch 1991; Di Paolo, Buhrmann, and Barandiaran 2017), and ecological psychologists have been critical of enactivism (e.g., Swenson and Turvey 1991). Moreover, ecological psychology and enactivism differ in emphasis. Ecological psychology focuses on the nature of the environment that animals perceive and act in; enactivism focuses on the organism as an agent. This suggests that combining the two might provide a complete picture of cognition: an enactive story of agency, and an ecological story of the environment with which the agent is coupled. Indeed, such a unification has been called for by many philosophers (Chemero 2009; McGann 2014; Baggs and Chemero 2018, 2020; Kiverstein and Rietveld 2018). A special journal issue of *Frontiers in Cognitive Science*, published in 2020, focuses on the possibility of reconciling these two forms of radical embodied cognitive science (Di Paolo et al. 2020).

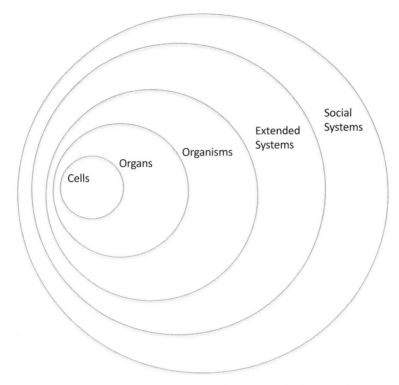

Figure 13.4 Cognition as a nested, self-organized, dynamical system
Source: Authors' own

This conceivable reconciliation points to the possibility of a more unified future for scientific phenomenology, centered on the idea of nested,
self-organized, dynamical systems (Chemero 2008; Kelso 2009). (See
Figure 13.4.) At the foundation of this conception is the autopoietic
cell. The cell is a self-organizing system, that maintains itself. Just as
being components in a self-organized whirlpool affects the behavior of
the water molecules that are its components, so the cells that are the
components of organs are constrained in their activity by being components of organs. That is, organs, such as livers or brains, are comparably
macro-scaled, self-organized systems with cells as their components.
Just like cells, they are autonomous systems with endogenous dynamics.
Similarly, organisms are self-organized systems, with organs as components. There are also self-organized organism-plus-tool systems, such
as the human-plus-computer system studied by Dotov et al. Moreover,
there are self-organized *social* systems, with individual humans as components (Schmidt, Carello, and Turvey 1990; Richardson et al. 2007;

Walton et al. 2018). Each of these self-organized systems, from the cell up to the social, will be temporary; each will exist only as long as there is energy expended to maintain its endogenous activity by constraining the activity of the comparatively micro components that comprise it. These self-organized systems will be explained using dynamical systems theory, and we should expect 1/f scaling at every scale in the nested hierarchy. We should also expect them to be explainable without ascribing representations at any scale.

This vision of the future of scientific phenomenology captures many of the features that Heidegger, Merleau-Ponty, Gibson, and the enactivists take to be central to human experience. Humans are lived bodies, and their way of being includes both transparent use of equipment and being with others in that their connections to equipment and to other humans are not different in kind from the connections that allow them to be unified systems themselves. That is, human organisms are self-organized systems of components just as humans-plus-tools and humans-plus-humans are. There is also one way in which today's practitioners of scientific phenomenology disagree with Heidegger and Merleau-Ponty. It is now widely assumed that the relevant concept of experience also applies to non-human animals. (Wheeler [2005] makes this point forcefully.) In this respect, future scientific phenomenology will be more naturalistic than the views of Heidegger and Merleau-Ponty, and more in line with Gibson's or enactivism's version of phenomenology. This concession matches the now-widespread acceptance of the evolutionary continuity of humans with other species, and is essential if future scientific phenomenology is to be scientific. The success of this future phenomenology depends upon the willingness of cognitive scientists to take phenomenology seriously and their willingness to collaborate with philosophers. Many of the scientists discussed in this chapter actively collaborate and publish works co-authored with philosophers. There is every reason to believe that these philosophers and scientists will continue to front-load phenomenology in the design of their experiments and in the analysis of their data, and every reason to be confident in the future of phenomenological cognitive science.

Key terms

action-oriented representations – mental representations that simultaneously describe the world and the appropriate behavioral response to it. Action-oriented representations are often seen as representations of affordances.

dynamical systems theory – a branch of calculus focused on change over time.

endogenous dynamics – a built-in tendency of a system to behave in a particular pattern when not perturbed by the environment.

frame problem – an outstanding problem for artificial intelligence concerned with relevance. How is a machine to know which of the roughly infinite number of possible actions is relevant at any time, without checking them all to see if they are relevant? In contrast, humans just know what is relevant.

front-loading phenomenology – designing scientific experiments specifically in order to test hypotheses concerning phenomenology.

Haken–Kelso–Bunz (HKB) model – an early dynamical model of self-organized human behavior.

Heideggerian cognitive science – a variety of cognitive science inspired by Heidegger's phenomenological philosophy.

neurophenomenology – the use of neuroscientific methods to test phenomenological hypotheses.

pink noise – the same as 1/f scaling.

radical embodied cognitive science – a combination of Gibsonian ecological psychology and dynamical systems theory. Unlike embodied cognitive science, radical embodied cognitive science denies that cognition is a form of computation.

self-organization – the tendency of physical systems that are open to the flow of energy to sometimes spontaneously form ordered states.

wide computationalism – a computationalist version of embodied, extended cognition, in which features of the environment play a role in the computational processes that make up cognition.

1/f scaling – a pattern of variability that is indicative of a properly functioning physiological system. The presence of 1/f scaling in a system's activity shows that the system's parts are so tightly coupled with one another that they form a single, unified system.

Further reading

Chemero, A. (2009). *Radical Embodied Cognitive Science*. Cambridge, MA: MIT Press.

Di Paolo, E., A. Chemero, M. Heras-Escribano, and M. McGann, eds. (2020). *Enactivism and Ecological Psychology: Convergences and Complementarities*. Special Issue of *Frontiers in Psychology*. https://www.frontiersin.org/research-topics/10973/enaction-and-ecological-psychology-convergences-and-complementarities

Gallagher, S. and D. Zahavi (2008). *The Phenomenological Mind*. New York: Routledge.

Kelso, J. A. S. (1995). *Dynamic Patterns*. Cambridge, MA: MIT Press.

Wheeler, M. (2005). *Reconstructing the Cognitive World*. Cambridge, MA: MIT Press.

References

Agre, P. (1997). *Computation and Human Experience*. New York: Oxford.

Agre, P. and D. Chapman (1987). "Pengi: An implementation of a theory of activity." *Proceedings of the Sixth National Conference on Artificial Intelligence*, 268–72. Menlo Park, CA: AAAI Press.

Alcoff, L. M. (2006). *Visible Identities: Race, Gender, and the Self*. New York: Oxford University Press.

Amazeen, E. L., D. Sternad, and M. T. Turvey (1996). "Predicting the nonlinear shift of stable equilibria in interlimb rhythmic coordination." *Human Movement Science*, 15: 521–42.

Amazeen, E. L. and M. T. Turvey (1996). "Weight perception and the haptic size–weight illusion are functions of the inertia tensor." *Journal of Experimental Psychology: Human Perception and Performance*, 22: 213–32.

Anderson, M. (2014). *After Phrenology*. Cambridge, MA: MIT Press.

Ash, M. (1998). *Gestalt Psychology in German Culture 1890–1967: Holism and the Quest for Objectivity*. Cambridge: Cambridge University Press.

Auvray, M., C. Lenay, and J. Stewart (2009). "Perceptual interactions in a minimalist virtual environment." *New Ideas in Psychology*, 27: 32–47.

Auvray, M. and E. Myin (2009). "Perception with compensatory devices: From sensory substitution to sensorimotor extension." *Cognitive Science*, 33(6): 1036–58.

Bach-y-Rita, P. and S. W. Kercel (2003). "Sensory substitution and the human–machine interface." *Trends in Cognitive Sciences*, 7(12): 541–6.

Baggs, E. and A. Chemero (2018). "Radical embodiment in two directions." *Synthese*. https://doi.org/10.1007/s11229-018-02020-9

Baggs, E. and A. Chemero (2020). "The third sense of environment," in J. B. Wagman and J. J. C. Blau (eds.), *Perception as Information Detection: Reflections on Gibson's Ecological Approach to Visual Perception*. New York: Taylor and Francis.

Beauvoir, S. de (1947/1976). *Ethics of Ambiguity*, trans. B. Frechtman. New York: Citadel Press.

– (1949/1984). *The Second Sex*, trans. H. M. Pashley. Harmondsworth: Penguin.

Beer, R. (1995). "Computational and dynamical languages for autonomous agents," in R. Port and T. van Gelder (eds.), *Mind as Motion*. Cambridge, MA: MIT Press.

Bettcher, T. (2012). "Trans women and the meaning of 'woman'," in N. Power, R. Halwani, and A. Soble (eds.), *The Philosophy of Sex: Contemporary Readings* (6th edn.). New York: Rowman & Littlefield.

Bickhard, M. (2013). "Toward a model of functional brain processes." Unpublished manuscript.

Blattner, W. (1999). *Heidegger's Temporal Idealism*. Cambridge: Cambridge University Press.

– (2006). *Heidegger's* Being and Time: *A Reader's Guide*. London: Continuum.

Brentano, F. (1874). *Psychologie vom Empirischen Standpunkte*. Leipzig: Von Duncker & Humblot.

Brooks, R. (1991). "Intelligence without representation." *Artificial Intelligence*, 47: 139–59.

Calogero, R. M., S. E. Tantleff-Dunn, and J. Thompson, eds. (2011). *Self-Objectification in Women: Causes, Consequences, and Counteractions*. Washington, DC: American Psychological Association.

Chalmers, D. (1996). *The Conscious Mind*. New York: Oxford University Press.

Chapman, D. (1991). *Vision, Instruction, Action*. Cambridge, MA: MIT Press.

Charles, E. (2012). *A New Look at New Realism: The Psychology and Philosophy of E. B. Holt*. Edison: Transaction.

Charpentier, A. (1891). "Analyse expérimentale de quelques elements de la sensation de poids." *Archives Physiologique Normals and Pathologiques*, 18: 79–87.

Chemero, A. (2008). "Self-organization, writ large." *Ecological Psychology*.

– (2009). *Radical Embodied Cognitive Science*. Cambridge, MA: MIT Press.

Chomsky, N. (1959). "A review of B. F. Skinner's *Verbal Behavior.*" *Language*, 35(1): 26–58.

– (1966). *Cartesian Linguistics: A Chapter in the History of Rationalist Thought.* New York: Harper and Row.

Clark, A. (1997). *Being There.* Cambridge, MA: MIT Press.

– (2000). *Mindware.* New York: Oxford University Press.

– (2013). *Mindware,* 2nd edn. New York: Oxford University Press.

Clark, A. and D. Chalmers (1998). "The extended mind." *Analysis*, 58(1): 7–19.

Clark, K. B. and M. P. Clark (1947). "Racial identification and preference among negro children," in E. L. Hartley (ed.), *Readings in Social Psychology.* New York: Holt, Reinhart, and Winston.

Conrad, K. (1933). "Das Körperschema: Eine kritische Studie und der Versuch einer Revision." *Zeitschrift für die gesamte Neurologie und Psychiatrie*, 147: 346–69.

Cope, D. (1996). *Experiments in Musical Intelligence.* Madison: A-R Editions.

Cuffari, E., E. Di Paolo, and H. De Jaegher (2015). "From participatory sense-making to language: There and back again." *Phenomenology and the Cognitive Sciences*, 14: 1089–125.

Cummins, F. (2018). *The Ground from Which We Speak.* Newcastle upon Tyne: Cambridge Scholars.

De Jaegher, H. and E. Di Paolo (2007). "Participatory sense-making." *Cognitive Systems Research*, 11: 367–77.

De Jaegher, H., E. Di Paolo, and S. Gallagher (2010). "Can social interaction constitute social cognition?" *Trends in Cognitive Sciences*, 14: 441–7.

Dennett, D. (1987). "Cognitive wheels: The frame problem in artificial intelligence," in Z. W. Pylyshyn (ed.), *The Robot's Dilemma: The Frame Problem in Artificial Intelligence.* Norwood: Ablex.

– (1991). *Consciousness Explained.* Boston: Little, Brown.

Descartes, R. (1641/1985). *Meditations on First Philosophy*, in *The Philosophical Writings of Descartes*, 2, trans. J. Cottingham, R. Stoothoff, and D. Murdoch. Cambridge: Cambridge University Press,

– (1644/1985). *Principles of Philosophy*, in *The Philosophical Writings of Descartes 1*, trans. J. Cottingham, R. Stoothoff, and D. Murdoch. Cambridge: Cambridge University Press.

– (1664/1985). *Treatise on Man*, in *The Philosophical Writings of Descartes 1*, trans. J. Cottingham, R. Stoothoff, and D. Murdoch. Cambridge: Cambridge University Press,

Dewey, J. (1896). "The reflex arc concept in psychology." *Psychological Review*, 3: 357–70.

Di Paolo, E. (2008). "Extended life." *Topoi*, 28: 9–21.

Di Paolo, E., T. Buhrmann, and X. Barandiaran (2017). *Sensorimotor Life: An Enactive Proposal.* New York: Oxford University Press.

Di Paolo, E., A. Chemero, M. Heras-Escribano, and M. McGann, eds. (2020). *Enactivism and Ecological Psychology: Convergences and Complementarities*. Special Issue of *Frontiers in Psychology*. https://www.frontiersin.org/research-topics/10973/enaction-and-ecological-psychology-convergences-and-complementarities

Di Paolo, E., E. Cuffari, and H. De Jaegher (2018). *Linguistic Bodies*. Cambridge, MA: MIT Press.

Dotov, D., L. Nie, and A. Chemero (2010). "A demonstration of the transition from readiness-to-hand to unreadiness-to-hand." *PLoSONE*, 5: e9433.

Dotov, D., L. Nie, K. Wojcik, A. Jinks, X. Yu, and A. Chemero (2017). "Cognitive and movement measures reflect the transition to presence-at-hand." *New Ideas in Psychology*, 45, 1–10.

Drayson, Z. (2010). "Extended cognition and the metaphysics of mind." *Cognitive Systems Research*, 4: 367–77.

Dreyfus, H. (1965). "Alchemy and artificial intelligence." Rand Paper P-3244.

– (1972/1979/1992). *What Computers (Still) Can't Do*. New York: Harper and Row.

– (2007). "Why Heideggerian AI failed, and why fixing it would require making it more Heideggerian." *Philosophical Psychology*, 20: 247–68.

Egbert, M. D., X. E. Barandiaran, and E. A. Di Paolo (2011). "Behavioral metabolution: The adaptive and evolutionary potential of metabolism-based chemotaxis." *Artificial Life*, 18: 1–25.

Ehrenfels, C. (1890/1988). "On Gestalt qualities," in B. Smith (ed. and trans.), *Foundations of Gestalt Theory*. Munich and Vienna: Philosophia, 1988. (Original work published as "Über Gestaltqualitäten,'Vierteljahrsschrift für wissenschaftliche'." *Philosophie*, 14, 1890: 249–92.)

Embree, L. (1980). "Merleau-Ponty's examination of Gestalt psychology." *Research in Phenomenology*, 10: 89–121.

– (2009). "Biographical sketch of Aron Gurwitsch," in A. Gurwitsch, *The Collected Works of Aron Gurwitsch (1901–1973). Volume I: Constitutive Phenomenology in Historical Perspective*, ed. J. García-Gómez. Dordrecht: Springer.

Fancher, R. (1995). *Pioneers of Psychology*, 3rd edn. New York: Norton.

Fanon, F. (1952/1967). *Black Skin, White Masks*, trans. C. L. Markmann. New York: Grove Press, 1967.

– (1961/1963). *The Wretched of the Earth*, trans C. Farrington. New York: Grove Weidenfeld, 1963.

Fechner, G. T. (1860/1912). *Elements of Psychophysics, Sections VII ("Measurement of Sensation") and XVI ("The Fundamental Formula and the Measurement Formula")*, trans. H. S. Langfeld. (Translation originally published in B. Rand (ed.), *The Classical Psychologists*. Boston: Houghton Mifflin, 1912.)

Fodor, J. (1980). "Methodological solipsism considered as a research strategy in cognitive science." *Behavioral and Brain Sciences*, 3: 63–109.

– (1987). *Psychosemantics*. Cambridge, MA: MIT Press.

Fredrickson, B. L. and T. Roberts (1997). "Objectification theory: Toward understanding women's lived experiences and mental health risks." *Psychology of Women Quarterly*, 21: 173–206.

Freeman, W. J. (2000). *Neurodynamics: An Exploration in Mesoscopic Brain Dynamics*. London: Springer.

– (2006). "Origin, structure, and role of background EEG activity. Part 4: Neural frame simulation." *Clinical Neurophysiology*, 117: 572–89.

Freeman, W. J. and C. Skarda (1990). "Representations: Who needs them?" in J. L. McGaugh, N. Weinberger, and G. Lynch (eds.), *Brain Organization and Memory Cells, Systems, and Circuits*. New York: Oxford University Press.

Frege, G. (1894). "Rezension von Dr. E. G. Husserl: Philosophie der Arithmetik. Psychologische und logische Untersuchung. Erster Band." *Zeitschrift für Philosophie und philosophische Kritik*, 103: 313–32. (Reprinted in *Kleine Schriften*, ed. I. Angelelli. Darmstadt: Wissenschaftliche Buchgesellschaft; Hildesheim: G. Olms. Trans. E. W. Kluge (1972) as "Review of Dr. E. Husserl's Philosophy of Arithmetic." *Mind*, 81(323): 321–37.)

Froese, T., and E. A. Di Paolo (2010). "Modelling social interaction as perceptual crossing: An investigation into the dynamics of the interaction process." *Connection Science*, 22: 43–68.

Froese, T., H. Iizuka, and T. Ikegami (2014). "Embodied social interaction constitutes social cognition in pairs of humans: A minimalist virtual reality experiment." *Scientific Reports*, 4, article 3672.

Froese, T. and T. Ziemke (2009). "Enactive artificial intelligence: Investigating the systemic organization of life and mind." *Artificial Intelligence*, 173: 466–500.

Fuchs, T. and H. De Jaegher (2009). "Enactive intersubjectivity: Participatory sense-making and mutual incorporation." *Phenomenology and the Cognitive Sciences*, 8: 465–86.

Gallagher, S. (2017). *Enactivist Interventions*. New York: Oxford University Press.

Gallagher, S. and D. Zahavi (2008). *The Phenomenological Mind*. New York: Routledge.

Gibson, J. J. (1950). *The Perception of the Visual World*. Boston: Houghton Mifflin.

– (1962). "Observations on active touch." *Psychological Review*, 69(6): 477–91.

– (1966). *The Senses Considered as Perceptual Systems*. Boston: Houghton Mifflin.

– (1967). "James J. Gibson," in E. G. Boring and G. Lindzey (eds.), *A History of Psychology in Autobiography. Vol. 5*. New York: Appleton-Century-Crofts.

– (1979). *The Ecological Approach to Visual Perception*. Boston: Houghton Mifflin.

Gibson, J. J. and L. Crooks (1938). "A theoretical field-analysis of automobile-driving." *The American Journal of Psychology*, 51: 453–71.

Gibson, J. J. and E. Gibson (1955). "Perceptual learning: Differentiation or enrichment?" *Psychological Review*, 62: 32–41.

Godfrey-Smith, P. (2001). "On the status and explanatory structure of developmental systems theory," in S. Oyama, P. Griffiths, and P. Gray (eds.), *Cycles of Contingency: Developmental Systems and Evolution*. Cambridge, MA: MIT Press.

Gordon, L. (2015). *What Fanon Said*. New York: Fordham University Press.

Guenther, L. (2020). "Critical phenomenology," in G. Weiss, A. Murphy, and G. Salamon (eds.), *50 Concepts for a Critical Phenomenology*. Chicago: Northwestern University Press.

Gurwitsch, A. (1929/1966). *Phenomenology of Thematics and of the Pure Ego: Studies of the Relation between Gestalt Theory and Phenomenology*, in A. Gurwitsch, *Studies in Phenomenology and Psychology*. Chicago: Northwestern University Press, 1966.

– (1931/1976). *Die mitmenschlichen Begegnungen in der Milieuwelt*, ed. A. Métraux. New York: De Gruyter, 1976.

– (1941/1966). "A non-egological conception of consciousness." *Philosophy and Phenomenological Research*, 1: 325–38. (Reprinted in A. Gurwitsch, *Studies in Phenomenology and Psychology*. Chicago: Northwestern University Press, 1966.)

– (1957/2010). *The Collected Works of Aron Gurwitsch (1901–1973). Volume III: The Field of Consciousness: Phenomenology of Theme, Thematic Field, and Marginal Consciousness*, ed. R. M. Zaner and L. Embree. Dordrecht: Springer, 2010.

– (2009). *The Collected Works of Aron Gurwitsch (1901–1973). Volume I: Constitutive Phenomenology in Historical Perspective*, ed. J. García-Gómez. Dordrecht: Springer.

Haken, H., J. A. S. Kelso, and H. Bunz (1985). "A theoretical model of phase transitions in human hand movements." *Biological Cybernetics*, 51: 347–56.

Hall, J. A. (1984). *Nonverbal sex Differences: Accuracy of Communication and Expressive Style*. Baltimore: Johns Hopkins University Press.

Harrison, S. and M. Richardson (2009). "Horsing around: Spontaneous four-legged coordination." *Journal of Motor Behavior*, 41: 519–24.

Hasson, U., S. A. Nastase, and A. Goldstein (2020). "Direct fit to nature:

An evolutionary perspective on biological and artificial neural networks." *Neuron*, 105: 416–34.

Haugeland, J. (1979). "Understanding natural language." *Journal of Philosophy*, 76: 619–32.

– (1985). *Artificial Intelligence: The Very Idea*. Cambridge, MA: MIT Press.

Heft, H. (2001). *Ecological Psychology in Context: James Gibson, Roger Barker, and the Legacy of William James's Radical Empiricism*. Mahwah: Erlbaum.

Hegel, G. W. F. (1807/1979). *Phänomenologie des Geistes*. Trans. as: *Phenomenology of Spirit*, by A. V. Miller. Oxford: Oxford University Press, 1979.

Heidegger, M. (1927/1928/1977). *Phänomenologische Interpretation von Kants Kritik der reinen Vernunft*, ed. I. Görland, in *Gesamtausgabe. Vol. 25*. Frankfurt: Klostermann, 1977.

– (1927/1975/1982). *Die Grundprobleme der Phänomenologie*, ed. F.-W. von Herrmann, in *Gesamtausgabe. Vol. 24*. Frankfurt: Klostermann, 1975. Trans. as: *The Basic Problems of Phenomenology*, by A. Hofstadter. Indianapolis: Indiana University Press, 1982.

– (1927/1977/1993, cited as *SZ*). *Sein und Zeit*. 17th edn. Tübingen: Max Niemeyer, 1993.

– (1929/1991). *Kant und das Problem der Metaphysik*, ed. F.-W. von Herrmann, 5th edn. Frankfurt: Klostermann, 1991.

Heidegger, M. and K. Jaspers (1992). *Briefwechsel 1920–1963*, ed. W. Biemel and H. Saner. Munich: Piper.

Hurley, S. L. (2002). *Consciousness in Action*. Cambridge, MA: Harvard University Press.

Hurley, S. L. and A. Noë (2003). "Neural plasticity and consciousness." *Biology and Philosophy*, 18(1): 131–68.

Husbands, P., I. Harvey, and D. Cliff (1993). "Circle in the round: State space attractors for evolved sighted robots," in L. Steels (ed.), *The Biology and Technology of Intelligent Autonomous Agents*. Berlin: Springer.

Husserl, E. (1891/1992/2003). *Philosophie der Arithmetik*, ed. E. Ströker, in *Gesammelte Schriften. Vol. 1*. Hamburg: Felix Meiner, 1992. Trans. as: *Philosophy of Arithmetic: Psychological and Logical Investigations with Supplementary Texts from 1887–1901*, by D. Willard. Dordrecht: Kluwer, 2003.

– (1900/1992). *Logische Untersuchungen. Erster Band: Prolegomena zur reinen Logik*, ed. E. Ströker, in *Gesammelte Schriften. Vol. 2*. Hamburg: Felix Meiner, 1992.

– (1901a/1992). *Logische Untersuchungen. Zweiter Band. I. Teil: Untersuchungen zur Phänomenologie und Theorie der Erkenntnis*, ed. E. Ströker, in *Gesammelte Schriften. Vol. 3*. Hamburg: Felix Meiner, 1992.

– (1901b/1992). *Logische Untersuchungen. Zweiter Band. II. Teil:*

Untersuchungen zur Phänomenologie und Theorie der Erkenntnis, ed. E. Ströker, in *Gesammelte Schriften*. Vol. 4. Hamburg: Felix Meiner, 1992.

– (1907/1973). *Ding und Raum. Vorlesungen 1907*, ed. U. Claesges, in *Husserliana*. Vol. 16. The Hague: Martinus Nijhoff, 1973.

– (1911). "Philosophie as strenge Wissenschaft," in G. Mehlis (ed.), *Logos: Internationale Zeitschrift für Philosophie der Kultur*. Bd. 1. Tübingen: J. C. B. Mohr.

– (1913/1992). *Ideen zu einer reinen Phänomenologie und phänomenologischen Philosophie*, ed. E. Ströker, in *Gesammelte Schriften*. Vol. 5. Hamburg: Felix Meiner, 1992.

– (1928/1991). "Edmund Husserls Vorlesungen zur Phänomenologie des Inneren Zeitbewusstseins," in M. Heidegger (ed.), *Jahrbuch für Philosophie und phänomenologische Forschung*. Bd. IX. Halle: Max Niemeyer. Trans. as: *Edmund Husserl on the Phenomenology of the Consciousness of Internal Time*, by J. Brough. Dordrecht: Kluwer, 1991.

– (1936/1954/1970). *Die Krisis der europäischen Wissenschaften und die transzendentale Phänomenologie: Eine Einleitung in die phänomenologische Philosophie*, ed. W. Biemel. The Hague: Martinus Nijhoff, 1954. Trans. as: *The Crisis of European Sciences and Transcendental Phenomenology*, by D. Carr. Evanston: Northwestern University Press, 1970.

– (1952). *Ideen zu einer reinen Phänomenologie und phänomenologischen Philosophie. Zweites Buch: Phänomenologische Untersuchungen zur Konstitution*, ed. M. Biemel, in *Husserliana*. Vol. 4. The Hague: Martinus Nijhoff, 1952.

Hutto, D. and E. Myin (2013). *Radicalizing Enactivism*. Cambridge, MA: MIT Press.

– (2017). *Evolving Enactivism*. Cambridge, MA: MIT Press.

James, W. (1890). *The Principles of Psychology*. Boston: Henry Holt.

– (1904). "Does consciousness exist?" *Journal of Philosophy, Psychology, and Scientific Methods*, 1: 477–91.

– (1909). *The Meaning of Truth*. New York: Longman Green.

Jiang, Y. and L. Mark (1994). "The effect of gap depth on the perception of whether a gap is crossable." *Perception and Psychophysics*, 56: 691–700.

Kant, I. (1781/1997). *Kritik der reinen Vernunf*. Riga: J. F. Hartknoch, 1781. [A-edn (Ak. 4:5–252); B-edn (Ak. 3:2–552).] Trans. as: *Critique of Pure Reason*, by P. Guyer and A. W. Wood. Cambridge: Cambridge University Press, 1997.

– (1786/1800/1985, cited as *MFNS*). *Metaphysische Anfangsgründe der Naturwissenschaften*. Riga: Johann Friedrich Hartknoch, 1786. [Ak. 4: 467–565.] Trans. as: *Metaphysical Foundations of Natural Science* by J. W. Ellington, in *Immanuel Kant: Philosophy of Material Nature*. Indianapolis: Hackett, 1985.

– (1798/1907). *Anthropology from a Pragmatic Point of View*, trans. O. Külpe, ed. Königlichen Preußischen (later Deutschen) Akademie der Wissenschaften, in *Kants gesammelte Schriften*. Berlin: Georg Reimer (later Walter de Gruyter), 1900–.

Katz, D. (1925). *Der Aufbau der Tastwelt*. Leipzig: Johann Ambrosius Barth.

– (1930). *Der Aufbau der Farbwelt*. Leipzig: Johann Ambrosius Barth.

Kelso, J. A. S. (1995). *Dynamic Patterns*. Cambridge, MA: MIT Press.

– (2009). "Synergies: Atoms of brain and behavior," in D. Sternad (ed.), *Progress in Motor Control*. Heidelberg: Springer.

Kelso, J. A. S., A. Fuchs, R. Lancaster, T. Holroyd, D. Cheyne, and H. Weinberg (1998). "Dynamic cortical activity in the human brain reveals motor equivalence." *Nature*, 392(6678): 814–18.

Kiverstein, J. (2012). "What is Heideggerian cognitive science?" in J. Kiverstein and M. Wheeler (eds.), *Heidegger and Cognitive Science*. Basingstoke: Palgrave Macmillan.

Kiverstein, J. D. and E. Rietveld (2018). "Reconceiving representation-hungry cognition: An ecological-enactive proposal." *Adaptive Behavior*, 26: 147–63.

Klahr, P. and D. Waterman (1986). "Artificial Intelligence: A Rand Perspective." Rand Paper P-7172.

Koffka, K. (1923). "Perception: An introduction to the *Gestalt-Theorie*." *Psychological Bulletin*, 19: 531–85.

Köhler, W. (1913). "Über unbemerkte Empfindungen und Urteilstäuschungen." *Zeitschrift für Psychologie*, 66: 51–80.

– (1917/1925). *The Mentality of Apes*, trans. E. Winter from the 2nd German edn. London: Kegan, Trench; New York: Harcourt, Brace and World. (Original work published as *Intelligenzprüfungen an Anthropoiden*. Berlin: Königlichen Akademie der Wissenschaften, 1917.)

Kono, T. (2010). "The extended mind approach for a new paradigm for psychology." *Integrated Psychological and Behavioral Science*, 44: 329–39.

Kreisler, H. and H. Dreyfus. (2005). "Meaning, relevance, and the limits of technology: A conversation with Hubert Dreyfus." Institutes of International Study, University College Berkeley. http://globetrotter.berkeley.edu/people5/Dreyfus/dreyfus-con0.html

Kugler, P. N., J. A. S. Kelso, and M. T. Turvey (1980). "Coordinative structures as dissipative structures. I: Theoretical lines of convergence," in G. E. Stelmach and J. Requin (eds.), *Tutorials in Motor Behavior*. Amsterdam: North-Holland.

Leahey, T. H. (2000). *A History of Modern Psychology*, 3rd edn. New York: Pearson.

Lee, D. N. (1980). "The optic flow-field: The foundation of vision." *Philosophical Transactions of the Royal Society London B*, 290: 169–79.

– (2006). "How movement is guided." http://www.perception-in-action. ed.ac.uk/PDF_s/Howmovementisguided.pdf

Lee, D. N. and P. E. Reddish (1981). "Plummeting gannets: A paradigm of ecological optics." *Nature*, 293: 293–4.

Lewin, K. (1936). *Principles of Topological Psychology*. York, PA: McGraw-Hill.

Lutz, A., J. P. Lachaux, J. Martinerie, and F. J. Varela (2002). "Guiding the study of brain dynamics by using first-person data: Synchrony patterns correlate with ongoing conscious states during a simple visual task." *Proceedings of the National Academy of Sciences*, 99: 1586–91.

Mach, E. (1865/1965). "On the effect of the spatial distribution of the light stimulus on the retina," in F. Ratliff, *Mach Bands: Quantitative Studies on Neural Networks in the Retina*. San Francisco: Holden-Day, 1965.

– (1886/1897). *The Analysis of Sensations and the Relation of the Physical to the Psychical*, trans. C. K. Williams. La Salle: Open Court.

Marcus, G. (2014). "What comes after the Turing test?" *The New Yorker*, June 9.

Maturana, H. (1978). "The biology of language: The epistemology of reality," in G. Miller and E. Lenneberg (eds.), *Psychology and Biology of Language and Thought*. New York: Academic Press.

Maturana, H. and F. Varela (1973). *De Máquinas y Seres Vivos: Una teoría sobre la organización biológica*. Santiago: Editorial Universitaria.

– (1987). *The Tree of Knowledge: The Biological Roots of Human Understanding*. Boston: Shambala.

McCarthy, J. and P. J. Hayes (1969). "Some philosophical problems from the standpoint of artificial intelligence." *Machine Intelligence*, 4: 463–502.

McClamrock, R. (1995). *Existential Cognition*. Chicago: University of Chicago Press.

McGann, M. (2014). "Enacting a social ecology: Radically embodied intersubjectivity." *Frontiers in Psychology*. https://doi.org/10.3389/fpsyg.2014.01321

Menary, R. (2010). *The Extended Mind*. Cambridge, MA: MIT Press.

Merleau-Ponty, M. (1942/1963). *The Structure of Behavior*, trans. A. Fisher. Pittsburgh: Duquesne University Press, 1963.

– (1945/2012, cited as *PP*). *Phenomenology of Perception*, trans. D. Landes. Abingdon: Routledge, 2012.

Mulvey, L. (1975). "Visual pleasure and narrative cinema." *Screen*, 16(3): 6–18.

Noë, A. (2004). *Action in Perception*. Cambridge, MA: MIT Press.

– (2009). *Out of Our Heads: Why You Are Not Your Brain and Other Lessons from the Biology of Consciousness*. New York: Hill and Wang.

O'Regan, J. K. (2011). *Why Red Looks Red instead of Sounding like a Bell: The Feel of Consciousness*. New York: Oxford University Press.

O'Regan, J. K. and A. Noë (2001). "A sensorimotor account of vision and visual consciousness." *Behavioral and Brain Sciences*, 24(5): 883–917.

Oyama, S., P. E. Griffiths, and R. D. Gray, eds. (2001). *Cycles of Contingency: Developmental Systems and Evolution*. Cambridge, MA: MIT Press.

Pezzulo, G. and P. Cisek (2016). "Navigating the affordance landscape: Feedback control as a process model of behavior and cognition." *Trends in Cognitive Sciences*, 20(6): 414–24.

Port, R. F. (2003). "Meter and speech." *Journal of Phonetics*, 31(3): 599–611.

Preston, B. (1993). "Heidegger and artificial intelligence." *Philosophy and Phenomenological Research*, 53: 43–69.

Radloff, B. (2007). *Heidegger and the Question of National Socialism: Disclosure and Gestalt*. Toronto: University of Toronto Press.

Richardson, M., K. Marsh, R. Isenhower, J. Goodman, and R. Schmidt (2007). "Rocking together: Dynamics of intentional and unintentional interpersonal coordination." *Human Movement Science*, 26: 867–91.

Rietveld, E. (2008). "Situated normativity." *Mind*, 117: 973–1001.

– (2012). "Context-switching and responsiveness to real relevance," in J. Kiverstein and M. Wheeler (eds.), *Heidegger and Cognitive Science: New Directions in Cognitive Science and Philosophy*. Basingstoke: Palgrave Macmillan.

Riley, M. and J. Holden (2012). "Dynamics of cognition." *WIREs Cogn Sci* 2012. https://doi.org/10.1002/wcs.1200

Robbins, D. (2019). *The Bourdieu Paradigm*. Manchester: Manchester University Press.

Rubin, E. (1921). *Visuell Wahrgenommene Figuren: Studien in Psychologischer Analyse*. Copenhagen: Gyldendalske Boghandel.

Rubin, H. (2003). *Self-Made Men*. Nashville: Vanderbilt University Press.

Salamon, G. (2010). *Assuming a Body*. New York: Columbia University Press.

Sanches de Oliveira, G., C. Riehm, and C. Annand (2019). "Bee-ing in the world: Phenomenology, cognitive science, and interactivity in a novel insect-tracking task," in C. Freksa, A. Goel, and C. Seifert (eds.), *Proceedings of the 41st Annual Meeting of the Cognitive Science Society*, 1008–13.

Sartre, J.-P. (1962). *The Transcendence of the Ego*, trans. F. Williams and R. Kirkpatrick. New York: Noonday Press. (Original version published in *Recherches philosophiques*, 6, 1936–7.)

– (1936/2012). *The Imagination*, trans. K. Williford and D. Rudrauf. New York: Routledge.

– (1940/2010). *The Imaginary*, trans. J. Webber. New York: Routledge.

– (1943/1984, cited as *BN*). *Being and Nothingness*, trans. H. Barnes. New York: Washington Square Press.

– (1948). "Orphée Noir," in L. S. Senghor (ed.), *Anthologie de la nouvelle poésie nègre et malgache de langue française*. Paris: Presses Universitaires de France.

Schilder, P. (1923). *Das Körperschema: Ein Beitrag zur Lehre vom Bewusstsein des Eigenen Körpers*. Berlin: Springer.

Schmidt, R., C. Carello, and M. Turvey (1990). "Phase transitions and critical fluctuations in the visual coordination of rhythmic movements between people." *Journal of Experimental Psychology: Human Perception and Performance*, 16: 227–47.

Scholz, J. and J. A. S. Kelso (1990). "Intentional switching between patterns of bimanual coordination depends on the intrinsic dynamics of the patterns." *Journal of Motor Behavior*, 22: 98–124.

Sedgewick, H. (1973). "The visible horizon." Unpublished doctoral dissertation, Cornell University.

Senghor, L.S., ed. (1948). *Anthologie de la nouvelle poésie nègre et malgache de langue française*. Paris: Presses Universitaires de France.

Shockley, K., C. Carello, and M. T. Turvey (2004). "Metamers in the haptic perception of heaviness and moveableness." *Perception and Psychophysics*, 66: 731–42.

Shockley, K. and M. T. Turvey (2005). "Encoding and retrieval during bimanual rhythmic coordination." *Journal of Experimental Psychology: Learning, Memory, and Cognition*, 31(5): 980–90.

Simon, H. and A. Newell (1958). "Heuristic problem solving." *Operations Research*, 6: 1–10.

Skarda, C. and W. Freeman (1987). "How the brain makes chaos in order to make sense of the world." *Behavioral and Brain Sciences*, 10: 161–95.

Smith, B., ed. and trans. (1988). *Foundations of Gestalt Theory*. Munich and Vienna: Philosophia.

Steele, C. M. (1997). "A threat in the air: How stereotypes shape intellectual identity and performance." *American Psychologist*, 52(6): 613–29.

Stern, W. (1897). "Psychische Präsenzzeit." *Zeitschrift für Psychologie und Physiologie der Sinnesorgane*, 13: 325–49.

Straus, E. (1966). *Phenomenological Psychology*. New York: Basic Books.

Swenson, R. and M. T. Turvey (1991). "Thermodynamic reasons for perception–action cycles." *Ecological Psychology*, 3: 317–48.

Thompson, E. (2004). "Life and mind: From autopoiesis to neurophenomenology. A tribute to Francisco Varela." *Phenomenology and Cognitive Science*, 3: 381–98.

– (2007). *Mind in Life*. Cambridge, MA: Harvard University Press.

Thompson, E. and M. Stapleton (2008). "Making sense of sense making." *Topoi*. https://doi.org/10.1007/s11245-008-9043-2

Titchener, E. B. (1895). "Simple reactions." *Mind*, 4: 74–81.

– (1898a). "The postulates of a structural psychology." *Philosophical Review*, 7: 449–65.

– (1898b). *A Primer of Psychology*. New York: Macmillan.

Treffner, P. and M. Turvey (1995). "Symmetry, broken symmetry, and handedness in bimanual coordination dynamics." *Experimental Brain Research*, 107: 163–78.

Turing, A. M. (1950). "Computing machinery and intelligence." *Mind*, 59: 433–60.

van Gelder, T. (1998). "The dynamical hypothesis in cognitive science." *Behavioral and Brain Sciences*, 21: 615–28.

Varela, F. J. (1979). *Principles of Biological Autonomy*. New York: Elsevier.

– (1996). "Neurophenomenology: A methodological remedy for the hard problem." *Journal of Consciousness Studies*, 3(4): 330–49.

– (1999). "The specious present: A neurophenomenology of time consciousness," in J. Petitot, F. J. Varela, B. Pachoud, and J.-M. Roy (eds.), *Naturalizing Phenomenology: Issues in Contemporary Phenomenology and Cognitive Science*. Stanford: Stanford University Press.

Varela, F., J. P. Lachaux, E. Rodriguez, and J. Martinerie (2001). "The brainweb: Phase synchronization and large-scale integration." *Nature Reviews Neuroscience*, 2: 229–39.

Varela, F. J., H. R. Maturana, and R. Uribe (1974). "Autopoiesis: The organization of living systems, its characterization and a model." *Currents in Modern Biology*, 5(4): 187–96.

Varela, F. J., E. Thompson, and E. Rosch (1991). *The Embodied Mind*. Cambridge, MA: MIT Press.

Walton, A. E., A. Washburn, P. Langland-Hassan, A. Chemero, H. Kloos, H., and M. J. Richardson (2018). "Creating time: Social collaboration in music improvisation." *Topics in Cognitive Science*, 10: 95–119.

Warren, W. H. (1984). "Perceiving affordances: Visual guidance of stair climbing." *Journal of Experimental Psychology: Human Perception and Performance*, 10: 683–703.

Weiss, G., A. Murphy, and G. Salamon (2020). *50 Concepts for a Critical Phenomenology*. Chicago: Northwestern University Press.

Wertheimer, M. (1912/1979). "On perceptual organization into wholes and gestalt psychology," in R. Watson (ed.), *Basic Writings in the History of Psychology*. New York: Oxford University Press. (Original work published as "Experimentelle Studien über das Sehen von Bewegung." *Zeitschrift fur Psychologie*, 61, 1912: 161–265.)

– (1923/1938). "Laws of organization in perceptual forms," in W. Ellis (ed. and trans.), *A Source Book of Gestalt Psychology*. London: Routledge and Kegan Paul, 1938. (Original work published in 1923 as "Untersuchungen zur Lehre von der Gestalt II." *Psychologische Forschung*, 4: 301–50.)

West, B. J. (2006). *Where Medicine Went Wrong: Rediscovering the Path to Complexity*. New York: World Scientific.

Wheeler, M. (1996). "From robots to Rothko," in M. Boden (ed.), *The Philosophy of Artificial Life*. New York: Oxford University Press.

– (2005). *Reconstructing the Cognitive World*. Cambridge, MA: MIT Press.

– (2010). "In defense of extended functionalism," in R. Menary (ed.), *The Extended Mind*. Cambridge, MA: MIT Press.

Wilson, R. (1995). *Cartesian Psychology and Physical Minds*. Cambridge: Cambridge University Press.

– (2004). *Boundaries of the Mind*. Cambridge: Cambridge University Press.

Withagen, R., H. J. de Poel, D. Araújo, and G. J. Pepping (2012). "Affordances can invite behavior." *New Ideas in Psychology*, 30: 250–8.

Wundt, W. M. (1874/1902/1904). *Principles of Physiological Psychology*, trans. E. B. Titchener from the 5th German edn., published 1902. (Original German edn. published 1874.)

– (1912/1916). *Völkerpsychologie*. Trans. as: *Elements of Folk-Psychology*, by E. L. Schaub. London: Allen, 1916.

Young, I. M. (1980/2005). "Throwing like a girl: A phenomenology of feminine body comportment, motility, and spatiality." *Human Studies*, 3: 137–56. (Reprinted in I. M. Young, *On Female Body Experience: "Throwing Like a Girl" and Other Essays*. New York: Oxford University Press, 2005.)

Index